Living LITERATURE

EXPLORING ADVANCED LEVEL
English Literature

Frank Myszor & Jackie Baker

Edited by
John Shuttleworth
With a foreword by George Keith

Hodder & Stoughton
A MEMBER OF THE HODDER HEADLINE GROUP

For Sonia, Julian, Nicholas and Jacob.

With thanks to the staff and students of Itchen College and Stanbridge Earls School, and to Richard Baker and Emma Myszor for practical and moral support.

Orders: please contact Bookpoint Ltd, 78 Milton Park, Abingdon, Oxon OX14 4TD. Telephone: (44) 01235 827720, Fax: (44) 01235 400454. Lines are open from 9.00–6.00, Monday to Saturday, with a 24 hour message answering service. Email address: orders@bookpoint.co.uk

British Library Cataloguing in Publication Data
A catalogue record for this title is available from The British Library

ISBN 0 340 77208 5
First published 2000
Impression number   10 9 8 7 6 5 4 3 2 1
Year   2005 2004 2003 2002 2001 2000

Cover photo from The Ronald Grant Archive
P 67 illustrations by Doug Gray/The Art Business
Typeset by Fakenham Photosetting Limited, Fakenham, Norfolk NR21 8NN
Printed in Great Britain for Hodder & Stoughton Educational, a division of Hodder Headline Plc, 338 Euston Road, London NW1 3BH by J. W. Arrowsmith Ltd, Bristol.

Contents

FOREWORD

'For a start I like this poem. I like its humour and I suppose I recognise the kind of experience I might have had as a child, although, as yet, I cannot claim to fully understand it. I know that it tells a simple story of the finding of a tyre and its mysterious disappearance. But I expect the poem to be saying something more than this . . . so I will look for it'.

[comments on a poem by Simon Armitage]

In the last year of the twentieth century a flurry of new books appeared with ominous titles like *The Death of Literature, Literature Lost, Literature: an Embattled Profession, The Rise and Fall of English* and *What's Happened to Literature?*

All sorts of arguments were put forward: English Literature teachers are too conservative for modern students; students don't read anyway; there's too much literary theory; there's not enough literary theory; syllabuses pay too much attention to minority authors; syllabuses pay too much attention to hidebound texts; the print medium has been superseded; the print medium is entering a new era, and so on – contradiction after contradiction. But the general drift was, and still is, pessimistic.

The truth is, literature in English (and in Englishes worldwide), is very alive and very well, living in all sorts of places not least in the book you are now reading. Its authors though, would be the first to disclaim any literary kinship with the writers they celebrate and illuminate. What they do, is repeatedly turn the reader away from their own book, toward texts ancient and modern, on which they throw so much light. And that is the best kind of literary criticism as well as the best kind of English teaching.

It is worth remembering that English Literature as an academic subject in Britain is little more than a hundred years old. The first English degree course was established at Oxford in 1894, though the Americans beat us to it in 1876 in Harvard. In terms of eras of cultural history, the study of English Literature has just reached adolescence, with all the energy, radical conservatism, wild flights of fancy and linguistic unpredictability of a 13 year old. If the quality of poetry, novels and TV drama written over the past 20 years, along with a continuing pleasure in the classics, are anything to go by, students of A level English Literature have much to look forward to in the next 20 years.

Candidates in examinations have long relied on three traditional aspects of literary criticism taught in schools and colleges for the past 50 years: theme, character and alliteration. Sometimes there is a stab at metaphor and irony, and that is about it. Of course, themes and character are interesting and exciting, while alliteration is very noticeable – almost too noticeable. With only 21 consonant letters in the alphabet, and half a million or so words to choose from, it's not surprising that alliteration is so frequent. But it is often accidental rather than intended, and is, in any case, only a part of the web of poetic language that includes assonance, rhythm, rhyme and syllable stress.

Themes and assessment of character need to be well rooted in texts and contexts; they always have been, and they always will be. Otherwise, the 'theme' can easily take over from the book itself, while characters are mistakenly treated as real people with a real psychology to speculate about, rather than appreciated as highly imaginative constructs and fictions that are all the more valuable for being so.

Metaphor and irony are not just features to be quarried out of the text to 'show' something about character and theme; they are a subtle, fascinating part of the web of language that binds a reader and a writer together, once a reader has started to read the text.

Living Literature combines the qualities of traditional literary criticism with a modern understanding of the nature of written texts. It is in our ideas of what texts are, and of what goes into their construction, that the biggest changes in literary criticism have occurred over the last 40 years or so. The old meaning of the Latin word 'text' is still appropriate, 'something woven together' (as in 'texture' and 'textiles'). But woven out of many elements, not just the words on the page.

Living Literature helps readers to understand the part they play as readers, in constructing meanings in texts. Texts exist in readers' minds as well as in writers' minds. Today is the age of the reader, but that doesn't mean the writer is somehow put in second place. The writer, the text itself and the reader too, all form part of the meaning making process. The right attention to each one of these is what earns marks in examinations.

In the quotation at the beginning of this foreword, the authors point out how important it is for readers/exam candidates to be able to say 'I am unsure', to consider their own expectations and to press on, looking ever more closely at the language in the text, rather than parrot a set of notes that have already been pre-packed for instant consumption and regurgitation.

Living Literature also stresses, quite rightly, the importance of two kinds of context, that of the writer and that of the reader. Bits of Shakespeare don't just have meaning according to the bigger bits of context they have been quoted from; the whole text of the play now has an existence in the social context of its own times and in the contexts that modern actors, directors, film makers and modern readers bring to it, two hundred, three, four hundred years later. Enjoying, disagreeing with, other people's interpretations, points of view and contexts are all part of modern A level English studies.

What is especially timely about this book, is not just the clarity with which it explains new critical approaches to literary texts and how to use them, but also the care with which it addresses assessment objectives laid down by the Qualifications and Curriculum Authority for all A level examinations in English Literature. The plain fact is that you cannot even pass an A level examination on just being a good reader. You have to write your way to success, and the authors, both experienced teachers, are well aware of the importance of not just communicating, but of knowing how to communicate engagement and expertise in what new millennium examiners are required to assess.

If Literature is dead, all one can say is, 'long live literature'.

GEORGE R. KEITH
February 2000

1 Introducing AS and A Level English Literature

'Books are a load of crap – get stewed' – Philip Larkin

Who are you?

If you are reading this book, then you:
- are probably studying AS and/or A level English Literature
- are a little experienced in the study of English Literature
- are aware of some of the relevant terms and concepts, or
- may be a teacher looking for ideas.

Living Literature will help you if you are studying the following courses: AS or A level English Literature; AS or A level English Language and Literature. For English Language courses you should read *Living Language*, and for a more direct focus on Language and Literature see *Living Language and Literature*, both by George Keith and John Shuttleworth (Hodder & Stoughton, 2000).

In this chapter we explain:

- the differences between GCSE and A level
- how this book relates to the current Assessment Objectives – these are the seven statements common to all A level specifications (the concept formerly known as 'syllabus')
- how this book is organised
- the context of writing literature and the context of reading literature – two important concepts
- what literature is

Bridging the gap: from GCSE to A level

You will find that moving from GCSE to A level is a big step, but it is not as big a step as it used to be. This is because from September 2000 new A level examinations have been in place. These new examinations introduced an intermediate stage into A level which means that everyone can gain an 'AS' qualification at the end of one year. The AS exam (Advanced Supplementary) is pitched at a level between A level and GCSE, the net effect being that at the beginning of an A level course, you are faced with less of a mountain to climb. In order to get your full A level you must also have taken AS level. In short, the gap has been bridged so that the one big step has become less of a mountain!

English Literature exams are now connected like this:

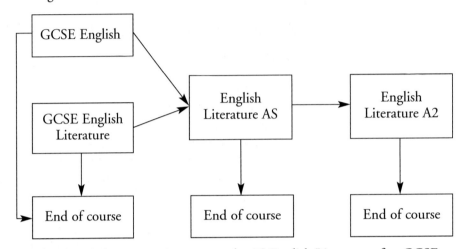

This means that you can go on to take AS English Literature after GCSE English or GCSE English Literature.

A summary of the content of each course is shown below. Where the statements are clarified later in this book, they are followed by the appropriate page number.

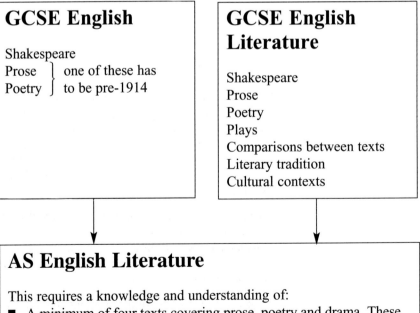

GCSE English

Shakespeare
Prose ⎱ one of these has
Poetry ⎰ to be pre-1914

GCSE English Literature

Shakespeare
Prose
Poetry
Plays
Comparisons between texts
Literary tradition
Cultural contexts

AS English Literature

This requires a knowledge and understanding of:
■ A minimum of four texts covering prose, poetry and drama. These must include Shakespeare and one other text published before 1900.
■ how texts relate to the context in which they were written (Chapter 3)

- the different ways in which texts are interpreted by different readers, acknowledging that literary texts have a range of meanings and the significance of these is related to the readers' knowledge, experience and ideas (Chapter 4).

A Level English Literature (in addition to AS requirements)

Knowledge and understanding of:
- a minimum of four further texts, covering prose, poetry and drama. At least one work should be pre-1770 (pre-Romantic) and at least one other should be pre-1900
- how texts relate to the context in which they were written, including the importance of cultural and historical influences on literary works and the relevance of the author's biography ... and other works (Chapter 3);
- the significance of literary traditions, periods and movements in relation to texts studied (Chapters 3 and 8);
- the ways in which texts have been interpeted and valued by different readers at different times, acknowledging that interpretation of literary texts can depend on a reader's assumptions and stance (Chapter 4);
- the connections and comparisons between texts and how texts relate to one another (Chapter 12).

So how is GCSE different from AS and A level? The answer to this depends on whether you are discussing English or English Literature GCSE. One thing to remember is that because there is a lot of literature in English GCSE, you don't need to have studied GCSE English Literature in order to go on to AS/A level. Obviously some major differences are that the AS and A level require the study of more literature than English GCSE and there is no component that can be called personal writing. But there is also a great deal of familiar ground.

As one would expect, there is much continuity with English Literature GCSE, where you had to show some knowledge of the historical and cultural context in which a text was written as well as an understanding of the literary tradition. Both of these feature again at AS and A level.

In general terms, to succeed beyond GCSE you obviously need to enjoy studying literature. You will also need to be prepared to examine texts from outside your own time and culture, thus expanding your literary horizons. As you continue your studies, the methods you use will become just as important as the content of the course. This is why *how* you approach a text is just as important as *what* you say about it. Above all, you will need to be able to make your own judgements about what you read, coming closer to being an *independent informed reader,* especially as you progress through A2. This is an important term for the whole course. It suggests that you can develop your own ideas about what you read but also use other sources such as criticism to support your ideas.

Here are the assessment criteria in full for AS and A level. The right hand column of the chart offers some explanations.

	Assessment Objectives	Explanation
AO1	Communicate clearly the knowledge, understanding and insight appropriate to literary study, using appropriate terminology and accurate and coherent written expression.	Write accurately and use some technical terms.
AO2i (AS)	Respond with knowledge and understanding to literary texts of different types and periods.	Show that you know about old texts and ones from other cultures.
AO2ii (A2)	Respond with knowledge and understanding to literary texts of different types and periods, exploring and commenting on relationships and comparisons between literary texts.	As above but you must also be able to compare texts.
AO3	Show detailed understanding of the ways in which writers' choices of form, structure and language shape meanings.	For example show that you know why the writer has used certain language or chapter organisation.
AO4	Articulate informed, independent opinions and judgements, showing understanding of different interpretations of literary texts by different readers.	Think for yourself but make use of what others have said about a literary work.
AO5i (AS)	Show understanding of the contexts in which literary texts are written and understood.	See Chapter 3.
AO5ii (A2)	Evaluate the significance of cultural, historical and contextual influences on literary texts.	See Chapter 3.

Notice in particular that AO2 and AO5 are split into two parts, one of which applies to AS and the other to A2.

Key skills

The National Qualification in key skills requires all AS and A level students to take the following key skills:

- Application of Number
- Communication
- Information Technology.

English Literature is relevant to two of these: Communication and Information Technology.

The **Communication** Unit includes:

- **discussion**
- making a **presentation**
- selecting and synthesising information (**reading**)
- **writing** different kinds of texts.

The **Information Technology** Unit includes:

- Plan and use **different sources** to search for and select information
- Explore, develop and exchange **information**, and derive new information
- **Present information**, including text, numbers and images.

You can be credited with key skills through any of the A levels or GNVQs that you are studying. This book indicates when an activity is relevant to the key skills of Communication or Information Technology. Here is how this is shown in the text:

Example from page 133

ACTIVITY 116

Find out if the play you are studying has had alternative endings and what they were. Discuss the significance of this.

Key skills: Communication – reading/discussion

Example from page 213

ACTIVITY 187

Find out more detail about the lives of the Brontës and how their books reflect their experiences – if they do!

Key skills: Information Technology – different sources

An introductory text such as this can only give a brief indication of how the activities relate to key skills. For more detailed information you will need to look at key skills documents and, in consultation with a teacher, check the kinds of details given in the example below. You may then need to make adjustments to the activity as suggested in the right hand column.

Extract from Key Skills communication Unit level 3	Activity	Commentary
Read and synthesise information from two extended documents about a complex subject. One of these documents should include at least one image. ■ Select and read material that contains the information you need; ■ Identify accurately, and compare, the line of reasoning and main points from texts and images; ■ Synthesise the key information in a form that is relevant to your purpose.	Compare the above history of English poetry with the contents page of a historical book about English poetry. Look carefully at (a) how each age is labelled (e.g. by the style of the poetry, by the name of the monarch, etc); (b) the similarities and differences between each account; and (c) any bias that seems to emerge (from page 172).	■ The activity could be extended to look at more than one contents page. ■ If there are no images in the written sources, the Internet could be used. ■ The activity does not specify how the work is to be presented. You should choose your own way, consulting a teacher if necessary.

How this book is organised

The book is roughly divided into two halves. The first half covers the methods you use for studying literature. It is about developing approaches and acquiring specific techniques for getting into texts, in line with the A level specifications. The second half is geared towards literature itself – different periods in literary history and different genres such as plays, poetry and novels. Although this may look like a division between theory and practice, you will find plenty of examples and practical activities in both sections.

The book is closely linked to the Assessment Objectives on page 4. The most important word here is *context* because it crops up explicitly or implicitly in most of the objectives. It is this word that has strongly influenced the organisation of this book.

There are two kinds of context. Texts have to be written and texts have to be read. Writing and reading cannot take place in a vacuum; they are inevitably affected by the time and place in which they occur. So, if you wish to study a literary text you will need to consider both its context of writing and its context of reading – as well as the text itself. These three elements – context of writing, text, and context of reading – describe a kind of process which means they can be put next to each other on a diagram like this:

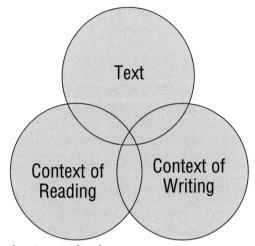

These three overlapping circles show:

■ that all three elements are closely linked to each other
■ that emphasis can be put on any one of them
■ that texts cannot be separated from their contexts
■ that contexts of writing and reading are connected.

You will find that the overlapping circles feature throughout the book. At the beginning of each chapter, one, two or three of the circles will be shaded to show the emphasis of that particular chapter.

The separation of what goes on in each circle is a little artificial. In practice you will deal with more than one at a time, as implied by the overlapping areas.

In summary, the main emphases in the chapters are as follows:

Chapter	Context of writing	Text	Context of reading
1	+	+	+
2		+	
3	+		
4			+
5			+
6		+	
7	+	+	+
8	+	+	+
9	+	+	+
10	+	+	+
11	+	+	+
12	+	+	+

What have these three overlapping circles got to do with the Assessment Objectives (AOs)?

The diagram overleaf suggests how the two are related. Each assessment objective is given a main focus, with some AOs applying to more than one circle.

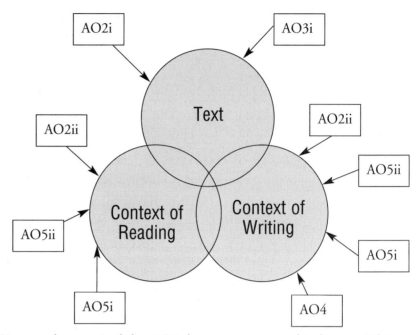

You may have noticed that AO1 does not appear on this diagram. This is because it is not about the literature you are studying but about how you express yourself.

AS and A2: How are they dealt with in the text?

- the chapters tend to move towards more difficult activities as they progress
- the final chapter, which covers synoptic assessment, is aimed at A2
- most of the activities are not formally assessed and can therefore be useful for A or AS, according to your needs.

What does 'Context of Writing' mean?

ACTIVITY 1

The two lists below contain specific events from the context of writing and facts about the writing itself. With a partner connect the items from the first list with those of the second. There are specific answers but you may also be able to justify alternative answers. Write a number from the first list followed by a letter from the second e.g. 2A and then add your reasons.

How many kinds of contexts can you identify? For example, biographical, psychological, etc.

Key skills: Communication – discussion/reading

1 The country beheads its king.
2 The writer's wife commits suicide.
3 Changes in the law make it easy for the police to stop and search.
4 The government bans certain kinds of writing.
5 Women are not allowed to vote.
6 The writer suffers from arthritis.

7 Other writers of the period experiment with style.

8 The writer's country was invaded by foreigners several hundred years before.

9 The writer's ancestors were forcibly taken from their homes and made to work for nothing.

10 War breaks out.

11 The writer is thought to be schizophrenic.

12 People like happy endings.

A Over 30 years later the poet writes a series of poems about their relationship.

B Young black British poets begin to write.

C A poet gives up writing poetry for several years and writes political pamphlets instead.

D Novels depicting the suicide of a female character are written.

E A writer tries to capture how people really think in a novel.

F Black British poets write in their own dialect.

G A novel about a sexual relationship uses language considered to be obscene.

H The novelist rewrites part of his book.

I The poet is not interested in being Poet Laureate.

J The poet's drug-taking influences the nature of his poetry.

K Several young men write poetry about their experiences.

L The writer's first collection of short stories helps to convince the authorities that she is sane.

COMMENTARY

1 Charles I was beheaded in 1649. Returning from abroad, the great English poet John Milton then devoted himself to political writing for the next 20 years.

2 Ted Hughes was married to Sylvia Plath when she committed suicide in 1963. Their relationship was the subject of speculation for decades. The profound effect of this on Hughes was largely unexpressed in his poetry until his collection *Birthday Letters* was published in 1998.

3 In the 1980s, laws that made it easier for the police to stop and search people increased the black community's feelings of racial discrimination. These feelings are expressed in the works of many young black poets such as Benjamin Zephaniah.

4 There are numerous examples of the way that censorship has influenced writers. In 1960 the ban on D.H. Lawrence's *Lady Chatterley's Lover* was lifted, and the effect of this was to change what was possible to write and read, characterising, to some extent, the 'swinging' sixties. In this case and many others, censorship involved language. In Shakespeare's time a religious group called the Puritans would allow no blasphemy in plays and so expressions such as 'zounds' were invented to disguise their religious origins ('zounds' was short for 'God's wounds').

5 In the years leading up to the end of the 19th century calls for women to be given the vote were on the increase. At the time, several novels seemed to express the restriction and frustration of being a woman by creating plot structures that led to the suicide of the main (female) character. For example, Tolstoy's *Anna Karenin* and Kate Chopin's *The Awakening*.

6 Coleridge was forced to take opium because of his arthritis and other ailments; this influenced his writing, notably of *Kubla Khan* which he claimed to have written during an opium induced sleep. Here it should be noted that his style was also influenced much more significantly by the literary movement known as the Romantic.

7 In the early decades of the 20th century writers began to experiment with the way in which they represented the consciousness of their characters. Instead of just describing what characters thought, they began to use words to reflect the fragmented way in which people's thoughts shift rapidly from one topic to the next without apparent organisation.

8 Literature has been profoundly influenced by movements of people due to war, slavery, invasion and emigration. Seamus Heaney, from Northern Ireland, found himself a possible candidate for the Poet Laureateship. Although technically British, having his roots in a country that had been invaded by the British several hundred years ago made it difficult for him to consider the position.

9 Grace Nichols' poetry reflects both the psychology of being black and a woman, as well as the slavery of her ancestors. In her case it gave rise to works written in Standard English with the occasional peppering of the creole of the Caribbean Islands. In other cases it has led to dialect poetry; for example, that of Merle Collins.

10 Janet Frame, New Zealand's best known novelist, was released from a mental asylum when she wrote *The Lagoon*, her first collection of short stories.

11 Many novelists are known to have changed the endings to their works because of public pressure for happy endings. The best known case is probably that of Charles Dickens and *Great Expectations*.

For a discussion of different kinds of contexts, see Chapter 3.

The answers to the first task can be found at the end of this chapter.

Questions you might ask about the context of writing:

Was the writer a recognised member of a literary movement that wrote in a particular way or that had particular beliefs about the world?

Was the period in which the piece was written dominated by a particular way of thinking, e.g. religious, philosophical, political?

Was the writer experiencing anything in his or her life at the time that significantly influenced the writing, e.g. mental breakdown, conversion to a religion, going blind, in love, etc?

Was anything happening in the world at the time, that significantly influenced the writer, e.g. revolution, industrialisation, war, censorship?

1 Discuss with a partner whether or not the word 'reader' could be substituted for the word 'writer' in the questions above. Try to explain your views.
2 Research. Using the above questions, investigate the following writers and poets: Charlotte Brontë, Alexander Pope, Merle Collins, Joseph Conrad, Pat Barker, Gillian Clarke, Vikram Seth, Maya Angelou, or a writer of your own choice.

Key skills: Communication – discussion/reading

Living literature: the Context of Reading

To many people, literature perhaps suggests something that is dead, something associated with dead writers, something only brought back from the dead in the lavish productions of classic novels seen on television. This is a mistaken view: literature lives in the process of its making, in the society in which it was written and in the life of the writer, who after months or years of intense struggle finally fixes it on the page. But literature also remains alive in you. It re-lives every time you read a book, play or poem, every time you discuss these things over a cup of coffee, every time you hand in an essay. In short, readers help to create books as much as writers do and this is true in a number of senses:

- readers literally activate what they read in their imagination.
- without readers books would not sell, they would not be read.
- readers judge books: they condemn them, they praise them.
- different kinds of readers help to give a book its qualities.
- readers can keep a book alive for centuries.
- readers remember and recall what they read.

A book is read in a different way by different individuals or by different groups of people. The following example should clarify this point.

The context in which someone reads a text exerts a strong influence over the meanings that the reader creates. Here is an extreme example. In 1949 China experienced the Communist Revolution. The result of this revolution was that all forms of individuality within Chinese society were suppressed, so that, for example, everyone wore the same clothes – the uniform issued by the government. For several decades no Western plays were performed in China. The following extract from Arthur Miller's diary illustrates the influence that the Chinese attitude towards clothes had on the choice of costume in a Chinese production of Miller's *Death of A Salesman* in 1983.

The sight of the two women whom Happy picks up in the bar reminds me of where I am. Letta ... has been imprisoned in a rose-patterned dress with a large bow across the chest, a high-waisted bodice, and folds of material down almost to her ankles, a veritable British aunt a few months after the World War One armistice ... Letta's look strikes fear in my heart. 'My dear' – I address the now sunken costumier, whose glances barely rise off the floor – 'this girl Letta is twenty years old, but this dress is for a sixty year old who is trying to hide the shape she is in.' I break off in a collapse of all hope, aware again that they simply have had no contact with any clothing except the national uniform of jacket and ballooning trousers for more than thirty years, more than the lifetimes of most of them. (Miller 1983, page 200)

One way of looking at this is to say that Miller's cast simply did not have the appropriate experience by which to interpret the play. They had absorbed images from Hollywood films but these were highly stereotypical – Westerners were often played using loutish walks and outrageous red hair. The example also shows that aspects of theatrical performance are readings of a text – this is a point that will be taken up in Chapter 11.

How does cultural context affect the way in which a play is received? In this section an extreme example has shown that what one political ideology (Western capitalism) takes for granted, has completely different meanings for another.

Questions you might ask about the context of reading:

Who is the reader?

Are the readers aware of themselves as a member of a particular group, e.g. race, gender, sexual orientation, social class?

Is the age in which the text is read dominated by a particular way of thinking, e.g. that capitalism is wrong?

Is the reader likely to be influenced by a major contemporary event, e.g. war?

What is literature?

Questions about writers, texts and readers have already been raised. Behind these questions has been an assumption about the nature of literature itself and this is the topic that will be addressed in this section.

ACTIVITY 3

The aim of this exercise is to set you thinking about the question 'what is literature?'. You will already have some assumptions about what sort of writing can be called 'literature' and what cannot. Work through the following questions with a partner and write down your responses in as much detail as you can.

Key skills: Communication – discussion

Text A

When You Make a Call

First check the code (if any) and number.
   Lift the receiver and listen for dialing tone (a continuous purring).
Dial carefully and allow the dial to return freely.
Then wait for another tone:
Ringing tone (burr-burr) the number is being called.
Engaged tone (a repeated single note) try again a few minutes later.
Number unobtainable tone (steady note) replace receiver, recheck the code and number, and then re-dial.
After dialing a trunk call there will be a pause before you hear the tone; during this time the trunk equipment will be connecting your call.
At the end of the call, replace the receiver securely because timing of calls stops when the caller hangs up.
(extract from *General Post Office: Dialing Instructions and Call Charges* (GPO, 1970)

What kind of writing is Text A? What is its purpose and audience? Would you call this text 'literature?' Comment on how it is set out on the page.

Text B

Extract from *A Martian Sends a Postcard Home* – by Craig Raine

In homes, a haunted apparatus sleeps
that snores when you pick it up.

If the ghost cries, they carry it
to their lips and soothe it to sleep

with sounds, and yet, they wake it up
deliberately, by tickling with a finger.

What kind of writing is Text B? What are its distinctive features? Compare it with Text A.

Now read Texts C and D carefully and then respond to the questions that follow.

(Note that the reference is to Bethlehem, USA)

Text C

Sad Tragedy at Bethlehem
Raymond Fitzgerald a Victim
of Fatal Accident

Raymond Tracy Fitzgerald, one of the twin sons of Michael G. and Margaret Fitzgerald of Bethlehem, died at his home Thursday afternoon, March 24, as the result of an accident by which one of his hands was badly hurt in a sawing machine. The young man was assisting in sawing up some wood in his own dooryard with a sawing machine and accidentally hit the loose pulley, causing the saw to descend upon his hand, cutting and lacerating it badly. Raymond was taken into the house and a physician was immediately summoned, but he died very suddenly from the effects of the shock, which produced heart failure. . . . (The *Littleton Courier*, 1901)

Text D

'Out, Out –' by Robert Frost

The buzz saw snarled and rattled in the yard
And made dust and dropped stove-length sticks of wood,
Sweet-scented stuff when the breeze drew across it.
And from there those that lifted eyes could count
Five mountain ranges one behind the other
Under the sunset far into Vermont.
And the saw snarled and rattled, snarled and rattled,
As it ran light or had to bear a load.
And nothing happened: day was all but done.
Call it a day, I wish they might have said
To please the boy by giving him the half hour
That a boy counts so much when saved from work.
His sister stood beside them in her apron
To tell them 'Supper.' At the word, the saw,
As if to prove saws knew what supper meant,
Leaped out at the boy's hand, or seemed to leap –
He must have given the hand. However it was,
Neither refused the meeting. But the hand!
The boy's first outcry was a rueful laugh,
As he swung toward them holding up the hand,
Half in appeal, but half as if to keep
The life from spilling. Then the boy saw all –
Since he was old enough to know, big boy
Doing a man's work, though a child at heart –
He saw all spoiled. 'Don't let him cut my hand off –
The doctor, when he comes. Don't let him, sister!'
So. But the hand was gone already.
The doctor put him in the dark of ether.
He lay and puffed his lips out with his breath.
And then – the watcher at his pulse took fright.
No one believed. They listened at his heart.
Little – less – nothing! – and that ended it.
No more to build on there. And they, since they
Were not the one dead, turned to their affairs.

As you have noticed these texts cover the same subject but in very different ways. Identify the differences. (Hints: What is the purpose of each text? Look at how the boy and the saw are described. Which text is more emotional and which is more factual? Refer closely to the texts using quotations to prove your points. What feeling or atmosphere is created by each text?)

Text E

Five Ways to Kill a Man – by Edwin Brock

There are many cumbersome ways to kill a man:
you can make him carry a plank of wood
to the top of a hill and nail him to it. To do this
properly you require a crowd of people
wearing sandals, a cock that crows, a cloak

to dissect, a sponge, some vinegar and one
man to hammer the nails home.

Or you can take a length of steel,
shaped and chased in a traditional way,
and attempt to pierce the metal cage he wears
But for this you need white horses,
English trees, men with bows and arrows,
at least two flags, a prince and
castle to hold your banquet in.

Dispensing with nobility, you may, if the wind
allows, blow gas at him. But then you need
a mile of mud sliced through with ditches,
not to mention black boots, bomb craters,
more mud, a plague of rats, a dozen songs
and some round hats made of steel.

In an age of aeroplanes, you may fly
miles above your victim and dispose of him by
pressing one small switch. All you then
require is an ocean to separate you, two
systems of government, a nation's scientists,
several factories, a psychopath and
land that no one needs for several years.

These are, as I began, cumbersome ways
to kill a man. Simpler, direct and much more neat
is to see that he is living somewhere in the middle
of the twentieth century, and leave him there.

Although this looks like a set of instructions, it is obviously not! Briefly describe what each verse is about, paying particular attention to the final verse. Is this text poetry? Justify your answer. It should help if you say how it is different from Text A.

Text F

Too Much Love

Marianne, Ian's mother, arrived just as I was pressing Ian's suit.
'Hallo, Angie,' she said, noting the jacket draped over the ironing board. 'Are you two going somewhere special?'
'No, I just like Ian's clothes to look nice, that's all,' I replied. She chuckled. 'Well, he didn't get attention like that when he lived at home, I can tell you! And what's that I can smell in the oven? Something delicious. You spoil that lad rotten, do you know that?'
I grinned back. 'Yes, and it's fun.' (Source: Walter Nash, 1990)

Where do you think Text F comes from? Do you think it could be classified as literature? Explain your answer.

Text G

***All There is to Know About Adolph Eichmann* – by Leonard Cohen**

EYES: .... Medium

HAIR: .... Medium

WEIGHT .... Medium

HEIGHT: .... Medium

DISTINGUISHING FEATURES: .... None

NUMBER OF FINGERS: .... Ten

NUMBER OF TOES: .... Ten

INTELLIGENCE: .... Medium

What did you expect?
Talons?
Oversize incisors?
Green saliva?
Madness?

Is Text G literature? Is it a poem? What do you
think its purpose is?

COMMENTARY You probably came up with comments like these.

Text A is a set of instructions for using an old-fashioned telephone. It tells
you how to do something and there is an expectation that you will follow
these instructions. It is written for someone who has recently acquired a
telephone. It is a straightforward text with no imagery or figurative use of
language. There is no emotional engagement. It is set out in lines each of
which begins with a capital letter. In fact, if you just glanced at it you
might think it was poetry. However, it is not considered literature.

You probably considered that **Text B** is a poem. It is set out in verses but it
does not rhyme. The telephone is described in an imaginative way both as
a person and a ghost. This text looks at an ordinary event from an original
perspective. A and B could both be said to look like poetry but only Text B
uses poetic techniques.

Both **Texts C** and **Text D** cover the tragic story of a boy who dies after his
hand has been injured in an accident with a saw. C (a newspaper report)
gives the precise information while D (a poem) gives an emotional account.
D also adds an extra dimension with the ideas expressed in the final two
lines. 'No more to build on there. And they, since they/Were not the one
dead, turned to their affairs.' In D the saw is described figuratively as a
hungry beast. Although we are given the name of the boy in text C, he
really only comes alive to us in D where we hear him speak. We hear the
emotion in his voice as he repeats, 'Don't let him . . .' The cold factual tone

of C is replaced with the regretful sad atmosphere of D. C would be considered non-literary.

In **Text E** you should have been able to identify the different methods of killing. You may have been uncomfortable if you found yourself smiling at some of the ideas. The final verse has a twist to it suggesting that in modern times we·do not have to do anything specific to kill people as we are naturally destroying ourselves. The text looks like poetry. It takes a well-established subject and looks at it from a new perspective, which makes us feel involved and also uncomfortable. There is no implication that we should actually use any of the instructions in the poem. Its purpose is not the same as Text A. Text E would be considered literature.

Text F might have been the most controversial of the texts presented here. As a short story from a women's magazine, you could argue that it doesn't count as literature on the grounds of quality.

Text G is an example of how literature can borrow from the language of any situation it likes; in this case the format of passport details. The subject matter is in fact far removed from its surface features.

ACTIVITY 4

Now study these extracts and, in the light of the commentary above, discuss whether you think these extracts are literature or not. The texts from which these extracts are taken are given at the end of the chapter.

Key skills: Communication – discussion

Text H

Imagine that men are from Mars and women are from Venus. One day long ago the Martians, looking through their telescopes, discovered the Venusians. Just glimpsing the Venusians awakened feelings they had never known. They fell in love and quickly invented space travel and flew to Venus.

The Venusians welcomed the Martians with open arms. They had intuitively known that this day would come. Their hearts opened wide to a love they had never felt before.

The love between the Venusians and Martians was magical. They delighted in being together, doing things together and sharing. Together, though from different worlds, they reveled in their differences. They spent months learning about each other, exploring and appreciating their different needs, preferences, and behavior patterns. For years they lived together in love and harmony.

Then they decided to fly to Earth. In the beginning everything was wonderful and beautiful. But the effects of Earth's atmosphere took hold, and one morning everyone woke up with a peculiar kind of *amnesia—selective amnesia!*

Both the Martians and the Venusians forgot they were from different planets and were supposed to be different. In one morning everything they had learned about their differences was erased from their memory. And since that day men and women have been in conflict.

Text I

That time of year thou mayst in me behold
When yellow leaves, or none, or few, do hang
Upon those boughs which shake against the cold,
Bare ruin'd choirs where late the sweet birds sang.
In me thou seest the twilight of such day
As after sunset fadeth in the west,
Which by and by black night doth take away,
Death's second self, that seals up all in rest.
In me thou seest the glowing of such fire
That on the ashes of his youth doth lie,
As the deathbed whereon it must expire,
Consum'd with that which it was nourished by.
This thou perceiv'st, which makes thy love more strong,
To love that well that thou must leave ere long.

Text J

I was set down from the carrier's cart at the age of three; and there with a sense of bewilderment and terror my life in the village began.

The June grass, amongst which I stood, was taller than I was, and I wept. I had never been so close to grass before. It towered above me and all around me, each blade tattooed with tiger-skins of sunlight. It was knife-edged, dark and wicked green, thick as a forest and alive with grasshoppers that chirped and chattered and leapt through the air like monkeys.

I was lost and didn't know where to move. A tropic heat oozed up from the ground, rank with sharp odours of roots and nettles. Snowclouds of elder-blossom banked in the sky, showering upon me the fumes and flakes of their sweet and giddy suffocation. High overhead ran frenzied larks, screaming, as though the sky were tearing apart.

For the first time in my life I was out of the sight of humans. For the first time in my life I was alone in a world whose behaviour I could neither predict nor fathom: a world of birds that squealed, of plants that stank, of insects that sprang about without warning. I was lost and I did not expect to be found again. I put back my head and howled, and the sun hit me smartly on the face, like a bully.

From this daylight nightmare I was awakened, as from many another, by the appearance of my sisters. They came scrambling and calling up the steep rough bank, and parting the long grass found me. Faces of rose, familiar, living; huge shining faces hung up like shields between me and the sky; faces with grins and white teeth (some broken) to be conjured up like genii with a howl, brushing off terror with their broad scoldings and affection. They leaned over me – one, two, three, their mouths smeared with red currants and their hands dripping with juice.

Text K

Strategically, the Battle of the Somme was an unredeemed defeat. It is supposed to have worn down the spirit of the German army. So no doubt it did, though not to the point of crippling that army as a fighting machine. The German spirit was not the only one to suffer. The British were worn down also. Idealism perished on the Somme. The enthusiastic volunteers were enthusiastic no longer. They had lost faith in their cause, in their leaders, in everything except loyalty to their fighting comrades. The war ceased to have a purpose. It went on for its own sake, as a contest of endurance. Rupert Brooke had symbolized the British soldier at the beginning of the war. Now his place was taken by Old Bill, a veteran of 1915, who crouched in a shell crater for want of 'a better 'ole to go to'. The Somme set the picture by which future generations saw the First World War; brave helpless soldiers; blundering obstinate generals; nothing achieved. After the Somme men decided that the war would go on forever.

ACTIVITY 5

Using the preceding activity as a basis, make a list of possible criteria for literature and be prepared to justify your answers.

Compare your criteria with the ones suggested in the table below. Then as a research activity try to complete the chart by putting evidence against each criterion in the left-hand column, and evidence for each criterion in the right-hand column. Evidence is likely to be texts that obviously do or do not count as literature. Some suggestions have already been made using the texts in this chapter. You can use texts with which you are familiar, as well as the ones you have encountered in this chapter.

Evidence against	Criteria for literature	Evidence for
	It provides an unusual perspective	*A Martian Sends a Postcard Home* (Text B)
	It has to reach certain quality standards	
	Decided by powerful people (academics, critics, etc)	The Booker Prize
	It has to educate in some way	
	It has to put the reader through some kind of experience	
Newspaper reports use metaphor	It contains special use of language, e.g. metaphor	
	It does not make people do things in the real world	
	It uses special conventions of layout	
Too Much Love (Text F)	Anything can be read as literature	
	It must be about a 'serious' topic	
	It involves the imagination	

This chapter has outlined what is entailed in the AS and A level specifications for English Literature, giving an overview of the relationship between these exams and GCSE English. It has explained the part played by Key skills in the examination system and in this book. The central idea of the book – context – is explained, and divided into 'context of writing' and 'context of reading', which influence the whole organisation of the book. Finally, there was a chance to consider the question: 'What is literature?'.

Answers to Activity 1

1C 2A 3B 4G 5D 6J 7E 8I 9F 10K 11L 12H

Texts used in Activity 4

Text H: *Men are from Mars, Women are from Venus* – John Gray
Text I: *Sonnet 73*, Shakespeare
Text J: *Cider with Rosie* – Laurie Lee's autobiography
Text K: *A History of Europe* – H.A.L. Fisher

2 Ways into Texts

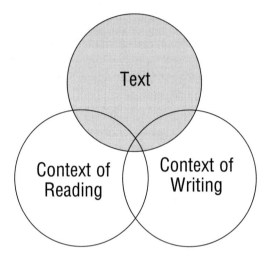

This chapter is an introduction to the study of literary texts and, as such, it relates to all of the Assessment Objectives. The main aim here is to suggest techniques for study that will enable to you to make your own judgements about the texts you are reading (Assessment Objective 4).

This section looks at practical ways of getting into texts of various kinds. By texts we mean novels, short stories, poems and plays. These are methods that can be used independently by you but might also be used by a teacher to help you with particular work. So why read texts in different ways? Common sense tells us that there is only one way to read a text – from start to finish – but this is far from true. Alternative methods of reading can open up new ways of perceiving texts. In particular, you shouldn't think of texts as fixed things that cannot be changed. Texts change all the time – in a sense, they change every time they are read by a new reader because that reader brings something new to the text, new experiences and new ideas. For example, you might tend to think of Shakespeare's works as fixed for all time but even these have changed in several ways over the years:

■ they were originally written down in various forms because actors pirated their own versions of the plays in order to perform them in rival theatres

- every time a play is produced directors decide to omit certain lines. For example, some productions of *The Merchant of Venice* that try to be sympathetic towards the Jewish money-lender, Shylock, miss out some of his most damning lines
- some words were changed to get around censorship laws in the 17th century
- the endings of some plays have been changed in times when Shakespeare's endings were thought to be too bleak. This happened to *King Lear* in Nahum Tate's 17th century version – which ends with a marriage and not quite so much death!

The conclusion you should draw from this is that texts don't have to be treated with that much respect. That doesn't mean that you can go around changing the endings of Shakespeare's plays because you don't like them, but it does mean that you should actively 'play' with texts in various ways in order to get into them.

In alphabetical order, here are some suggested ways into texts:

Asking questions

This is a very basic method that can be applied to any kind of text. As you read a text for the first, second or third time, write down questions in the margin. Here are one student's questions on *Out Out –* (see page 14):

ACTIVITY 6

Categorise these questions into types by examining what each one has in common. For example, one category might be that some of the questions are about the meanings of specific words. How many types of question are there?

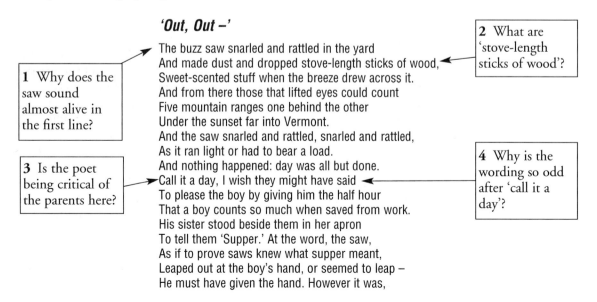

'Out, Out –'

The buzz saw snarled and rattled in the yard
And made dust and dropped stove-length sticks of wood,
Sweet-scented stuff when the breeze drew across it.
And from there those that lifted eyes could count
Five mountain ranges one behind the other
Under the sunset far into Vermont.
And the saw snarled and rattled, snarled and rattled,
As it ran light or had to bear a load.
And nothing happened: day was all but done.
Call it a day, I wish they might have said
To please the boy by giving him the half hour
That a boy counts so much when saved from work.
His sister stood beside them in her apron
To tell them 'Supper.' At the word, the saw,
As if to prove saws knew what supper meant,
Leaped out at the boy's hand, or seemed to leap –
He must have given the hand. However it was,

1 Why does the saw sound almost alive in the first line?

2 What are 'stove-length sticks of wood'?

3 Is the poet being critical of the parents here?

4 Why is the wording so odd after 'call it a day'?

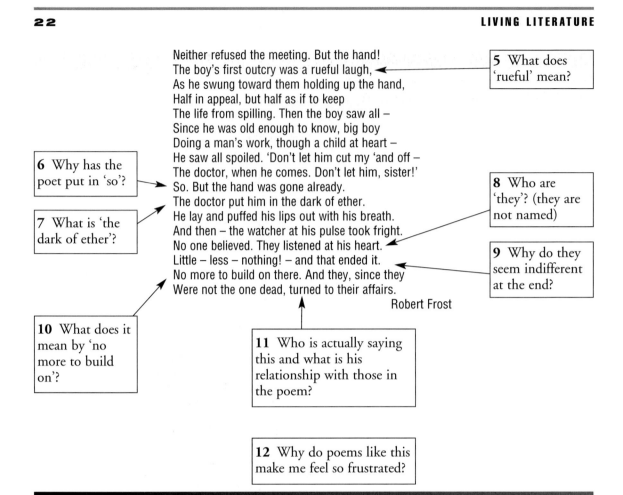

Neither refused the meeting. But the hand!
The boy's first outcry was a rueful laugh,
As he swung toward them holding up the hand,
Half in appeal, but half as if to keep
The life from spilling. Then the boy saw all –
Since he was old enough to know, big boy
Doing a man's work, though a child at heart –
He saw all spoiled. 'Don't let him cut my 'and off –
The doctor, when he comes. Don't let him, sister!'
So. But the hand was gone already.
The doctor put him in the dark of ether.
He lay and puffed his lips out with his breath.
And then – the watcher at his pulse took fright.
No one believed. They listened at his heart.
Little – less – nothing! – and that ended it.
No more to build on there. And they, since they
Were not the one dead, turned to their affairs.

Robert Frost

5 What does 'rueful' mean?

6 Why has the poet put in 'so'?

7 What is 'the dark of ether'?

8 Who are 'they'? (they are not named)

9 Why do they seem indifferent at the end?

10 What does it mean by 'no more to build on'?

11 Who is actually saying this and what is his relationship with those in the poem?

12 Why do poems like this make me feel so frustrated?

COMMENTARY Questions 2, 5 and 7 are simply about reference; that is, the student simply wants to know what these words refer to. Some of the questions seem to be about the effect the poem is having on the reader. Question 1 means that the reader has noticed the metaphor ('snarled') that compares the saw with an animal; he/she should now go on to find out if this is followed up elsewhere in the poem. Another 'effect' question is question 4, but the student should not regard the 'oddness' as a problem but rather as something to be explained in relation to what is happening in the poem at that moment. Another category of question is 'language': the student has clearly noticed the strangeness of the words 'build on' and the pronoun 'they' – the poet never tells us who they are. Question 11 is about the 'voice' represented in the poem – an important category. Finally, the last question is about the reader's own feelings in relation to the poem. It is important to address those feelings directly. Overall there is quite a range of questions although there will be other kinds and you should practise expanding your repertoire to make the most of your response.

ACTIVITY 7

Write your own questions in response to the
poem below. These can then be developed in
later activities.

The Wheel

[In Tobago, in the West Indies, a gigantic iron wheel, now reclaimed by nature, is
almost all that remains of what was once a sugar mill]

A wheel
of absurd dimensions
A thing of dire consequences
cane rust caked and molassed
lies in the rut where the tributaries
of history flowed
When all the rivulets merged
it should have vanished
with the evening
melted back into the past
It stood silhouetted against the sky
drawing in the pain and suffering
began to turn
revolving knowledge of how it was
Pressure building up inside my head
forced its own path
Steam hissed through the channels
pierced for escape
The night noises came too soon
bringing with them sounds so different
from the ones I thought to hear
The wheel
Vibrates as all
Who knew their place in life
Are pulled towards this field
magnetic hold
Emancipated souls hang
Grimly hub to rim
Locked in a web
of fate
Equal now and free
planters and slaves
fight to control
their circle of destiny
Their only claim of space
in time
Possession
of
the wheel

Amryl Johnson

Colour coding of semantic fields

Semantic fields are, roughly speaking, topic areas of related words such as 'knife', 'fork', 'spoon' etc. They are also known as 'lexical fields'. This technique is good for poems that seem dense and difficult to untangle. It involves searching for words and phrases that are linked by topic (as in – spade, fork, digging, etc) or by use (e.g. slang) and then working out how the topics are connected. You might begin by noticing one or two words in a semantic field and you then systematically search for more, colour coding each field. For example, in William Blake's *The Tyger* you might look for parts of body, light/dark, or references to animals. The fields that you find in a poem can often lead to the right kinds of question about the underlying influences on the poem and the poet. This technique is applied to the beginning of a novel on page 105.

ACTIVITY 8

The words below all come from Coleridge's poem *Kubla Khan*.

1 Colour code the semantic fields
2 Sub-divide them into further semantic fields. e.g. why might you put together 'sacred river' and 'fertile ground'?

3 Without looking at the poem, make some predictions about it and its underlying ideas.
4 Get hold of a copy of the poem to test your ideas, taking into account any further semantic fields that may emerge.

sacred river	deep romantic chasm
caverns	green hill
sunless sea	cedarn
fertile ground	waning moon
gardens bright	this chasm
incense-bearing tree	this rebounding hail
forests	chaffy grain
the hills	dancing rocks
greenery	sacred river
wood and dale	caves of ice
the sacred river	air
the caverns	caves of ice
lifeless ocean	honey-dew
the waves	milk of Paradise
the caves	

ACTIVITY 9

Colour code the semantic fields in *The Wheel* (above) and move towards an interpretation of the poem. How easy was it to do this and what problems did you encounter? How do the problems help us to interpret the poem?

Computer manipulation

Take a poem and type it out onto a computer screen. This works well if the poem is firstly seen as a piece of prose. Then begin to change the layout and typography of the poem to show what it means to you. This means that you can show similarities between parts of the poem, how the poem should be read aloud (in terms of volume, pitch, pauses, etc), important words, the feel of the words, and so forth. Features that you can use are: size of print; upper or lower case; underlining; spatial arrangement of words; font style; word art; etc.

Thaw by Edward Thomas

Here is the poem set out as prose:

Over the land freckled with snow half-thawed the speculating rooks at their nests cawed and saw from elm-tops, delicate as flower of grass, what we below could not see, Winter pass.

Manipulated poem

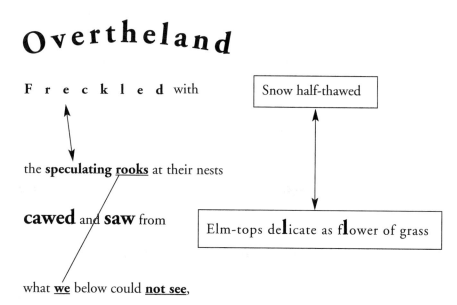

[With acknowledgement to Andrew Stibbs.]

ACTIVITY 10

Read the above manipulated poem and explain
why the writer has set it out as he has.

COMMENTARY   The first three words are joined together, 'arched' and spread out to give
the sense of a panorama. In a similar way 'freckled' implies the marks
spread out over the land. The link with 'speculating' is pointed out because
it is the rooks who can see that it is freckled – this is something that is
echoed in the repetition of the –'eck' sound. 'Snow half-thawed' and
'Elm-tops delicate as flower of grass' are linked as units because of their
similar grammatical structure. They are both noun phrases with the noun
at the beginning ('snow' and 'elm tops') followed by descriptive phrases
('half-thawed' and 'delicate . . .') The 'l's in the latter are enlarged because
they help to create the sense of delicacy implied by those lines. Moving to
the end, the larger space before 'winter pass' suggests a pause before these
significant words. The words themselves get smaller to imply the gradual
passing of winter which isn't as sudden as those two short words suggest.

ACTIVITY 11

Create your own manipulated poem using
either *Thaw* or a poem of your choice.

Key skills: IT – present information

Considering alternatives

This is a powerful method of approaching any piece of literature. Try
rewriting parts of a poem and observe the difference. It is probably a good
idea to do this physically rather than just in your head. Type out the poem
with the alternative words put in. For example, the beginning of
Shakespeare's famous sonnet becomes:

'Shall I draw a parallel between yourself and twenty-four hours during the hot season?'

("Shall I compare thee to a summer's day?")

This sounds like a recipe for creating a parody of the original but it can
draw your attention to: rhythm (see page 181); the poet's choice of
individual word – look closely at the connotations of the word the poet has
chosen (see page 105); for example, in *Thaw* above, what does 'freckled'
suggest that 'speckled' or 'spotted' don't, and how does it fit in better with
the other words in the poem? Here, 'freckled' has the living quality of
'speckled' but it is softer, creating alliteration with 'half-thawed' and
suggestive of the softness of snow.

A challenge that can extend this idea is to try changing as many of the
words in the poem as possible whilst keeping the 'meaning' the same.
Ignore grammatical words such as 'the' and 'so', etc. – concentrate on the
main content-carrying words. The technique works best with poetry, where
choice of vocabulary, rhythm and other sound qualities are all crucial, but
it can also be used with prose.

ACTIVITY 12

The poem below has been paraphrased using a thesaurus. Decide which of the two versions is the original and then explain what the paraphrase loses in each line and overall. The answer can be found at the end of the chapter.

Daniel 1

Bubbling with talk
And a fourteen-year old's
Anxious confidence,
you fend off the grim line
of your father's tight lip
and the advancing tide-mark of evidence
assembled by polite firemen
in your parents'
burned, pink bedroom.

Daniel 2

Boiling with speech
And a teenager's
Apprehensive conviction
you reject the unyielding line
of your father's firm edge of mouth
and the stains of signs
Put together by nice fire-fighters
In your father and mother's
Scorched off-red sleeping quarters.

Martin Turner

ACTIVITY 13

Do the same as the above with a poem of your own choice. It is best to choose a poem that is well within your grasp and it will help to use a thesaurus. Try giving the poem and its original to friends – can they distinguish the original from the new 'poem'?

Counting things

This sounds ridiculous and against the spirit of literature, but a great deal can be achieved by simply counting the number of times something occurs in a piece of writing. It is often the starting point for more significant thinking about the text. The stylistic approach in Chapter 6, where you look at specific linguistic features, is the most likely context for using this method. You might, for example, count the number of times adjectives or nouns are used in order to say something about the writer's style. In a play you can count the kinds of things said by each character. Who asks the questions? Are answers given? Who gives the orders? And so forth. If a feature is used a lot, it's probably important. If it's not used at all, it may also be important. This last statement may sound rather strange but it's just as important to find out what the author left out as to count what he or she put in.

In the following short short story, look closely at the dialogue. What each character says is called an utterance. Consider the following kinds of utterance: statements, questions, answers, advice. Count who says what kind of utterance and explain how this helps to build up to the story's climax. (This method can also be used with plays.)

Bedtime Story

'Careful, honey, it's loaded,'
he said, re-entering the bedroom.
Her back rested against the
headboard. 'This for your wife?'
'No. Too chancy. I'm hiring a
professional.'
'How about me?'
He smirked. 'Cute. But who'd
be dumb enough to hire a lady
hit man?'
She wet her lips, sighting along
the barrel.
'Your wife.'

[Jeffrey Whitmore, in *The World's Shortest Stories*, Ed Steve Moss]

Deletion

This technique can be used in at least two ways:

1 Using the technique known as cloze procedure, some words are deleted from a text and the reader has to work out what they are. Working in pairs you could devise a cloze on the same text for each other. The real advantage here is that the reader goes through something like the same process as the writer in making word choices. There is an example of a cloze activity on page 105.

2 Try taking it in turns to delete words from a poem (or story) that you think are unimportant.
   In *Thaw* on page 25, for example, you might consider deleting 'the' and 'and' first. There are many possible variations on this, for example, convert to haiku. A haiku is a three line Japanese poem with five syllables in the first line, seven syllables in the second line and five syllables in the third line. *Thaw* might look like this:

> High in elm-nests, rooks
> Saw what we below could not –
> Snow melt; winter pass

> (Andrew Stibbs)

The point of this is that a poem or short story could be reduced to its bare essentials. This would then allow different readings to be compared.

De-lineation/re-lineation

This involves taking poetry out of its layout and presenting it like prose – see *Thaw* on page 25. With a partner you can swap poems to be put back into some kind of shape which must then be justified. 'Finding' the poem's original shape is not the point but it does make for an interesting comparison once you have created your own poem. This idea is explored further on page 38.

Diagramming

This technique is not the same as computer manipulation. It involves looking at a section of a novel, play, etc. and converting an idea in the text into diagrammatic form. Here are some suggestions for diagrams:

- Time line – this is particularly effective when the text does not deal with events in chronological order. The purpose of the time line is to show the chronological order of events and how the author manipulates it. The first act of Tennessee Williams' play *Cat on a Hot Tin Roof* works well. See page 30.
- Various graphs showing changes over time – this applies particularly well to novels. One axis of the graph is 'time', the other might be 'how a character's fortunes go up or down' or 'how a character's courage changes.' The graph is best accompanied by a commentary explaining and justifying its content. The example on page 31 shows how one student responded to the task of producing a graph based on Emily Brontë's *Wuthering Heights*. The vertical axis shows 'degree of sympathy for Heathcliff' when he first arrives at Wuthering Heights. The student's commentary is reproduced after the diagram on page 32.
- Sociograms – these are diagrams that show the relationships between characters by means of circles to represent characters and the distance between them to represent the closeness of their relationship.
- Schematic maps – these can be used when places are important. They can help to reveal the symbolic significance of the places used in the story. This technique would lend itself well to Thomas Hardy's novels. Or, for example, in *Wuthering Heights*, where the action centres around two houses, the novel's movement between them (noting events and their symbolic significance) can be mapped onto two columns representing the two houses. In E.M. Forster's *A Passage to India*, a novel about the English in India at the beginning of the 20th century, you can consider the different houses belonging to characters of various religions, as well as the different geographical locations. The big advantage of schematic maps is that they allow you to see an overall pattern spanning a great deal of text – they are especially useful when studying novels.

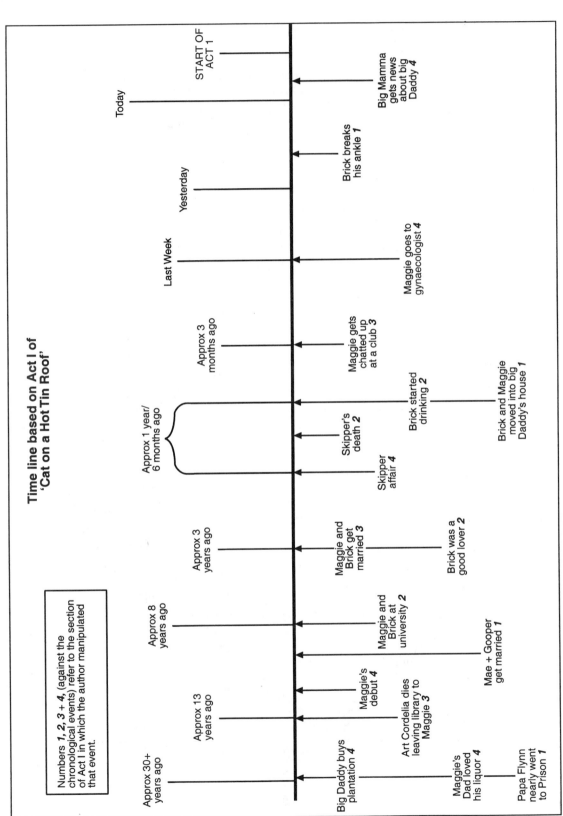

Time line based on Act I of 'Cat on a Hot Tin Roof'

Numbers *1*, *2*, *3* + *4*, (against the chronological events) refer to the section of Act I in which the author manipulated that event.

START OF ACT 1

Big Mamma gets news about big Daddy *4*

Today

Brick breaks his ankle *1*

Yesterday

Last Week — Maggie goes to gynaecologist *4*

Approx 3 months ago — Maggie gets chatted up at a club *3*

Approx 1 year/ 6 months ago
- Brick started drinking *2*
- Skipper's death *2*
- Skipper affair *4*
- Brick and Maggie moved into big Daddy's house *1*

Approx 3 years ago — Maggie and Brick get married *3*

Brick was a good lover *2*

Approx 8 years ago — Maggie and Brick at university *2*

Mae + Gooper get married *1*

Maggie's debut *4*

Approx 13 years ago — Art Cordelia dies leaving library to Maggie *3*

Big Daddy buys plantation *4*

Approx 30+ years ago

Maggie's Dad loved his liquor *4*

Papa Flynn nearly went to Prison *1*

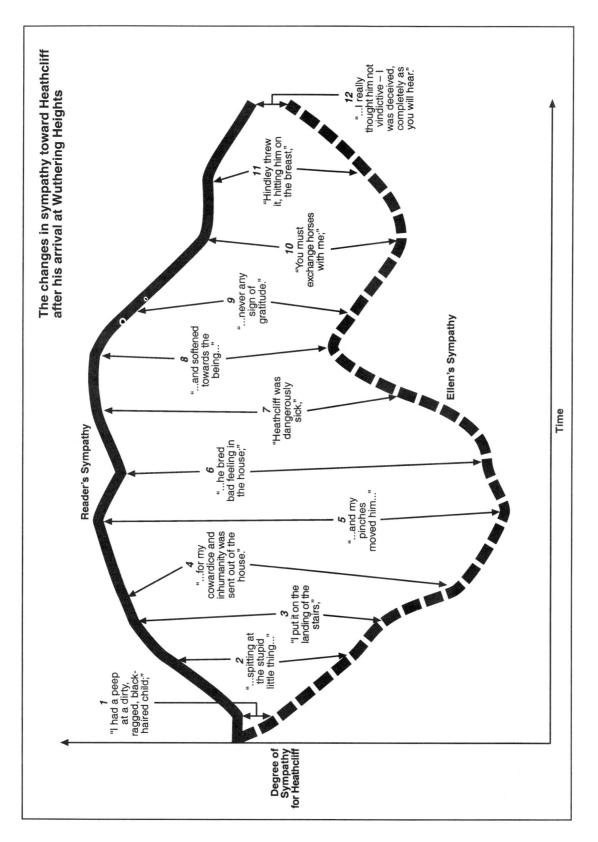

The changes in sympathy toward Heathcliff after his arrival at Wuthering Heights

Degree of Sympathy for Heathcliff

Time

Reader's Sympathy

Ellen's Sympathy

1 "I had a peep at a dirty, ragged, black-haired child;"

2 "...spitting at the stupid little thing...."

3 "I put it on the landing of the stairs,"

4 "...for my cowardice and inhumanity was sent out of the house."

5 "...and my pinches moved him..."

6 "...he bred bad feeling in the house;"

7 "Heathcliff was dangerously sick,"

8 "...and softened towards the being,..."

9 "...never any sign of gratitude."

10 "You must exchange horses with me,"

11 "Hindley threw it, hitting him on the breast,"

12 "...I really thought him not vindictive – I was deceived, completely as you will hear."

The story so far: Heathcliff has been adopted by Earnshaw as a young boy and has just arrived at Wuthering Heights. Hindley is Earnshaw's son (who immediately comes into conflict with Heathcliff) and Ellen appears as both the narrator and her younger self in the story – she is the housekeeper at Wuthering Heights.

Student commentary

After the arrival of Heathcliff at Wuthering Heights there are two different areas of sympathy towards him. These are the sympathy of Ellen, the narrator at the time, and the reader's sympathy about the same incidents. There are also areas where the sympathy of Ellen at the time of telling Lockwood the story, is obviously different from her actual sympathy at the time. However, because she already knows the entire story she has a fixed level of sympathy for Heathcliff. Therefore there is no record of this on the graph.

After the initial arrival of Heathcliff at Wuthering Heights, Ellen's level of sympathy decreases (**quotes *1–3***). She treats him badly, does not show any kindness. Heathcliff is referred to as 'it' by Ellen for a large section of this early segment of Heathcliff's life at Wuthering Heights (**quote *3***). The effect on the reader is likely to be sympathetic to him. On the graph therefore, any drops in sympathy during this early section on Ellen's part are mirrored by an increase in sympathy in the reader (**quotes *1–5***).

This continues into the section where Ellen is sent from the house (**quote *4***). Obviously the older, narrating Ellen understands her wrong-doings and is more sympathetic to Heathcliff than she was at the time. After this section, the young Ellen's sympathy drops to its lowest levels, reflected by the sympathy in the reader being one of its highest levels (**quote *5***).

The emotionless nature of Heathcliff has effects on the reader's sympathy mostly. The fact that he does not react to Hindley's blows or Ellen's pinches increases the reader's sympathy towards Heathcliff. However, the fact that Heathcliff never showed any gratitude to Earnshaw (**quote *9***) means that he is no longer treated with the same sympathy. The reader suspects he is not as innocent as they thought.

This idea is confirmed when Heathcliff demands to change horses (**quote *10***). The reader is now certain of his evil side. This is strengthened further when Ellen reveals that she was deceived by Heathcliff (**quote *12***).

ACTIVITY 15

Create a graph for a text or part of a text that you know well and write a commentary explaining it.

Key skills: Communication – writing

Empathic response/using creativity to get into texts

ACTIVITY 16

1 **Writing a parody**. For example, write a modern day parody of Wordsworth's *Upon Westminster Bridge*, suggesting for a 21st century audience that London isn't what it used to be. You could begin your poem with Wordsworth's line:

'Earth has not anything to show more fair'

Here is what one parodist did with Hamlet's famous soliloquy:

Toothache

To be, or not to be: that is the question:	To have it out or not? That is the question
Whether 'tis nobler in the mind to suffer	Whether 'tis better for the jaws to suffer
The slings and arrows of outrageous fortune,	The pangs and torments of an aching tooth,
Or to take arms against a sea of troubles,	Or to take steel against a host of troubles,
And by opposing end them? To die: to sleep;	And, by extracting, end them? To pull – to tug!
No more; and, by a sleep to say we end	No more: and by a tug to say we end
The heart-ache and the thousand natural shocks	The tooth-ache, and a thousand natural ills
That flesh is heir to, 'tis a consummation	The jaw is heir to. 'Tis a consummation
Devoutly to be wish'd. To die, to sleep;	Devoutly to be wished! To pull – to tug! –
To sleep: perchance to dream: ay, there's the rub;	To tug – perchance to break! Ay, there's the rub,
For in that sleep of death what dreams may come	For in that wrench what agonies may come,
When we have shuffled off this mortal coil,	When we have half-dislodged the stubborn foe,
Must give us pause.	Must give us pause.

(Anonymous)

ACTIVITY 17

- Examine the original and the parody above. List the features that the parodist attempts to imitate and draw a spider diagram advising how to write a parody.

- Attempt a parody of a piece of writing you are studying (or of this soliloquy) using the findings from the task above. Remember that a ridiculous subject often works well. Note that even if you are not too successful, what really helps is the close reading you have to do in making the attempt.

- Discuss with a partner why we find *Toothache* funny and what this has to do with the context in which a passage appears.

2 **Writing a creative extension**. For example: a scene or chapter from another character's point of view; writing a scene or chapter only mentioned or summarised in the original; rewriting in the style of a different author. There is an example of this technique on page 59.

Key skills: Communication – writing

Focus on a key word or line

This works better with some poems than with others. As readers, there is a tendency to focus on content words (words that carry significant images or ideas) such as 'days' or 'time' in the poem below. But a new train of thought about a poem can be opened up when an unusual or seemingly insignificant word is brought into focus. As you read Philip Larkin's poem *Days* below, consider what you think is the most significant word and justify your answer.

Days

What are days for?
Days are where we live.
They come, they wake us
Time and time over.
They are to be happy in:
Where can we live but days?

Ah, solving that question
Brings the priest and the doctor
In their long coats
Running over the fields.

Philip Larkin

Most readers tend to overlook the word 'ah' as just a filler before the important business of answering the question at the end of the first stanza. But if it becomes the focus of attention, the reader is forced to answer new questions such as: What is the purpose of 'ah'? How exactly is it meant to be read? The second of these leads to another kind of activity with dramatic potential:

ACTIVITY 18

Consider the following meanings of the word 'ah': *I've found the solution/surprise/oh dear/interest/disappointment/resignation/relief/won der/I'm going to tell you/I'm pleased about it.* With a partner devise short dramatic improvisations in order to illustrate each meaning and practise the intonation you will use for each one. Then choose the meaning which you think best fits the poem and read it aloud. Justify your reading of 'ah' with reference to the rest of the poem.

Key skills: Communication – discussion

ACTIVITY 19

With the rest of your group agree on a poem and find what you believe to be the most important word or line. Explore the meaning of this word using dramatic improvisation.

Label each stanza/paragraph using one word

Ask yourself how you would sum up each stanza in one word (or one sentence if you wish). This forces you to make generalisations about each stanza with respect to the whole poem. The technique can also raise interesting questions about the structure of a poem. For example, Lewis Carroll's *Jabberwocky* (which begins ' 'Twas brillig, and the slithy toves') has the following structure: stability, warning, the quest, the battle, the victory, celebration, stability. This works particularly well with ballads – poems that tell a story.

ACTIVITY 20

The poem on page 101, *Your Dad Did What?* can be broken down using the labels in the table below. Two possibilities are given.

Discuss which words best sum up each verse and justify your answers. You may wish to substitute your own words.

Key skills: Communication – discussion

Verse 1	task	problem
Verse 2	reaction	routine
Verse 3	confusion	frustration
Verse 4	solution	guilt

ACTIVITY 21

Read the following short story – a kind of mini-myth. Divide it into sections and label each one using (a) one word or (b) a sentence.

Death Speaks

There was a merchant in Baghdad who sent his servant to market to buy provisions and in a little while the servant came back, white and trembling, and said, 'Master, just now when I was in the market place I was jostled by a woman in the crowd and when I turned I saw that it was Death that jostled me. She looked at me and made a threatening gesture; now, lend me your horse, and I will ride away from this city and avoid Death. I will go to Samarra and there Death will not find me. Then the merchant went down to the market place and he saw me standing in the crowd and he came to me and said, 'Why did you make a threatening gesture to my servant when you saw him this morning?'

'This was not a threatening gesture,' I said, 'it was only a start of surprise. I was astonished to see him in Baghdad, for I had an appointment with him tonight in Samarra.

This method prepares for a structuralist approach to literature – see page 91.

Reading as drafting

This is not so much a method of reading as an attitude. In the last decade or so students of A level literature have become used to drafting and redrafting their writing for coursework assignments. The idea of reading as drafting has been slower to take off. How often are you asked for an opinion on a text and how often do you reply, 'But it's only my first draft'? Just as writing should take more than one draft to get the way you want it, so should reading.

Reading in slow motion

This sounds laborious and against the spirit of literature but, in fact, if you cover up the rest of the poem or story whilst exposing it line by line, you are forced into focusing very closely only on what appears in front of you. This method also reveals the process of reading, showing that your reading will change and develop as you expose more text. Taken to an extreme, this technique can involve revealing a text word by word, which can also force you into predicting what will come next. This will in turn make you ask questions about a writer's use of grammar and the extent to which conventional grammatical patterns are broken for effect (see pages 107–110 for grammar). The following example illustrates how reading in slow motion works.

ACTIVITY 22

Re-read *Bedtime Story* on page 28 in slow motion, jotting down comments on what is implied by each word (or group of words) as you come to it. Here is a start. Notice that as this is a second reading you can 'think forward' to later implications.

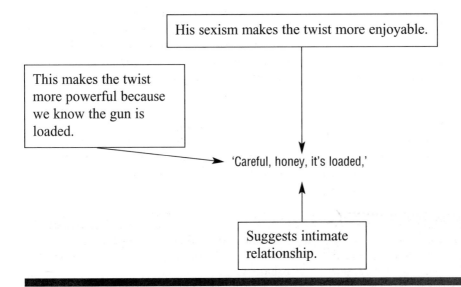

His sexism makes the twist more enjoyable.

This makes the twist more powerful because we know the gun is loaded.

'Careful, honey, it's loaded,'

Suggests intimate relationship.

Response diary

In the case of a novel, this can involve writing an honest diary style piece as you go along or at the end of each chapter. This is a less demanding task with short stories or poems. Here is an example of this kind of writing in response to Charles Dickens' novel *Bleak House*. It doesn't matter if you don't know the novel. What we are interested in here is the technique of responding in diary form.

My overall reaction to Esther is confused, and even seems to encompass a variety of emotions. Much of what Esther does I consider to be game playing. I am disturbed myself when I as well as others resort to this. I also find myself making excuses for Esther's behaviour, yet as the novel progresses, I find these excuses wearing thin. I feel as if I should be sympathetic to Esther throughout the novel as I was at the beginning, but instead I find my tolerance for her behaviour vanishing. I do not consider her a very interesting character and sometimes wish that she would do something daring. Yet I feel so guilty that I am so annoyed with her.

I was happy for Esther when she was at Greenleaf, because she seemed to be happy, well liked, and accepted. However, shortly after that point, my impatience started growing. I became royally sick and tired of her letting me know how nice everyone was to her and how well liked she was. She seemed to do this under the guise of trying to make other characters look kind and charitable, but from my own experiences I have found that people describe the kindness of others in at least two ways: 1) 'They were so kind.' 2) 'They were so kind to me.' Those who use the second expression are trying to praise themselves by using someone else's kindness as an excuse to do this. This is where I have a problem with Esther. It seems as if she talks about how kind other people are to her with the ulterior and overriding desire to let me know how wonderful she really is. I am irritated and annoyed with this behaviour and consider it to be a kind of game. I don't like to see it in my friends or in myself. It is almost an insult to the listener's intelligence. (in *Stories of Reading (Subjectivity and Literary Understanding)* David Bleich, Johns Hopkins, 1989, page 72)

The advantage of using the diary method is that you can acknowledge the part played by your personal experiences in forming your response. The danger here is that you allow your personal experiences too much prominence in your final response to the work. It is therefore important to remember that your initial diary forms the foundation for a more informed response. The essay that you produce may not bear much direct evidence of the diary that informed it. Response diaries are favoured by critics who believe in a reader response approach (see page 82). For AS and A level purposes it is important to remember that personal response should be informed by both the text and academic study and, when appropriate, by the context of writing and the context of reading. This could mean, for example, that you test out the ideas of a particular critic on a chapter or poem as you read. Or that you respond from the point of view of a woman reader or a reader from the 18th century. The key phrase is clearly 'informed personal response'.

ACTIVITY 23

Does the above response use both the text itself and the reader's personal experience? Re-read the response underlining sections that refer to text and sections that refer to personal experience. Do you think this reader has got the balance right?

Sequencing

In pairs, one person photocopies a poem or short story and chops it up in one of several ways:

- line by line (this works well with *He Wishes for Cloths of Heaven* William Yeats)
- by stanza (*Five Ways to Kill a Man* Edwin Brock see page 14)
- word by word (*Days* Philip Larkin see page 34).

The other person must then re-assemble the pieces to make a poem and justify what they have done. You can practise using this technique at the beginning of Chapter 6 on page 97.

Summaries

Writing a summary of any kind of text used to be standard practice. It then came to be frowned upon by many because it does not encourage much engagement with the text on the part of the reader. However, in recent years it has been resurrected as a way of highlighting what different readers share about a text. Working with a partner, summarise a text separately in an agreed number of words or sentences. Short stories or poems can often be summarised in about three lines. Novels may take a few more words.

There are two distinct ways of using this technique:

1 Summarise the action of the story in a statement that begins: 'This is the story of ...'
2 Summarise the point of a story in a statement that begins: 'This story is about ...'

Here are two examples of 2 applied to *The Visitor*, a short story by Elizabeth Bowen:

'It's about a boy whose life has been disturbed by the imminent death of his mother. At the end he remains trapped by his idealised image of his mother.'

'It's about a boy growing up through the Oedipal phase (he loves his mother and hates his father). At the end his problem is resolved through his acceptance of his mother's death.'

The differences between these two summaries will lead you back into the text and to a discussion of the differences. For example, what is the evidence that his problem is resolved at the end or that he remains trapped?

ACTIVITY 24

Apply the summarising method to *Pattern* (page 71) or another story of your choice.

Voicing the unspoken

Many literary texts work by somehow limiting what you the reader (or other characters) are allowed to see or experience. Consider, for example, all of the things that are unspoken in the short story *Bedtime Story* on page 28 – the man's smug lack of awareness of what is about to happen, the woman's conscious teasing of the man, etc. Filling out what is unspoken in a particular way can be a useful way in. Here are some possibilities:

■ writing down what the characters are really thinking (rather than saying)
■ considering what other characters are thinking about a character
■ what the reader is supposed to be thinking
■ what the characters do not know at a particular point.

ACTIVITY 25

Alan Bennett's monologues *Talking Heads* feature characters talking to an audience or a camera. What the audience comes to understand about the characters works largely through the limitation of the point of view. The audience quickly comes to understand things about the character that they themselves don't. Here, in *Her Big Chance*, Lesley is a small part actress who takes a part in a low grade porn film. She is unaware that this is all she is. In fact she believes she is a star and tries to behave as if this were true.

In the extract below, concentrate on what the reader is supposed to be thinking. What features reveal that Lesley is not what she thinks she is? What aspects of her language are important in this respect? What is Spud thinking during this episode and what enables the reader to see what she cannot? Read the passage several times.

Key skills: Communication – reading

'The parts I get offered tend to be fun-loving girls who take life as it comes and aren't afraid of a good time should the opportunity arise type-thing. I'd call them vivacious if that didn't carry overtones of the outdoor life. In a nutshell I play the kind of girl who's very much at home on a bar stool and who seldom has to light her own cigarette. That couldn't be more different from me because for a start I'm not a smoker. I mean, I can smoke if a part requires it. I'm a professional and you need as many strings to your bow as you can in this game. But, having said that, I'm not a natural smoker and what's more I surprise my friends by not being much of a party-goer either. (Rather curl up with a book quite frankly.) However, this particular party I'd made an exception. Thing was I'd met this ex-graphic designer who was quitting the rat race and going off to Zimbabwe and he was having a little farewell do in the flat of an air hostess friend of his in Mitcham, would I go? I thought, well it's not every day you get somebody going off to Zimbabwe, so I said 'Yes' and I'm glad I did because that's how I got the audition.

Now my hobby is people. I collect people. So when I saw this interesting-looking man in the corner, next thing is I find myself talking to him. I said, 'You look an interesting person. I'm interested in interesting people. Hello.' He said, 'Hello.' I said, 'What do you do?' He said, 'I'm in films.' I said, 'Oh, that's interesting, anything in the pipeline?' He said, 'As a matter of fact, yes,' and starts telling me about this project he's involved in making videos for the overseas market, targeted chiefly on West Germany. I said, 'Are you the producer?' He said, 'No, but I'm on the production side, the name's Spud.' I said, 'Spud! That's an interesting name, mine's Lesley.' He said, 'As it happens, Lesley, we've got a problem at the moment. Our main girl has to drop out because her back's packed in. Are you an actress?' I said, 'Well, Spud, interesting that you should ask because as a matter of fact I am.' He said, 'Will you excuse me one moment, Lesley?' I said, 'Why, Spud, where are you going?' He said, 'I am going to go away, Lesley, and make one phone call.'

It transpires the director is seeing possible replacements the very next day, at an address in West London. Spud said, 'It's interesting because I'm based at Ealing.' I said, 'Isn't that West London?' He said, 'It is. Where's your stamping ground?' I said, 'Bromley, for my sins.' He said, 'That's a far-ish cry. Why not bed down at my place?' I said, 'Thank you, kind sir, but I didn't fall off the Christmas tree yesterday.' He said, 'Lesley, I have a son studying hotel management and a daughter with one kidney. Besides, I've got my sister-in-law staying. She's come up for the Ideal Home Exhibition.'

The penny began to drop when I saw the tattoo. My experience of tattoos is that they're generally confined to the lower echelons, and when I saw his vest it had electrician written all over it. I never even saw the sister-in-law. Still traipsing around Olympia probably.'

COMMENTARY

As is often the case with literature, the end helps to point to earlier features that may have passed us by first time. By the end of this passage it is clear that the reader ought to be thinking about how she got to see the tattoo. In short, the references to 'vest' and the sister-in-law make it clear that Lesley has slept with Spud. We might wonder at her naivety – in spite of seeming to know what he is up to she still succumbs to Spud's offer, still believing the story about the sister-in-law and thinking that seeing through him is working out that he is an electrician. The opening paragraph can now be seen in a new light. When Lesley describes the kinds of parts she plays, she is, in effect, describing herself using euphemisms: 'fun-loving girl', 'at home on a bar stool', and so forth. Her claims at professionalism are based on the trivial (smoking when required) and now appear empty and rather pathetic. Her use of cliches ('in a nutshell,' 'in the pipeline') also only go to highlight the limitations of her point of view and the vast gulf between it and what she thinks of herself. Lesley can see none of this.

When Lesley meets Spud we can assume that he sees through her immediately, repeating her word 'interesting' and wasting no time in sleeping with her. There are a number of signals that speak to the reader, if not to Lesley, in telling us what Spud does for a living: 'overseas market', 'West Germany,' and 'main girl' suggest the pornography business.

ACTIVITY 26

Use the same activity to analyse part of another text that you are studying. Choose a text where the point of view is limited in some way.

Write the last stanza

This works well when the form of a poem is highly predictable, as, for example in the case of ballads which use a regular rhyme scheme and rhythm. One possibility is for the last stanza simply to be missed off and the other person tries to write it using the pattern of the poem up to that point. An alternative is for one person in a pair to provide an outline of the last stanza, describing it as helpfully as possible, and the other person to write the stanza. This will test both your ability to describe the poem accurately and your partner's ability to interpret what you have written.

ACTIVITY 27

Below is a writing frame for the last stanza of *Five Ways to Kill a Man* (page 14). Using this as a starting point, compose your own writing frame for the last stanza of a poem you are studying. Try it out on a friend!

> The last stanza brings the reader to the twentieth century. Building on the idea of cumbersome ways of killing and reversing the idea, the poet explains that death comes much more easily in the twentieth century. He hints at spiritual death rather than just physical death using language that is not descriptive like the previous verses but matter of fact. The stanza is half the length of the others and the instructional style is continued.

ACTIVITY 28

Look back over the activities in this chapter. Draw up a chart and decide which of them works best with which forms of writing: poetry, plays, novels and short stories.

Key skills: Communication – writing

This chapter has provided an introduction to literary study at AS and A level. It has introduced you to just some of the methods available for reading various forms of literature. It is important that you choose the right method of getting into a text as this will affect the way you read it. The emphasis here has been on creativity and active involvement with texts. These practical approaches will help you to understand the more theoretical approaches that appear later in the book.

Answer to Activity 12:

Daniel 1 is the original poem.

3 Contexts of Writing

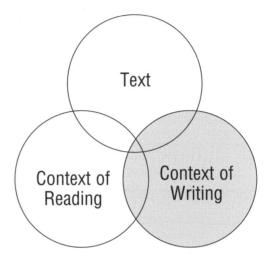

In Chapter One some examples of the contexts of writing literature were given. These were mainly historical and personal in nature. Here several other kinds of contexts of writing will be considered. This chapter sets out to explore just what are contexts, the wide variety of contexts and how they can influence literary texts. It suggests ideas for writing about contexts and works through some historical examples. Finally it shows how texts themselves can reveal a great deal about the context in which they were written.

Where does this fit in?

Contexts of writing are important for both AS and A level.
For AS level you are required to:

Show understanding of the contexts in which literary texts are written and understood (AS Assessment Objective 5i)

For A level you are required to:
Evaluate the significance of cultural, historical and other contextual influences on literary texts and study (A2 Assessment Objective 5ii)

Notice that both of these Assessment Objectives suggest the context of writing and reading together. In this book these two are dealt with separately because they are such important aspects of the A level specifications. Notice too that A level is more demanding for two reasons: first because you are asked to evaluate how important the contextual factors are; and second because a number of different kinds of contexts are specified.

What are contexts?

The simplest way of thinking about contexts is visually. According to this way of thinking, context is the space in which something stands:

It is also worth noting that 'text' and 'context' come from the same origin (as does 'texture') – the Latin word 'texere' which means 'to weave'. You might like to consider the connections between these words, bearing in mind that the prefix 'con-' means 'together'.

ACTIVITY 29

It seems reasonable to suggest that context might influence text. Context of writing refers to any of the circumstances of the writing of a literary text. In a small group copy the diagram below and suggest possible contexts of writing, putting them on the ends of the arrows.

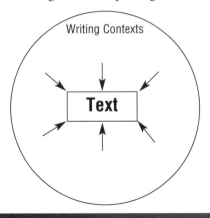

The following example shows quite clearly how context can influence text in a non-literary situation.

ACTIVITY 30

Read the text in the triangle below, firstly to yourself, then aloud, then slowly line by line. Try to explain what happened when you read these words the first time. What influenced the way you read them?

PARIS
IN THE
THE SPRING

COMMENTARY

Most people who look at these words see 'Paris in the Spring' without noticing that 'the' is repeated. This happens partly because of the way that the eye is guided by the triangle but also because 'Paris in the Spring' is a well-known phrase that is easily recognised when you read. So the reading of the individual words ('the') is affected by the context in which those words appear – in this case, in the context of a well-known phrase. Here the context is limited to a few words but in works of literature contexts operate on a much grander scale, including factors such as the life of the writer and the political beliefs of the time in which he lived. As with the phrase 'Paris in the Spring', contextual factors such as history and culture can influence readers into ignoring certain parts of a text and emphasising others. For example, for much of literary history, people's views of women meant that readers ignored the ways in which women were represented in fiction.

In literary studies the context of writing can be seen as a means by which texts are linked together. One of the exam board specifications defines context as: 'significant facts or processes of different kinds which shaped the writing and understanding of literary works.'

Varieties of context

The following activity shows some of the kinds of contexts that might influence the writing of a literary text.

ACTIVITY 31

Twelve different contexts of writing are described below. The labels for each context are given at the beginning. Read the descriptions of the contexts of writing and match them with the labels. For example, description (a) clearly emphasises biography and therefore goes with label number 9.
Key skills: Communication – discussion/writing

Labels for contexts

1 Genre
2 Language
3 The process of writing
4 Mythology
5 Other works by the same writer
6 Intertextuality
7 The influence of other writers
8 Literary movements

9 Biography
10 Cultural influence
11 Historical influence
12 Psychology

Descriptions of writing contexts

a Here the writer's life provides a useful background to the work of literature. For example: Seamus Heaney's Northern Ireland upbringing helps to explain some of his early poetry; D.H. Lawrence's background as the son of a miner and a middle class mother is relevant to several of his stories and much of his characterisation.

b The means by which a writer actually wrote the published version of their work is often illuminating. Some writers make earlier drafts of a work available. Others publish more than one version. For example: earlier drafts of work by Wilfred Owen and Seamus Heaney are available and the Irish short story writer Frank O'Connor published several versions of some of his stories.

c Writing by one author can usually be connected in several ways: by theme, style, development of the writer, etc. For example, it is possible to compare the treatment of social class in several of Dickens' novels.

d This influence refers to groups of writers who share a common approach to literature. This may involve shared principles about the content, style or aims of any kind of literature. Some examples are: the Romantics (Coleridge, Wordsworth, Keats, etc.); the Imagists (Pound, Lowell, Williams, etc.); Modernists (James Joyce, Virginia Woolf, T.S. Eliot, etc.).

e A writer may be influenced by another who is not part of the same literary movement. Indeed the influence may come from hundreds of years before. For example, the 20th century poet T.S. Eliot acknowledged the influence of the 17th century Metaphysical poets on his style of writing even though they wrote several hundred years before him.

f This influence is difficult to define but roughly speaking it refers to the beliefs, understanding and values of a society. For example, a society at any one moment in history may value the freedom of the individual or it may have certain unspoken beliefs about the position of women in society. Caribbean poetry is sometimes said to come from a culture of dislocation – where a people has been separated from its roots in Africa because of slavery.

g This overlaps with cultural influence but it is more obviously linked to the events of a particular period. For example, a great deal of poetry emerged from the First World War; early Romantic poets such as William Blake were responding in part to the French Revolution's underlying philosophy.

h This approach is a refinement of the biographical approach in that it looks more deeply at the writer's personality in order to shed light on their writing. Examples are: D.H. Lawrence and his novel *Sons and Lovers*; Coleridge and *The Ancient Mariner*.

i This influence comes from basic stories which seem to exist across many cultures. The 'rags to riches' story or 'the green man' (Robin Hood) are examples of stories that can be adapted and re-told in new literature. Some critics believe that all of Dickens' novels are versions of Cinderella.

j Science fiction, romance, bildungsroman (the personal development of a character) and adventure are examples of this kind of influence. Writers consciously write texts according to various types, building on what has gone before and sometimes adding new elements.

k Here we might focus on a particular technique used by the writer or other connected writers e.g. the way in which Shakespeare makes use of 'thou' and 'you' to suggest the relationships between characters; in English, Latin based vocabulary (e.g. to masticate) usually has a different set of connotations from vocabulary based on Anglo-Saxon (e.g. to chew).

l All texts are related to each other; there are no new texts according to some theorists. Without getting too philosophical, this influence refers to the subtle and not so subtle ways in which different literary works draw on each other. This could mean that one work quotes an earlier one or that it builds on it without directly telling you. For example, Margaret Atwood's *The Handmaid's Tale* could be said to draw upon Chaucer's *Canterbury Tales*, various futuristic utopias and various Biblical stories. But these influences depend partly on the reader: many readers are not aware of references to *Coral Island* in *Lord of the Flies* until they are told, but it may trigger off references to their own childhood reading.

(Answers can be found at the end of the chapter).

ACTIVITY 32

One way of looking at context is to say that it is a way of making links between texts. For example, a context that emphasises the process of writing would link various drafts of a text. For each one of the above contexts, say which kinds of texts could be linked as part of a literature course. For 'biography' for example, you would compare the literary work with biography and autobiography.

Here are some examples of texts to help you although the list is not exhaustive:

poetry, novels, plays, autobiography, biography, criticism, early drafts and earlier versions of literary pieces, historical documents of various kinds (diaries, contemporary criticism, political pamphlets, etc.), scientific or medical texts, magazine articles, journal articles, etc.

You may well be able to discover more for yourself.

ACTIVITY 33

Investigating myth: find out about the myth of Oedipus and explain its connection with the story *Death Speaks* on page 35. Are there any films that are modern re-workings of well-known myths?

Further contexts of writing

Intratextuality

This rather daunting term hides a familiar idea. One of the simplest kinds of context is a passage or extract considered in relation to the whole work from which it is taken. Even when passages are presented as 'unseens', as they frequently are on exam papers, it is often important for the reader to get a sense of the whole work. Here are some of the things you should consider when looking at this kind of context:

- how the extract fits in with the structure of the literary work. For example, is it part of a turning point in a novel? Is it a flashback? (See page 205)
- how the extract compares linguistically with the rest of the work. Does it use more or less formal language? Does it use the same or different examples of metaphor and imagery?
- how the extract fulfils conventions of the literary work. In Shakespeare,

for example, is the extract written in poetry or prose and is that what the reader would expect? In a ballad such as *The Rime of the Ancient Mariner*, does the extract use the same rhyme scheme as the rest of the text?

Serialisation

The structure and general quality of a piece of literature are significantly determined by how they are to be published, in what form and for whom (under the above categorisation these things are grouped under 'process of writing'). Take soap operas for example: in the chart below, the left-hand column gives features of the context of production and the right-hand side suggests how those features might influence the structure and style of the programmes:

Context of production	Structure and style
30 minute episodes	End with a cliff-hanger
Must maintain interest	Cliff-hangers; several stories at different stages
Wide range of viewers	Wide range of characters
Viewers relaxing at home	Short scenes; fast-moving; easy to pick up again
Viewers talk about it a lot	Deal with topical issues (drugs, gays, etc.)

ACTIVITY 34

Analyse an episode of a television soap opera. Produce a chart like the one above showing how the context of production influenced that particular episode. You may wish to add further contexts to the left-hand column. The right-hand column should be specific to the episode you are studying.

ACTIVITY 35

Create a similar kind of chart for a text that you are studying. You will need to research the context of production of the text. Here are some examples:

- 19th century novels in serial form
- publication of poems in newspapers and journals
- short stories published in journals or periodicals.

How do contexts of writing influence reading?

How exactly do contexts of writing influence the way we read and write about literary texts? Often one of these contexts stands out as providing useful information about how to read a text. Sometimes you may be able to make use of several contexts, each offering different interpretations.

Biographical reading

There seems to be a natural impulse towards this kind of reading. Readers are very prompt to ask questions like: Did this happen to the author? Did she write this because she believed . . .? Or Shakespeare had an affair with an older woman, didn't he? In recent years there has been a move away from such biographical explanations – in the 1960s critics wrote of 'the death of the author', meaning that it was no longer important to consider the living author behind a piece of literature. For A level students the danger of biographical explanations is obvious: such explanations can give inexperienced readers the impression that all there is to reading is uncovering the hidden aspects of the writer's life. But a second danger is that readers are taken away from the text they are studying into texts describing the author's life, so that the literary text is merely servant to the biographical text.

These dangers still apply but to some extent authors have been resurrected. It is acceptable to write about authors and their life stories in literary criticism, as long as we exercise caution. New attitudes to history have recently suggested that we should not accept stories about the past without question – all accounts of the past are biased because they have to be told from someone's point of view. Biographical explanations should therefore be treated with caution and alternative explanations should be considered where possible. Remember that biographies are themselves interpretations. For example, the poet Philip Larkin's life was interpreted very differently when the contents of his letters were made public after his death in 1985.

Knowing the basic frame for reading

For some texts there is a minimum level of context required to understand the surface meaning of a literary work. The following activity should make this clear.

ACTIVITY 36

1 The poem below has had its title and author removed. Before finding out any further context, respond to the poem in any way you wish (you may like to choose one of the methods described in Chapter 2). Note that 'ere' means 'before'.

Discuss with a partner the difficulties of interpreting this poem.

When I consider how my light is spent,
Ere half my days in this dark world and wide,
And that one talent which it is death to hide
Lodged with me useless, though my soul more bent
To serve therewith my maker, and present
My true account, lest he returning chide;
'Doth God exact day-labour, light denied?'
I fondly ask. But Patience, to prevent
That murmur, soon replies, 'God doth not need
Either man's work or His own gifts. Who best
Bear his mild yoke, they served Him best. His state
Is kindly: thousands at his bidding speed,
And post o'er land and ocean without rest;
They also serve who only stand and wait.'

The basic background to the poem is given at the end of the chapter.

2 When you have looked up the background to the poem above respond to it again. This time consider:

a which particular words and phrases are clarified by this biographical information

b how your interpretation of the whole poem is affected

c how this fact about the poet affects your emotional reaction to the poem.

COMMENTARY

In cases like this, biographical information unlocks the poem and provides a template or context against which to interpret it. At a basic level, decoding of phrases such as 'my light is spent' and 'that one talent' is facilitated. Interpretation of the whole poem is thereby easier, but knowing that Milton was blind does not provide an 'answer' to the problem that the poem sets. The reader still has to work out Milton's attitude to his blindness as expressed in the relationship with God that he describes. Further contextual information such as people's attitudes to blindness in the 17th century would also be useful.

The fact that on this occasion the persona or character created by the poet is the poet himself, perhaps affects our emotional reaction to the poem. The things that the poet speaks of presumably affected the act of writing this poem so that there is a merging of the real and fictional worlds. For some readers this might add poignancy to the poem which it might not suggest if it were purely fictional.

Here are some words of advice about using biographical information in your critical writing:

- don't begin an essay with an account of part or whole of the author's life
- make sure that what you write bears a direct and obvious relationship to the text you are studying and the question at hand
- try to consider alternative ways of looking at the apparent biographical facts
- use biographical information to support your own independent judgements about the text. Don't let it replace them.

ACTIVITY 37

The following poem by Thomas Hardy refers to events in Hardy's life that are important for an understanding of the poem. A little basic research will reveal the kind of biographical information given afterwards. Using the above advice and the biographical information below write a short response to the poem. Incorporate the information carefully into your personal response, taking only what you need. From whose point of view do you think the poem is told?

Alike and Unlike (Great Orme's Head)

We watched the self-same scene on that long drive
Saw the magnificent purples, as one eye,
Of those near mountains; saw the storm arrive;
Laid up the sight in memory, you and I,
As if for joint recallings by and by.

But our eye-records, like in hue and line,
Had superimposed on them, that very day,
Gravings on your side deep, but slight on mine! –
Tending to sever us thenceforth alway;
Mine commonplace; yours tragic, gruesome, gray.

Entry in Hardy's diary for 18 May 1893:

'Left Euston by 9 o'clock morning train with E. for Llandudno, *en route* for Dublin. After arrival at Llandudno drove around Great Orme's Head. Magnificent deep purple-grey mountains, the fine colour being on account of an approaching storm.'

Extract from *The Penguin Poetry Library*: Hardy (Ed. David Wright)

'Like Hardy, Emma was musical; she played the harmonium in the church of St Juliot. Hardy was to commemorate this not long after her death. But Emma was a rung or two above Hardy in the social scale – a matter of more import then than now. An uncle of hers became an Archdeacon, who married them in 1874 when Hardy's ship came home with the success of *Far from the Madding Crowd*.

The marriage was happy enough to begin with. They honey-mooned on the Continent and set up house in London, later moving to Sturminster Newton, where they spent their two happiest years together (cf 'A Two Years' Idyll', 'The Musical Box'). Then things began to go wrong between them. There was no child; Emma's social snobbery became pronounced – she would not invite Hardy's parents or sisters to their house at Max Gate. She made it clear that she had married beneath her, but at the same time was exasperated by Hardy's social success in London, where his fame made him welcome at the houses of the great ... Near the end of their marriage the Hardys were in effect living separate lives at Max Gate, meeting only at meals; for Hardy (according to his second wife) there were 'long evenings spent alone in his study, insult and abuse his only enlivenment'. Yet Emma Hardy was a generous hostess, well liked by her friends and neighbours; the servants at Max Gate preferred her to the withdrawn and rather stingy master of the house.'
(page 25)

COMMENTARY   Some of the essential biographical facts that need to be referred to are:

- where they went
- the storm – link this with the metaphorical storm in their relationship
- the nature of their relationship and (briefly) the causes.

Some features of the poem that you may have mentioned are:

- the over-riding feeling of division between the two characters
- the differences between the two stanzas (the experience versus the interpretation)
- the expectation of the first stanza and the stark reality of the second
- one rhyme in the first stanza but two in the second
- the heaviness (depression?) suggested by the repeated 'g' in the last stanza
- the poem is told from the point of view of Hardy's wife, something implied in the second biographical extract. How does this influence your response to the poem?

In integrating these two sets of points, the biographical information should have supported your comments on the poem, and not vice-versa.

The next activity considers how several contexts of writing can influence the way that you write about a literary work.

ACTIVITY 38

Below are three examples of writing about D.H. Lawrence's short story *The Horse Dealer's Daughter*. Which contexts of writing does each one draw on? You may wish to consult the list on page 45 to help you. A commentary can be found at the end of the chapter.

Key skills: Communication – reading

Text A

The climax of Lawrence's short story The Horse Dealer's Daughter comes as an almost comic release from middle class gentility. Young Dr Ferguson has just rescued Mabel Pervin from the pond where she has attempted to drown herself. In an attempt to revive her, he removes her 'saturated, earthy-smelling' black clothing and wraps her in warm blankets. As she gains full awareness of her surroundings, she realises she is naked under the blankets and 'with wild eye' asks, 'Who undressed me?' Dr Ferguson can only reply, 'I did to bring you round'. Middle-class mores being what they were in Edwardian England, to have been viewed naked by a man can mean only one thing to Mabel. 'Do you love me then?'

This is almost comic, yet not at all. In Lawrence's hands the episode has an ache-in-the-throat poignancy, and, with Dr Ferguson, the reader's soul seems also 'to melt'. The reader can only be glad, then, when Mabel sheds her middle-class sense of propriety with her clothing and shuffles forward to clasp him around the knees as, heedless of her 'wild, bare, animal shoulders,' she acknowledges and responds to his love. Dr Ferguson lets 'his heart yield toward her' as he crosses 'over the gulf to her' while 'all [bachelorhood, loneliness, isolation, unhappiness] that he had left behind had shrivelled and become void'. Gentility – and with it stubborn pride and empty life – has been conquered by the passion of love.

Text B

Lawrence in 'Nottingham and the Mining Countryside' tells us that his father was a collier and characterises colliers as men who have neither ambition nor intellect, men who avoid a rational life. Joe Pervin in Lawrence's short story 'The Horse Dealer's Daughter' is a perfect embodiment of such working men, displaying the coarseness and vitality that Lawrence's mother taught him to abhor. He is a strong physical specimen, 'broad and handsome in a hot, flushed way,' but 'his bearing' is 'stupid.' He watches the horses leave on their last exercise with 'a certain stupor of downfall'. Because he is not intelligent, he will be controlled by others in the same way that the horses are. Lawrence links Joe specifically with the horses in a later passage: 'The horses were almost like his own body to him'. He is going to be married, but marriage will not provide the companionship that Mabel and Dr Ferguson will achieve later in the story: Joe 'would marry and go into harness. . . . He would be a subject animal now'.

Insensitive, helpless despite his strength, Joe Pervin represents the working class for which Lawrence, despite his schoolteacher mother, always felt a kinship.

Text C

Mabel Pervin's immersion in the pond in 'The Horse Dealer's Daughter' is a deliberate use by Lawrence of the archetypal significance of water as baptism, a rite involving the destruction of the old life and the birth of a new one. Mabel has chosen the pond as her means of committing suicide so that she can join her mother in death. Lawrence has already shown the reader enough of her current life for one to realize that it is a living death; isolated and destitute, Mabel has no plans and no hope. She marches steadily towards her goal of glorification by death; the doctor observes her walking 'slowly and deliberately' into the water and thence to the deep center of the pond. She has gone under by the time he reaches the bank, so he slowly and reluctantly wades out to find her. However, he cannot reach her until he too is submerged 'horribly, suffocating in the foul earthy water, struggling madly'. This 'baptism' of total immersion enables him to be reborn; after what seems an 'eternity' he 'rises' and 'gasps' and knows he is 'in the world.' The newly born man can be a saviour; he grasps Mabel who 'rises' near him and, after carrying her to shore, he is able to restore her to life. Having been reborn to an awareness of their humanity, it is only natural then, that in the next scene, they accept their love for each other.

[in Suzanne Cole and Jeff Lindemann '*Reading and Responding to Literature*' Harcourt Brace Jovanovich Inc, 1990, page 191]

Setting contexts – introductions

Introductions to anthologies of poetry can often reveal a great deal about the context in which a work was written (as well as the context in which it is read). The following extract is the introduction to a book by four black women poets called *A Dangerous Knowing*. The purpose of the introduction is to inform readers of what they can expect in the anthology, provide background to the publication of the collection and to explain what it stands for.

ACTIVITY 39

Read the following introduction to *A Dangerous Knowing*. Analyse its content following the examples given in the boxes alongside the text. Look for:

- Basic ingredients such as the quotation at the beginning.

- The order in which the introduction presents its information.
- The kind of language used to describe the contents of the book.

Key skills: Communication – reading

Begins with a quotation that expresses feelings of the poets.

'The furthest horizons of our hopes and fears are cobbled by our poems, carved from the rock experiences of our daily lives.' Audre Lorde, Sister Outsider.

Indeed it is these daily experiences, as much as the visions and imaginations of Black women, which form the substance of the poems you are about to read.

Makes connections with quotation and states subject of collection.

Classifies the work within a literary movement.

A Dangerous Knowing marks a unique and historic moment in feminist publishing. Here, for the first time in Britain, poetry written by four British based Black women is brought together.

States exactly what is new about the work.

Black women have been writing poetry for centuries but their words have often stayed within themselves; Black women as poets and writers have remained invisible. Racism in the publishing industry has ensured this invisibility by ignoring black women's creativity and denying them access to publishing, so many Black women have been reluctant to name themselves as poets. It is with courage that the four women in this book have taken this risk.

If poetry is an intense form of communication, creating new ways of seeing through imaginative uses of language, then these poets do that and more. Their ways of seeing reach out and touch all Black women's lives, for we can see our lives manifested in these words. These poets help create new images of black women and strengthen and encourage their Black sisters to write.

Long overdue, *A Dangerous Knowing* reflects the variety and depth of Black women's experiences. These poems leave us with a sense of the complexities of Black women's lives, sharing not only their fears, angers and sense of isolation with us, but also their hopes, joys, laughter, and the sensuality of being black women. It is a vision of black women's lives which confirms their uniqueness. With it goes a powerful presence: the spirit of resistance.

Write an introduction to an anthology of poetry of your choice using your analysis from Activity 36. Try to capture how the anthology would have been received at the time of writing.

Key skills: Communication – reading/writing

- Find a suitable quotation to start the introduction.
- Research the background to your chosen topic using a literary encyclopaedia.
- Follow the format of the above introduction closely.
- List its ingredients and adopt a similar style of writing.

You could choose an existing anthology that doesn't already have an introduction or one of the following possibilities:

- Romantic poetry by one or several authors (see pages 179–185)
- Metaphysical poetry
- A collection of short stories by gay men
- Poetry of the sixties
- 'Moon Country': Further Reports from Iceland – Simon Armitage and Glyn Maxwell (you will need to research Auden and MacNeice's 'Letters from Iceland' for this).

Texts create contexts

The previous section showed that introductions often help to describe the context of writing a particular text. In this section we move to the text itself and what it implies about the context in which it was written. The following extract from the beginning of *The Nightwatchman's Occurrence Book* by V.S. Naipaul, a short story, illustrates this:

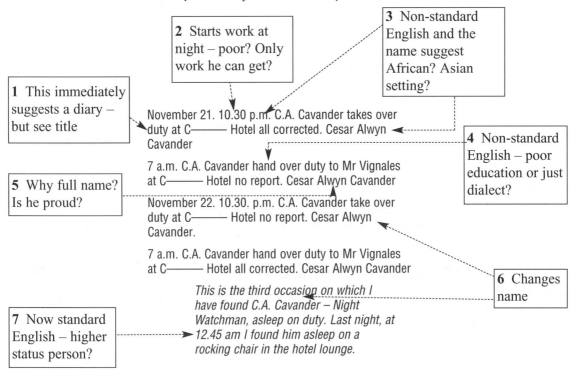

1 This immediately suggests a diary – but see title

2 Starts work at night – poor? Only work he can get?

3 Non-standard English and the name suggest African? Asian setting?

4 Non-standard English – poor education or just dialect?

5 Why full name? Is he proud?

6 Changes name

7 Now standard English – higher status person?

November 21. 10.30 p.m. C.A. Cavander takes over duty at C——— Hotel all corrected. Cesar Alwyn Cavander

7 a.m. C.A. Cavander hand over duty to Mr Vignales at C——— Hotel no report. Cesar Alwyn Cavander

November 22. 10.30. p.m. C.A. Cavander take over duty at C——— Hotel no report. Cesar Alwyn Cavander.

7 a.m. C.A. Cavander hand over duty to Mr Vignales at C——— Hotel all corrected. Cesar Alwyn Cavander

This is the third occasion on which I have found C.A. Cavander – Night Watchman, asleep on duty. Last night, at 12.45 am I found him asleep on a rocking chair in the hotel lounge.

COMMENTARY These show only a few of the possible responses to this passage – you may have others to suggest. Notice that the responses are both personal and tentative, although readers from the same culture are likely to respond in a similar way. What the reader is doing here is filling out a context for the story using his or her assumptions about the world although they will almost certainly have to be changed in the light of subsequent text.

Response 1: Here the reader is considering the basic form that the story is going to adopt. The reader probably knows a great deal about diary writing but a night watchman's report is likely to be much more limited in what it can say. How the story uses this form is likely to be very important to an overall reading.

Response 2: This is based on cultural assumptions about night work but it might usefully be connected with the position of some ethnic groups in the Caribbean (where the story is set) if, for example, some groups are forced into taking low paid work.

Response 3: This sows the seeds of understanding the cultural setting of the story and the relative status of the two characters.

Response 4: The reader uses intuitive knowledge of the significance of non-standard English; that is, non-standard means sub-standard. However, it may be possible that the author is making a political point about this assumption.

Response 5: The reader has some understanding of the way that names are used. This knowledge is used to begin characterising the night watchman.

Response 6: This change in the way the character is referred to is relevant to status. The second character (writing in italics) refers to the first character in a way that suggests his higher status.

Response 7: The reader's knowledge of the use of Standard English again comes into play.

These free responses can now be supplemented with the contextual information that they seem to be calling forth. That is:

- texts about language variation, standard and non-standard dialects in the Caribbean
- texts about social class and possibly ethnicity in the Caribbean
- diaries and/or reports, real or imagined, for comparison.

These ideas are followed up in the last chapter.

ACTIVITY 41

1 Annotate the following beginnings of short stories or novels in the same way as above. It may help to use a dictionary.

2 Work out what kind of contextual information would be necessary to fill out these responses.

Text A – *Dead Men's Path* – Chinua Achebe

Michael Obi's hopes were fulfilled much earlier than he had expected. He was appointed headmaster of Ndume Central School in January 1949. It had always been an unprogressive school, so the mission authorities decided to send a young and energetic man to run it. Obi accepted this responsibility with enthusiasm. He had many wonderful ideas and this was an opportunity to put them into practice. He had had sound secondary school educacion which designated him a 'pivotal teacher' in the official records and set him apart from the other headmasters in the mission field. He was outspoken in his condemnation of the narrow views of these older and often less educated ones. [from *Girls at War and other Stories*]

Text B – *An Occurrence at Owl Creek Bridge* – Ambrose Beirce

A man stood upon a railroad bridge in northern Alabama, looking down into the swift water twenty feet below. The man's hands were behind his back, the wrists bound with a cord. A rope closely encircled his neck. It was attached to a stout cross-timber above his head and the slack fell to the level of his knees. Some loose boards laid upon the sleepers supporting the metals of the railway supplied a footing for him and his executioners – two private soldiers of the Federal army, directed by a sergeant who, in civil life may have been a deputy sheriff. At a short remove upon the same temporary platform was an officer in the uniform of his rank, armed. A sentinel at each end of the bridge stood with his rifle in the position known as 'support', that is to say, vertical in front of the left shoulder, the hammer resting on the forearm thrown straight across the chest....

Text C – *Another World* – Pat Barker

Cars queue bumper to bumper, edge forward, stop, edge forward again. Resting his bare arm along the open window, Nick drums his fingers. The Bigg Market on a Friday night. Litter of chip cartons, crushed lager cans, a gang of lads with stubble heads and tattooed arms looking for trouble – and this is early, it hasn't got going yet. Two girls stroll past, one wearing a thin, almost transparent white cotton dress. At every stride her nipples show, dark circles beneath the cloth, fish rising. One of the lads calls her name: 'Julie!' She turns, and the two of them fall into each other's arms.

Nick watches, pretending not to.

What is love's highest aim?
Four buttocks on a stem.

Can't remember who said that – some poor sod made cynical by thwarted lust.

Movements as contexts of writing

On page 45 literary movements were named as one of the important contexts of writing. This is because authors rarely work in isolation from each other. They influence each other through the exchange of ideas, through reading and talking about their work. As a result writers often move in a similar direction – sometimes this is conscious like a club but sometimes it is unconscious, when writers are simply moved, by the spirit of the times in which they live, to write in a particular way.

One such movement that marked the change from 19th to 20th century thinking was Modernism which became most active in the years after the First World War. Modernism included the following:

- experiments with unusual ways of writing
- a concern with the psychological, conscious and unconscious
- a concern with metaphorical or symbolic ways of thinking
- a tendency to move away from chronological story telling.

ACTIVITY 42

Below are two lists of titles of novels. One contains titles of Victorian and Edwardian novels of the type that preceded the Modernist movement. The other contains titles of novels that were influenced by Modernism.

1 Work out, using an encyclopedia if necessary, which is which.
2 Explain how the two sets of titles are different from each other and how this relates to Modernism.

List 1: *Heart of Darkness; A Passage to India; The Rainbow; To the Lighthouse; Ulysses; The Shadow Line; The Wings of the Dove.*

List 2: *David Copperfield; Middlemarch; Barchester Towers; Kipps; The Forsyte Saga.*

ACTIVITY 43

This activity focuses on how two writers of the Modernist era represented thoughts and feelings in their writing. Neither Hemingway nor D.H. Lawrence were strongly Modernist but in their different ways they were both concerned to capture human emotion. Read the following two extracts from works by Hemingway and Lawrence.

1 With a partner decide which one best communicates the feelings of the characters involved and justify your views.
2 Describe how each author communicates feelings with specific reference to the language used.

Key skills: Communication – reading

D.H. Lawrence: from *The White Stocking*

The husband and wife are arguing about some valentine gifts that the woman has received from another man.

'But he had seen her standing there, a piteous, horrified thing, and he turned his face aside in shame and nausea. He went and sat heavily in his chair, and a curious ease, almost like sleep, came over his brain.
She walked away from the wall towards the fire, dizzy, white to the lips, mechanically wiping her small, bleeding mouth. He sat motionless. Then, gradually, her breath began to hiss, she shook, and was sobbing silently, in grief for herself. Without looking, he saw. It made his mad desire to destroy her come back.
At length he lifted his head. His eyes were glowing again, fixed on her.
'And what did he give them you for?' he asked, in a steady, unyielding voice.
Her crying dried up in a second. She also was tense.
'They came as valentines,' she replied, still not subjugated, even if beaten.
'When, today?'
'The pearl ear rings today – the amethyst brooch last year.'
'You've had it a year?'
'Yes'

She felt that now nothing would prevent him if he rose to kill her. She could not prevent him any more. She was yielded up to him. They both trembled on the balance, unconscious.

'What have you had to do with him?' he asked, in a barren voice.

'I've not had anything to do with him,' she quavered.

'You just kept'em because they were jewellery?' he said.

A weariness came over him. What was the worth of speaking any more of it? He did not care any more. He was dreary and sick.

She began to cry again, but he took no notice. She kept wiping her mouth on her handkerchief. He could see it, the blood-mark. It made him more sick and tired of the responsibility of it, the violence, the shame.

When she began to move about again, he raised his head once more from his dead, motionless position.

'Where are the things?' he said.

'They are upstairs,' she quavered. She knew the passion had gone down in him.

'Bring them down,' he said.

'I won't,' she wept, with rage. 'You're not going to bully me and hit me like that on the mouth.'

And she sobbed again. He looked at her in contempt and compassion and in rising anger.

'Where are they?' he said.

Ernest Hemingway: from *Hills Like White Elephants*

A young couple are waiting for a train in Spain. The woman is pregnant.

'. . . I said the hills looked like white elephants. Wasn't that bright?'

'That was bright.'

'I wanted to try this new drink. That's all we do, isn't it – look at things and try new drinks?'

'I guess so.'

The girl looked across at the hills.

'They're lovely hills,' she said. 'They don't really look like white elephants. I just meant the colour of their skin through the trees.'

'Should we have another drink?'

'All right.'

The warm wind blew the bead curtain against the table.

'The beer's nice and cool,' the man said.

'It's lovely,' the girl said.

'It's really an awfully simple operation, Jig,' the man said. It's not really an operation at all.'

The girl looked at the ground the table legs rested on.

'I know you wouldn't mind it, Jig. It's really not anything. It's just to let the air in.'

The girl did not say anything.

'I'll go with you and stay with you all the time. They just let the air in and then it's all perfectly natural.'

'Then what will we do afterwards?'

'We'll be fine afterwards. Just like we were before.'

'What makes you think so?'

'That's the only thing that bothers us. It's the only thing that's made us unhappy.'

The girl looked at the bead curtain, put her hands out and took hold of two of the strings of beads.

'And you think then we'll be all right and be happy.'

'I know we will. You don't have to be afraid. I've known lots of people that have done it.'

'So have I,' said the girl. 'And afterwards they were all so happy.'

COMMENTARY Lawrence tends to build up his descriptions using lists of adjectives ('piteous, horrified'; 'steady, unyielding') that often describe the emotion directly. Hemingway, on the other hand is much less direct, leaving us looking at his characters rather than being given an exposed view of their emotions. So, in Hemingway there is a great deal of speech followed by no speech tag at all or simply 'he said'. Hemingway's descriptions of his characters' actions are tantalisingly objective; that is, the reader sees only the outside, as in, 'The girl looked at the ground'. However, this is not to say that the Hemingway passage is emotionless or cold; in everyday life such body language speaks volumes without explanation, and in many ways Hemingway was anticipating the technique that would later be used by the cinema. Hemingway's dialogue also uses a large number of pronouns ('they', 'it') which is very naturalistic. Lawrence's dialogue is similar but he gives us much more information about his characters' inner feelings using metaphorical language ('in a barren voice'). Perhaps the most noticeable difference between these two writers is in Lawrence's apparent striving to put his finger on the right word to capture the emotion. Thus we have: 'silently, in grief for herself'; 'his mad desire to destroy'; 'dreary and sick'. Much of this striving comes out as abstract nouns standing for emotions: 'responsibility'; 'shame'; 'contempt'; 'compassion' etc. The two writers were both aware of the need to represent consciousness, a Modernist obsession. Lawrence plunged directly into it, Hemingway appeared to try and hide it.

There is more on movements in poetry on page 183.

ACTIVITY 44

Re-write the Lawrence passage in the style of Hemingway or vice-versa. Try, as far as is possible, to keep the meanings the same as in the original.

Key skills: Communication – writing

Answers to Activity 29:
1j, 2k, 3b, 4i, 5c, 6l, 7e, 8d, 9a, 10f, 11g, 12h.

Background to the poem in Activity 34:
The poem is called *On His Blindness* by John Milton (circa 1655). Milton was blind by 1651.

Commentary on Activity 36
Text A: Here there is an emphasis on social class and the time at which the story was written. The critic sees the story as one in which love overcomes the boundaries imposed by social class at that time.

Text B: The writer here makes comparisons between Lawrence's own family and the characters in the story useing them as a basis for understanding the parts in the story that are played by those characters. Notice that the reference to Lawrence's family is fleeting and the writer does not get drawn into giving unnecessary biographical details.

Text C: The word 'archetypal' essentially means 'symbolic' and this is a clue to the writer's purpose. The story is being connected to the myth of death and re-birth as used by Christianity in the ritual of baptism.

Further reading

e-magazine, Published by e-em. P.O. Box 6, Denbigh, North Wales, Ed. Peter Buckroyd and John Shuttleworth. Lively and trendy magazine with a keen eye for its audience. Covers language issues too.

The English Review, Philip Allan Publishers Limited.
Provides plenty of short articles. Aimed at students but can be a demanding read.

NATE Critical Reading series, Ed. Sue Dymoke (1998).
Includes: *The Handmaid's Tale* (Margaret Atwood); *Beloved* (Toni Morrison); *A Streetcar Named Desire* (Tennessee Williams); *Wuthering Heights* (Emily Brontë). These books contain useful contextual information on the texts.

4 Contexts of Reading

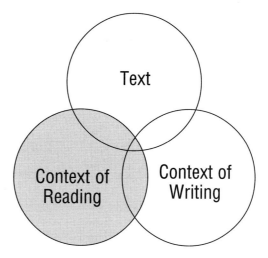

Where does this fit in?

‘**C**ontext’ is the most important new word in all A level literature specifications. Several of the Assessment Objectives imply context even when they don’t actually use the word:

AO2: ‘literary texts of different types and periods’
AO4: ‘different interpretations of literary texts by different readers.’

Some of the AOs are, however, explicit. Assessment Objective 5i (AS level) states:

‘show understanding of the contexts in which literary texts are written and understood.’

It is the word ‘understood’ that refers to the context of reading.
Assessment Objective 5ii (A2) states:

‘evaluate the significance of cultural, historical and other contextual influences on literary texts and study.’

All of this could be interpreted as addressing the context of reading, but especially the word ‘study’. The difference between AS and A2 is in the words ‘show understanding’ and ‘evaluate the significance of’. The former suggests that you will need to *use* contextual information in your studies whereas the latter implies that you will need to go much further, making *judgements* about the importance of those contextual factors.

ACTIVITY 45

This activity introduces you to different kinds of contexts of reading. Here are three ways in which a context of reading can emerge:

1 Presenting a text with another text
2 Changes in society cause a text to be re-interpreted
3 A group in society interprets a text in a particular way

Read the following examples of how real texts were affected by their contexts. Categorise them as types one, two or three above.

A In 1984 the American pop group 'The Cars' made a song called *Drive*. Some of the lyrics were as follows:

> Who's gonna tell you when
> it's too late
> who's gonna tell you things
> aren't so great
> you can't go on
> thinking nothing's wrong
> Who's gonna drive you home tonight?

There were many possible interpretations of this but it may have been about the relationship(s) of someone who is mentally unstable. Listeners felt that at least they could be sure of the kind of world being evoked by the words: a society that cares about its individuals and a context of young love in a car-dominated Western culture.

Then there was a famine in Ethiopia and a huge concert was organised in Wembley stadium – known as 'Live Aid'. Between two of the acts *Drive* was played over the loud speakers and a video showing scenes of famine accompanied it: horrifically thin children and babies; eyes wide and tear-filled, covered in flies; patient resignation in the face of imminent death, and

so forth. Suddenly *Drive* took on a completely new meaning. Suddenly it referred to a race of people in Africa with no one to care for them, with no one to care for their individual needs. The first few lines fitted easily – they seemed to become a call for awareness of what was wrong in Africa. But then the last line, apparently meaningless in this new context, was the most powerful of all. To ask these people who would drive them home tonight was to insult them with embarrassingly irrelevant questions. At the same time it embarrassed its Western audience who could afford to worry about romantic relationships without considering basic survival needs.

B 'Robin Hood, prince of thieves, was actually a gay outlaw who had been exiled from 'straight' society', reports *The Sunday Times*. Stephen Knight, a professor of English Literature at Cardiff University, claims that Little John, not Maid Marion, was his true love. He cites the fact that Robin and his men were 'all very male and lived exclusively without women', and that ballads about his life are filled with phallic images such as trees, arrows and quivers. Gay campaigner Peter Tatchell told the paper: 'His lifestyle alone was enough to provoke speculation.' [*The Week* 17th July, 1999]

This interpretation, if it can be taken seriously, is only possible in a society that has a significant enough gay minority for it to reclaim one of the country's mythical national heroes as their own.

C 'Late in the spring of 1986, a fundamentalist parent entered Mowat Junior High school in Panama City, Florida, to complain about her daughter's having to read *I am the Cheese*, a novel by Robert Cormier. ... The confrontation swelled and exploded early in 1987. A group of teachers and parents had filed a suit in the U.S. District Court. Rigid guidelines for book selection and retention were imposed unilaterally by the superintendent. In April, he threw out sixty-four books in current use in the high school English courses, noting that there was 'some profanity' in each one. All of Shakespeare's plays were removed; so were such classic works as *Oedipus Rex, Wuthering Heights, Animal Farm, Call of the Wild* and *The Red Badge of Courage*. [Hayhoe and Parker, 1990]

COMMENTARY The above are all examples of what this chapter will call contexts of reading. In the first example the meaning of the lyrics of the song *Drive* are changed by presenting them in a new context – by reading them alongside a different text – in this case images of the famine in Ethiopia. The second text presents a new way of reading an old text – the Robin Hood myth. It shows that changes in society, particularly in the attitudes of society, can lead to changes in the way a text is read. A good example of this is the rise of the women's movement over the last century; this has enabled us to read texts with gender a prime consideration. The third example illustrates some of the real consequences of reading texts in a particular way. People with extreme religious or moral views are apt to find reasons for rejecting texts that have become established parts of the curriculum. If such people have enough power and they read a book differently from you, they can influence the books you are allowed to study. In this case the context of reading is the particular religious beliefs held by that group of people.

This chapter aims to explain and illustrate what is meant by contexts of reading. It shows how the idea can expand one's ability to interpret texts, by opening up new possibilities. The chapter questions how much free play a reader has in interpreting texts. It gives examples of historical contexts of reading and shows how theory can be incorporated into an essay.

So what are contexts of reading?

At this point you might like to remind yourself what is meant by contexts of writing (see page 45). You will see that there, the focus was on the writers themselves, on the historical, psychological or cultural situations in which they are writing and so forth. Here we look at the other end of the process – the readers and their situations. An important question to ask in this respect is: what is it about readers and their situations that might influence the reading of the text? Consider the following possible answers:

- gender
- race
- sexual orientation
- the process of reading
- other readers' views (this is covered on page 187)
- historical/cultural/political context
- social class

ACTIVITY 46

Discuss how examples of each of the above might influence the reading of a text. For example, in the case of 'gender' you might consider that being a woman reader would make you reject some male characters because of the way they treat women. Think of as many examples as you can for each of the items in the list above. It will probably help if you think of specific texts.

COMMENTARY

Of course, none of this implies that you will need a sex change or have to change your sexual orientation in order to discuss a reading other than your own! 'Gender' means that you consider in theory how a man or woman (usually a woman) would read a text. This usually means reading like a feminist critic because of the rise of feminism in literary studies in the last hundred years. In the future it may become possible to read like a 'new man'. The Robin Hood article above is an example of a reading that focuses on sexual orientation. A reading that takes the race of the reader into account considers how black critics or ethnic minority groups might interpret a text. 'The process of reading' is about what happens when you read a text. As you read from beginning to end you gradually create your own personal context, and – if you are a good reader – you should reflect upon this context and its influence on your reading (see page 63). In a classroom situation this context is almost bound to expand into a consideration of the various opinions that are likely to emerge from studying the text. The example at the beginning of this chapter (the song *Drive* by 'The Cars') showed how awareness of a current world event – the Ethiopian famine – could influence the meaning of a text. Similarly, some critics would argue that Shakespeare's *The Merchant of Venice* can never be seen in the same light since the Jewish holocaust of the Second World War. This is because the play tells the story of a Jew's 'crimes' and eventual punishment. 'Social class' requires you to account for the portrayal of social class in a literary work, the implication being that the real subject of the text is the powerful taking advantage of the not-so-powerful – as, for example, in the novels of Charles Dickens and Elizabeth Gaskell. All of these are examples of how the context of reading can influence a reader's interpretation of a text.

Before looking at specific contexts of reading in more detail, the next two sections consider the part played by readers in reading literature.

Readers make meaning?

Students of A level English Literature frequently talk about the texts they are studying, whether to interested relatives or students from other colleges. The plays, poems and novels in the specification are clearly the subject under study. In an obvious way they define the content of English studies at A level. In this sense, the text itself is primary and is clearly more important than who is reading it. Most people would argue that texts play the most important part in creating the meanings that emerge from A level studies. It would be absurd to say that you were just studying your own readings and those of the other students in your class and not the texts. Yet it is also true to some extent, that readers do make meaning and some critics have gone to extreme lengths to show that this is true.

ACTIVITY 47

Before reading the following account, try making sense of the following poem used by American literary theorist, Stanley Fish. Can you produce a satisfying reading?

Jacobs-Rosenbaum
Levin
Thorne
Hayes
Ohman?

In his book entitled '*Is There a Text in this Class?*' Stanley Fish describes the story behind the book's title. Fish had delivered a lecture on linguistics and for this purpose had written the names of several distinguished linguists on the board – the question mark indicates that Fish was unsure of the spelling.

The next class to enter the lecture theatre had just been studying 17th century religious poetry and so you might say that they were in an appropriate 'mindset' for what followed. Fish told his students that what they saw on the board was a poem and they were to interpret it. The results were surprising. The students interpreted the text with a high degree of agreement, saying things such as: 'Jacob' refers to Jacob's ladder from the Old Testament, which often stands for the idea of Christian ascent into heaven. Here the ascent is by means of a tree – a 'rosenbaum' or rose tree which also symbolises the Virgin Mary. Fish's conclusion was that it is not texts that make meanings but readers.

ACTIVITY 48

In a small group discuss any objections to Fish's view that readers are more important than texts in making meaning.

COMMENTARY

The usual objections to Fish's arguments are that a text cannot mean anything you or a group of readers want it to – otherwise there would be no way of judging A level grades! One student's response would be just as valid as any other: if the text itself plays no part in deciding on its meanings then you might as well be studying blank pages for the exam. Most critics now acknowledge that a wide range of interpretations of literary texts are possible and developments in society in the future will almost certainly cause us to look at them again in a new light. But there are limitations: it is very difficult, for example, to read *Julius Caesar* from a feminist perspective because there are no female characters of note – or is this, itself, a feminist critique of the play?!

It is interesting to look at this idea from the point of view of an extreme 20th century literary movement. In the years following the First World War a group of artists and writers known as the Dadaists pitched themselves against all conventional artistic forms. They were so radical that the typical Dadaist poem was a random collection of words pulled from a hat. The purpose of the following activity is to explore in a practical way how much readers are responsible for making meaning in a text.

ACTIVITY 49

Create your own Dadaist poem by collecting together 50 or more words, putting them into a hat and pulling them out randomly. The way in which you select the words in the first place is, of course, crucial. Alternatively you could choose the seventh word on the seventh line of every page of a novel. Or you might consider investing in a 'magnetic poetry' kit available in bookshops. Whichever method you use, discuss the results with someone else. Attempt to interpret the resulting collection of words. Is it possible to call this a poem and can it be interpreted? How does interpreting this differ from interpreting conventional poems?

Key skills: Communication – writing

One clear benefit of working in this way from the point of view of the writer is that it enables you to discover original word combinations. These can then be interpreted by the writer and developed in more coherent ways.

Who makes meaning – the writer or the reader?

This question has plagued literary theorists for a long time and has become particularly heated during the last hundred years. The answer is, of course, both ... and neither! The writer in a sense puts certain limitations on possible readings of the text. The reader is able to give a personal response and consider how different kinds of readers might look at the same text. So both are responsible for providing some of the ingredients. But what is just as important is that neither the writer, nor the reader, nor the two combined are enough to complete the picture. Both writer and reader encounter the text in a situation or context and this helps to create both the original piece of writing and the reader's experience of the text. You should not think of literature as something the writer puts in and the reader takes out, with the teacher acting as a go-between. In other words the situation is *not* like the first diagram opposite; it is more like the second. (Idea adapted from 'Using English' from *Conversation to Canon*, edited by Janet Maybin and Neil Mercer, Routledge, 1996).

Meaning is transmitted from text to reader, mediated by authoritative teachers and critics.

Readers have complex dialogues with texts influenced by their ongoing dialogues with other people and texts.

Text presentation and contexts

You can learn a lot about the context of reading just by examining the way the text is presented. The way in which a piece of literature is presented often tells us a lot about the kind of reader and context that is expected. The following activities will clarify this.

ACTIVITY 50

1 Have a look in your library, local bookshop or English department stock cupboard and see if you can find different editions of texts that demonstrate how the same text may be promoted in different ways. For example, *Lord of the Flies* by William Golding used to feature a line drawing of a bedraggled boy surrounded by sketched trees. A more recent edition had a horrifying picture of a pig's head with rather startling blood dripping from it. Try to explain the differences that you find.

2 Different editions of Shakespeare suggest different contexts of reading because they present different information in slightly different ways; for example – footnotes (what do they contain?), pictures, introduction, etc. Find as many examples of different editions of the same play as you can and pool your findings with a small group. Discuss and make notes on what context of reading is implied by each text. The table below gives some starting points. You might like to continue the table and then write a brief description of the reading context implied by each edition.

Key skills: Communication – reading

Feature	Implied reading context (what are the readers like?)
Translation into contemporary English on opposite page	They can't understand it at all!
Lots of activities all the way through	They're reading it in school and the teacher won't be bothered to think them up. Shakespeare needs to be made practical.
Glossy and lively front cover	They won't pick it up unless you motivate them.

So far this creates a context in which:

- readers need to be encouraged to read and enjoy the text
- the text is being studied at school
- teachers are being saved work

- readers won't understand much unless a translation is provided.

(This activity is taken further in Chapter 7, Activity 120)

Texts can also suggest things about their readers in the blurb on the back of the book. These blurbs will promote a different aspect of the book depending on how the publishers see the readers, and texts are often interpreted in different ways during different historical periods. If you look at different editions of the same text you can see how the publishers have decided to promote the book in order to sell it.

ACTIVITY 51

Texts A to D are blurbs of the same novel, *Great Expectations* by Charles Dickens. This was originally written in serial form in 1860. These synopses are all modern. Take each text and list the key ideas that are expressed in each one. Decide what each writer feels is the main ingredient of the novel. Make a list of recurrent issues and ones which seem to occur only once. Note the different issues that are recorded. What are the main ingredients of the book? Which blurb would encourage you to read the book? Describe the kind of reader that each one seems to suggest.

Key skills: Communication – reading

Blurb A

Great Expectations (first published in 1860/61) is one of the most mature and serious of Dickens' novels. As Angus Calder points out in his introduction, it resembles a detective story – but in the sense in which Oedipus Rex also resembles one. From the first shock of the early pages, when Pip encounters the convict Magwitch, the mystery grips our attention and its psychological and moral truth holds us until the end. For, in discovering the secret of his 'great expectations', Pip also begins to discover the truth about himself.

[The Penguin English Library, 1965]

Blurb B

The central theme of *Great Expectations* – How do men know who they are? – is one that pre-occupied Dickens towards the end of his life.

The story of orphan Pip and the mysterious fortune which falls into his lap, his snobbish rejection of his old friends and his growth through pain and mishap into true maturity is the basis for a story where violence and guilt jostle with sharp and grotesque comedy. From the moment the child Pip meets Magwitch the convict on the eerie Kent marshes, to the last encounter with Estella, the beautiful, heartless woman who has so fruitlessly haunted Pip's emotions, the reader is sucked into a drama whose moral and psychological intensity never slackens.

Comic, tragic, vital, full of bitter pathos and haunting memories of childhood fairytales with an added twist, *Great Expectations* is a novel which, as Graham Greene comments, is full of secret prose giving us 'the sense of a mind speaking to itself with no one to listen.'

[Penguin Classics, 1965]

Blurb C

Great Expectations opens unforgettably in a twilit and overgrown churchyard on the eerie Kent Marshes.

There the orphan Pip is disturbed to meet an escaped convict, Magwitch, but gives him food, in an encounter that is to haunt both their lives. How Pip receives riches from a mysterious benefactor, snobbishly abandons his friends for London society and 'great expectations', and grows through misfortune and suffering to maturity is the theme of one of Dickens' best-loved novels.

In *Great Expectations* Dickens blends gripping drama with penetrating satire to give a compelling story rich in comedy and pathos: he has also created two of his finest, most haunting characters in Pip and Miss Havisham.

[Penguin Popular Classic, 1994]

Blurb D

Great Expectations is one of Dickens' most forcefully moral yet movingly human novels. The development of Philip ('Pip') Pirrip's character after he learns of 'great expectations' of wealth from a mysterious source shows that pride comes before a fall. But he is not the only character to learn from his errors: Estella, a young protegee of the half-deranged Miss Havisham, has used her beauty as a weapon and she suffers too. Dickens portrays repentance and forgiveness with skill, creating a novel of remarkable thematic strength. He changed his original ending on Bulwer-Lytton's advice; the rejected ending is offered in an appendix to this edition.

[Oxford University Press, 1989]

A commentary on this activity can be found on page 79.

Follow-up activities

ACTIVITY 52

1 Choose a text that a small group or a whole class has studied. Write the blurb for a new edition of this text – about five sentences will do. Make the blurb appeal to an A level audience and try to describe what is, for you, the essence of the book. Obviously you cannot include everything. Choose what you think will sell the book and also what you feel it is really about. In pairs compare the texts you have written and compile an agreed interpretation of what the book is about.

Discuss and change your text until you are both satisfied. Display the various versions around a room and on overheads. Note the similarities and differences and try to explain their significance.

2 Try the same activity but this time writing blurbs for different kinds of readers. For example: a school's edition; a simplified version; a TV tie-in edition; etc.

Key skills: Communication – writing

ACTIVITY 53

1 Dickens wrote many of his novels in serial form – that is, in weekly parts. See if you can find out how his stories were received at the time. See what you can find out about how he reacted to public pressure about the progress of his stories and whether he took any notice of public opinion. You may be able to find out on the Internet using the Victorian Web Overview (http://www.stg.brown.edu/projects/hypertext/landow/victorian/victov2.html) or a useful starting point might be Peter Ackroyd's biography of Charles Dickens (page 952

and the bibliography). Compare your findings with the public outcry to some soap operas.

2 Writers have often reacted to public opinion on the endings of their novels. This applies to Dickens, Hardy, Charlotte Brontë, Evelyn Waugh and Anthony Burgess. Compare the ways that some of these reacted and explain how the context in which they were writing influenced these reactions. David Lodge's book *Working with Structuralism* provides a useful starting point here.

ACTIVITY 54

Find other editions of a text you are studying. Either make a note of the blurb or bring the book in. Study the front cover too. Discuss if the blurb and cover fit your interpretation of the text. If you are artistic you might be able to

design a front cover for a text which will demonstrate what the text is about for you. You could also assemble a collection of objects which represent significant aspects of the text.

Using reading contexts

How does a reader actually arrive at readings like the ones at the beginning of this chapter? An important requirement is flexibility: you have to be prepared to consider alternatives if you are to take full advantage of the various contexts of reading. Perhaps the first question to ask is: what kind of contexts might affect the way that a particular literary work is read?

ACTIVITY 55

Read the story *Pattern* below and discuss which of the listed 'contexts' that follow might be useful for reading the story. In other words, do you think that the story could be read according to context 1, context 2, etc?

Key skills: Communication – reading

Pattern by Fred Brown

Miss Macy sniffed. 'Why is everyone worrying so? They're not doing anything to us, are they?'

In the cities, elsewhere, there was blind panic. But not in Miss Macy's garden. She looked up calmly at the monstrous mile-high figures of the invaders.

A week ago, they'd landed, in a spaceship a hundred miles long that had settled down gently in the Arizona desert. Almost a thousand of them had come out of that spaceship and were now walking around.

But, as Miss Macy pointed out, they hadn't hurt anything or anybody. They weren't quite substantial enough to affect people. When one stepped on you or stepped on a house you were in, there was sudden darkness and until he moved his foot and walked on you couldn't see; that was all.

They had paid no attention to human beings and all attempts to communicate with them had failed, as had all attacks on them by the army and the airforce. Shells fired at them exploded right inside them and didn't hurt them. Not even the H-bomb dropped on one of them while he was crossing a desert area had bothered him in the slightest.

They had paid no attention to us at all.

'And that,' said Miss Macy to her sister who was also Miss Macy since neither of them was married, 'is proof that they don't mean us any harm, isn't it?'

'I hope so, Amanda,' said Miss Macy's sister. 'But look what they're doing now.'

It was a clear day, or it had been one. The sky had been bright blue and the almost humanoid heads and shoulders of the giants, a mile up there, had been quite clearly visible. But now it was getting misty, Miss Macy saw as she followed her sister's gaze upward. Each of the two big figures in sight had a tank-like object in his hands and from these objects clouds of vaporous matter were emerging, settling slowly toward Earth.

Miss Macy sniffed again. 'Making clouds. Maybe that's how they have fun. Clouds can't hurt us. Why do people worry so?'

She went back to her work.

'Is that a liquid fertilizer you're spraying, Amanda?' her sister asked.

'No,' said Miss Macy. 'It's insecticide.'

[Fred Brown, from *Angels and Spaceships*]

Reading contexts:

1 The readers are interested in the historical relationship between jokes and short stories, particularly in the way that the story builds towards the 'twist in the tale'.
2 The readers are putting together an anthology of short stories about environmental issues.
3 The readers are champions of the working class and seek to show, in what they read, that the middle class often takes advantage of the working class.
4 The readers are concerned about the spread of ageism in society (e.g. older people finding it more difficult to get jobs) and often use this as a basis for understanding what they read.
5 The readers are women concerned about the promotion of sexist thinking in society.
6 The readers belong to a religious group determined that no offensive material should be used in schools.
7 The readers belong to a 'Science Fiction Writing Club' and are always on the look out for good examples of the genre.

COMMENTARY   Contexts one, two, four, five and seven can easily be applied to this story. Three and six are unlikely to be fruitful, although readers who like a challenge might want to build on the 'garden' versus 'the city' distinction as a way into comments about social class. The story can only be given religious significance if the aliens are seen as symbolic of some religious group or undesirable idea. It is best to focus on those kinds of readings that the text obviously has something to say about. So what is the textual evidence for some of these readings?

Context 1: reading for suspense and 'twist'

Here you might be interested in how the text gradually builds up to the final twist. 'Reading in slow motion' (as described on page 36) is a way into text that ought to be used. It is good for describing how a reader might react at various stages of the story. For example:

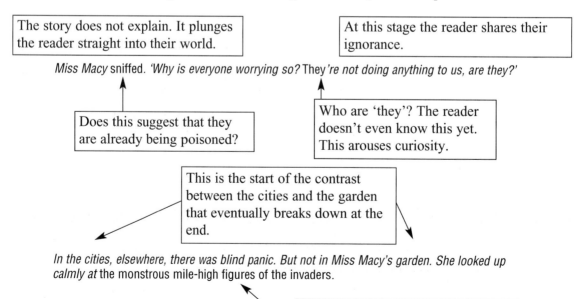

The story does not explain. It plunges the reader straight into their world.

At this stage the reader shares their ignorance.

Miss Macy sniffed. 'Why is everyone worrying so? They're not doing anything to us, are they?'

Does this suggest that they are already being poisoned?

Who are 'they'? The reader doesn't even know this yet. This arouses curiosity.

This is the start of the contrast between the cities and the garden that eventually breaks down at the end.

In the cities, elsewhere, there was blind panic. But not in Miss Macy's garden. She looked up calmly at the monstrous mile-high figures of the invaders.

This is the first note of science fiction and it immediately sets up further expectations.

ACTIVITY 56

Continue the above analysis, showing how the story builds up towards its climax. Pay attention to the following things:

- how curiosity is built up
- how the writer drops hints about the ending
- how the reader's position regarding the characters changes
- how the story is filled out
- the significance of the title
- how the punch line works

Context 2: reading in an environmentally aware context

Possible evidence:

- the contrast between 'city' and 'garden' (countryside?)
- references to deserts
- reference to H-bomb
- implied parallel between aliens treading on houses and people treading on ants
- references to clouds
- references to fun
- references to fertiliser and insecticide

Notice how textual evidence is built up before any kind of argument is produced.

Possible line of argument:

Miss Macy doesn't know the difference between fertiliser and insecticide. They are both just things you spray on the garden. She is punished for this.

The story shows how we can damage the environment at different levels – in the garden and using an H-bomb. They are equally dangerous to us.

Things that seem harmless are not (hence the use of the word 'fun').

Becoming self-sufficient and cutting oneself off from the 'city' will not help.

Thus, the story is an environmental warning.

ACTIVITY 57

Choose one of the other reading contexts and write about the story in the ways suggested above. Further information about reading from a woman's point of view is given on pages 85–89.

In a small group decide on five to six texts that you all know. Then consider the contexts of reading given so far in this chapter and say roughly how you might apply each one (although it is not always possible) to each of the texts. For example, a 'gendered'

interpretation of *Macbeth* would clearly focus on the power of the witches and Lady Macbeth over Macbeth. But could you read the play with social class or race as your main theme?

Key skills: Communication – presentation

Historical contexts of reading

Contexts of reading do not only include present day contexts. Equally important is how other readers at different times in history might have read various texts. The different attitudes of society at those times often meant that texts were read very differently from how they are read today.

Before attempting the next activity, explore your own views on marriage, in a mixed sex group if possible, considering the following aspects of it and any others you think are important.
- How important is it?
- Does it have religious significance?
- How important is it for children's welfare?
- Marriage and divorce.

Thomas Hardy's last novel, *Jude the Obscure*, published in 1895, is the story of failed marriage and failed education. Jude of the title dies wretchedly at the end having seen his partner, Sue, desert him, and his children hanged. Jude and Sue were never married and, because of this, experienced social disapproval.

Read the following two texts about *Jude the Obscure*.

1 Examine them critically so that you are able to pinpoint weaknesses in their arguments. For example, question what the writer assumes to be true; question the writer's logic.
2 Create a list of questions that you would want to ask about *Jude the Obscure* on the

basis of these texts if you were studying the novel.

Key skills: Communication – reading

Text 1:
The following review of *Jude the Obscure* was written in 1895. The right-hand column clarifies some of the points made.

Review 1895	Commentary
Sue and Jude may have been right in their detestation of the marriage tie – that is not the question: the point is that if they act as they did with their eyes open, it is absurd for them to repine because Society and Destiny do not accept their conduct in the same way that they do…There is no tragedy in the foolish weakness of their behaviour as displayed here – it is merely ludicrous …	The writer says that they might have been right in disapproving of marriage. They knew what they were doing when they decided to live together. To 'repine' is to 'lose heart'. Society and Destiny do not accept their non-marriage in the way that they do. Sue returns to a man she does not like and Jude takes to drink.
[Mr Hardy should not have written about] the marriage tie and its permanence. Not that the subject is in itself out of place in fiction; Mr Meredith has triumphantly shown that it is in its place; but lately so many of the inferior writers of novels have stirred up the mud with this controversy, that one would have been content if so great a writer as Mr Hardy had not touched it, if he was not going greatly to dignify it. [Nov 1895, The Athenaeum]	He does not deny that novelists can write about failure of marriage. Meredith was a highly successful writer of the time. Many inferior writers have written about marriage pessimistically so Hardy should have been optimistic.

Text 2:

Here is an extract from a letter by Thomas Hardy to a reviewer. Note that a 'purpose novel' is a novel with an obvious point to make about marriage.

'It is curious that some of the papers should look upon the novel as a manifesto on 'the marriage question' (although, of course, it involves it), seeing that it is concerned first with the labours of a poor student to get a university degree, and secondly with the tragic issues of two bad marriages, owing in the main to a doom or curse of hereditary temperament peculiar to the families of the parties. The only remarks which can be said to bear on the general marriage question occur in the dialogue, and comprise no more than half a dozen pages in a book of five hundred. And of these remarks I state that my own views are not expressed therein. I suppose the attitude of these critics is to be accounted for by the accident that, during the serial publication of my story, a sheaf of 'purpose' novels on the matter appeared.' (Hardy, 10th Nov 1895)

COMMENTARY   **Text 1**

Here the writer seems to assume that the two main characters acted with their eyes open, but it is worth considering the extent to which they are in fact given a choice in what they do. Secondly, he does not really argue that their behaviour is foolish weakness; he really asserts it. Two further assumptions should be questioned: Firstly, what exactly does the writer mean by tragedy? There are several different types of tragedy, so you would need to find out which, if any, fits this novel, and secondly, he calls Hardy a great writer – and this can hardly be challenged – but he makes all kinds of assumptions about what great writers can and cannot do in their works.

This last point leads to grounds for questioning the logic of the writer of Text 1. Firstly, if many inferior writers have made a point, can the same point not be made by a great writer without debasing himself? Secondly, if you consciously make a decision to do something and society rejects you for it, is it your fault? Are you displaying 'foolish weakness'? A comparison with people who put themselves out on a limb in today's society clearly needs to be made here.

Text 2

Hardy seems to think that it is enough to count the number of pages that are directly about the marriage question, i.e. in the dialogue. He overlooks the extent to which the plot may indirectly support these pages. Besides, does it matter whether or not Hardy's own views are expressed in this dialogue? Hardy's final comment about the popularity of marriage as a topic for novels suggests that, at the time, views were undergoing change and therefore Hardy's novel needs to be seen in the light of this broader issue.

Some of these questions move away from the text into context; others require specific answers from *Jude the Obscure* itself. These are some of the questions which the foregoing activity may have raised about the text:

- did the characters act with their eyes open?
- is their behaviour foolish weakness?
- is the novel a manifesto on the marriage question?
- are the only remarks on the general marriage question in the dialogue?

ACTIVITY 60

Write a paragraph in response to the above texts. Bring out some of your own opinions and those of the writers. Use expressions such as:

- One contemporary reviewer believed that...
- Hardy felt that ...
- A modern view might be that ...

ACTIVITY 61

Compare the following modern views of Dickens, following the procedure of Activity 57. Consider how the context of each text might have affected the writer's views.

Text A

Extract from *Great Writers – An Illustrated Companion to the Lives and Works of Britain's most Celebrated Writers* (1992)

'Charles Dickens was the greatest novelist of his time and is regarded by many as the greatest English writer after Shakespeare. The 'Dickensian' world is entirely his own, peopled with characters larger than life – Mr Micawber, Samuel Pickwick, Ebenezer Scrooge and a host of others. But Dickens was more than just a creator of memorable and colourful characters – he was essentially a subversive writer. He made his readers think and feel and *act* in a way that was new. Though he came to be embraced by the establishment of his own time, Dickens spent his life fighting its tyranny and injustice. When he died, a cabman's testimonial summed him up: 'Ah, Mr Dickens was a great man and a true friend of the poor.' (page 119)

Text B

Millennium Reputations: Which are the most overrated authors, or books, of the last 1,000 years? Continuing our series, the chairman of this year's Booker Prize, Gerald Kaufman, nominates Charles Dickens.

'... it is indubitably Dickens, who pulled a more successful con-trick ... by persuading millions – including the entire educational establishment – that the pulp fiction he penned was actually great literature.

Consider his plots: a stomach-turning mixture of melodrama, Grand Guignol and sloppy sentimentality. Consider the caricatures he called characters: the sturdy young chaps like Pip or Nickleby; the sickly (and sickening) waifs like Little Nell and Tiny Tim (God curse them, every one); the onomatopoeic villains, such as Murdstone, Squeers and, until his intolerable and unsatisfactory regeneration, Scrooge; the comic rude mechanicals – even more intolerable than Shakespeare's – like Sam Weller, with his excrutiating mispronunciation of 'v's and 'w's. Consider the anti-Semitism behind the creation of Fagin. Moreover, the evil that Dickens did lived after him, with *Oliver!,* one of the most gruesome musicals ever composed, and the nadir of Carol Reed's distinguished career. Today, adaptations of Dickens' novels provide a dreary G-string for the dumbed-down BBC. ...'

(Extract from *Sunday Telegraph* June 13th 1999, page 12).

Incorporating theory into an essay

Students often wonder how to structure a paragraph in an essay, or if they don't, they usually make up the essay as they go along – something that is definitely to be avoided! This section suggests a way of incorporating literary theory into a paragraph about two short stories, focusing in particular on how to structure the paragraph. Bear in mind, however, that it is not a straight-jacket – some variation is recommended.

The context of reading is often about using texts to judge each other. An obvious example of this is when you use a piece of criticism and a literary work together. The criticism helps you to assess the literature but you also use your reading of the literature to assess the criticism. The example that follows shows how a piece of theory can be incorporated into your reading of a text. It is based on two short stories from the collection *The Penguin Book of Modern Women's Short Stories* (edited by Susan Hill) and Frank O'Connor's theory of the short story. Frank O'Connor was an Irish short story writer who also wrote a book about the modern short story called *The Lonely Voice.*

For this activity it is not necessary to read the stories but you may wish to extend the activity by applying O'Connor's theory yourself, either to these stories or to one with which you are familiar.

Text 1: *The Visitor* – by Elizabeth Bowen.

This is the story of Roger, a young boy who has to stay with two old aunts because his mother is terminally ill. The story is told from Roger's point of view and it builds in tension as he awaits the tragic news.

Text 2: *A Fall from Grace* – by Sarah Maitland.

This is the story of two twin female trapeze artists who symbolically re-enact the myth of the Garden of Eden, in which Adam and Eve are expelled from the Garden.

Text 3: Frank O'Connor's theory of the short story says that short stories look at isolated individuals who undergo a frontier experience. Here, isolation can be physical, psychological or social, and a 'frontier experience' involves some kind of significant moment, like the experience of the death of a relative, that changes your perspective in some way.

ACTIVITY 62

How to structure a paragraph incorporating theory

In the extract below the text is the start of an essay that asks for Frank O'Connor's theory of the short story to be applied to the two short stories named above. In the right-hand column the labels for the different parts of the essay have been missed off. Match the labels below with the numbers in the right hand column.

The labels

Some of the labels used speak for themselves but most are explained:

A Advance organiser – this tells the reader what is about to come, in advance.
B Wider context – an argument becomes less specific in its application.
C Conclusion (links with topic sentence).

D Drawing ideas together.
E Topic sentence – this opens a paragraph and explains the subject of the sentence that follows.
F Either move on to the next story or the next aspect of O'Connor's theory.
G Evidence – this provides evidence from the text using paraphrase.
H Examples – these are more specific than evidence, and support the evidence.
I Contrast – this shows how ideas contrast with each other, possibly raising problems.
J Quotation.
K Expansion – an idea is taken a step further.

Answers at end of chapter. Some are already provided.
The forward slashes show how the text is to be divided up.

O'Connor's first requirement is that the main character is isolated in	1
some way./ In 'The Visitor' Roger is isolated in several senses./	2
Obviously he is physically separated from his parents by being sent	
to the Miss Emerys' house. Several aspects of this physical environment	3
reflect Roger's current state of mind./ For example, the reader is	4
constantly made aware of 'blackness', 'darkness' and 'shadows' with	
which Roger seems to have become obsessed./ These images suggest the	
shadow of his mother's impending death and yet they are also strangely	
comforting to him:/	5

'…obscuring the familiar town lights … making him feel distant and magnificently isolated …'/	6 J
This seems to suggest that he wants to remain 'alone, enisled with tragedy', fearing the news (of his mother's death) that will inevitably change his life./ Similarly, he gains comfort from the hall clock with its expressionless tick./ Not only are colours and sounds important here but so is Roger's need to count things, this perhaps suggesting his desire to regain control of his life, a control that he has clearly lost./ So in several subtle and interconnected ways, O'Connor's first condition is met./	7 8 9 10

Possible continuations:

Isolation in 'A Fall from Grace' takes a completely different form… OR The 'frontier experience' in 'The Visitor' is highlighted in both the title of the story and the arrival of Roger's father …	11 F

ACTIVITY 63

Either: Apply Frank O'Connor's theory of the short story to two stories that you are studying and write one of the paragraphs using the above format.

Or: Use the above format to write a paragraph about any piece of literature you are studying.

Key skills: Communication – reading

This chapter has made the following points:

- readers help to create the meaning of a literary work.
- they are influenced by the real or imagined context in which they read.
- contexts of reading change the meaning of a piece of literature.
- texts themselves tell us a lot about their readers.
- readers incorporate the views of other readers and critics into their own.

COMMENTARY ON ACTIVITY 51

Blurb A: This blurb suggests an intellectual audience – it expects its readers to be familiar with *Oedipus Rex* (a Greek tragedy) and perhaps to know other works by Dickens ('mature and serious' invites comparison with other books they have read). The blurb wants the reader to enjoy a good story but it expects them to be above anything that is merely a detective story. The allure of the plot ('mystery grips') is ultimately outweighed by the pleasures of insight into human nature ('psychological and moral truth', 'truth about himself').

Blurb B: This starts off philosophically with the reference to men knowing who they are and there is again familiarity with Dickens. There is more emphasis on plot, and particularly on Pip, as if the reader would be interested in his growing up. This is done through appeals to the emotions as in, 'orphan Pip', 'mysterious fortune', 'snobbish fortune', 'pain and mishap'. There is a definite sense that there is a soap opera viewer lurking behind 'violence and guilt', 'the beautiful and heartless woman', 'haunted

Pip's emotions'. This is perhaps supported by the fact that this blurb is the only one to mention romance. This can be contrasted with the reference to Graham Greene which suggests a specialist reader interested in the intricacies of style i.e. a student!

Blurb C: This is aimed at a less intellectual audience. It concentrates entirely on plot development and suggests that its audience is looking for an entertaining read, especially in the atmosphere suggested by the opening paragraph. The delights of the story are suggested in: 'gripping', 'compelling', 'haunting'.

Blurb D: It is more difficult to pinpoint a precise reader for this one. It has elements of a 'Hollywood blockbuster' audience in its use of cliché ('pride comes before a fall' and 'used her beauty as a weapon') but otherwise it is mainly abstract ('human novel', 'repentance and forgiveness') and gives away very little of the plot. Possibly the reference to the alternative ending suggests a study context.

Answers to Activity 62: 1E, 2A, 3G, 4H, 5I, 6J, 7K, 8D, 9B, 10C, 11F.

Further reading

'Jude the Obscure and the Marriage Problem' by Stephanie Forward in *The English Review*, Vol 10, No 1, Sept 1999.
An excellent example of how to raise questions using historical context.

Reading Fictions by B. Mellor, A. Patterson, M. O'Neill; Chalkface Press (1991).
An excellent practical book that explores context and literary theory. Packed with useful activities.

Reading Stories by B. Mellor, A. Patterson, M. O'Neill; Chalkface Press (1987).
Similar to the above.

Reading and Responding to Literature by Suzanne Cole and Jeff Lindemann; Harcourt Brace Jovanovich (1990).
Aimed at an American market but useful for different ways of reading.

5 Methodologies – An Introduction to Literary Theory

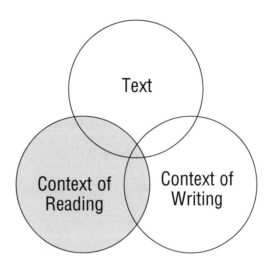

Where does this fit in?

In learning about different literary theories you will be thinking about different interpretations of literary texts by different readers (Assessment Objective 4).

These theories play an important part in how literary texts are understood and studied today (Assessment Objectives 5i and 5ii).

What are literary theories?

In simple terms, literary theories are theories about the ways that people read and interpret literature. A great deal of the work in this area was done in the 20th century and came about because of changes in the way that people thought about the world, reading and the nature of literary texts. Before embarking on this challenging topic however, it is worth considering for a while, how you read literature.

ACTIVITY 64

With a partner discuss which of the following statements apply to you. Rank order them from most to least preferred.

1 Readers read a text and just apply their common sense to it.

2 Readers read a text, gradually changing their opinions as they go.
3 Readers read by applying technical terminology to texts.
4 Readers are told what to think about a text by all of the great critics who have gone before.

5 Readers are influenced by the 'groups' to which they belong (e.g. women).
6 Texts give readers experiences which they must then try to understand.
7 Readers read by analysing the language of the text.

COMMENTARY

These statements are all to some extent true although it is the first one that this book attempts to challenge. You can go so far with common sense but your reading will be much richer if you go beyond it. This chapter builds on what has gone before in the preceding three chapters, so, although it sounds rather daunting we have tried to build you up slowly to what you are about to face here – some of the major literary theories of the 20th century.

There are, roughly speaking, three kinds of literary theory, depending on where you put the emphasis in reading.

Focus on text	Focus on the readers	Focus on society (context of reading and writing)
Structuralism	Reader response	Feminism
Stylistics		Marxism
←————— Deconstruction —————→		

The chart does not claim to be complete; it mentions only some theories that might be useful for A level purposes. The categorisation of the theories indicates their main area of focus in this respect.

Like the preceding chapter, this chapter continues to look at contexts of reading but in a way that becomes more specialised in literary studies. You will be introduced to theories that allow you to read texts in different ways. These are theories that have been developed during this century, such as feminism, Marxism etc. Daunting as they may sound, they are really only labels for taking into account a particular point of view when you read.

Focus on readers: reader response theories

There are many variations on this theme and you should be aware that most of this book takes a reader response approach to some extent. Here only some of the basic principles will be covered.

Several decades ago critics realised that the meaning of a piece of literature was not simply put into it by the author, waiting to be pulled out by the reader. The solution to this problem lay in paying close attention to the words on the page and letting them speak for themselves. Then critics realised that the words on the page didn't always mean the same thing – the meaning depended on who was reading them. It then became apparent that readers don't just read in a vacuum – they are influenced by the context (the society and all that it entails) in which they read. Reader response theories tend to focus on the individual reader but have increasingly taken into account the wider context. A more recent addition to all of this is the theory New Historicism which again focuses on the writer, but this time on the context in which the writer worked; in this respect things have moved a full circle. Chronologically then, critics' attention has moved like this:

The writer → The text → The reader → The context

Reader response theory says that the reader, to a greater or lesser degree, plays a part in creating the meaning of a work of literature. How is this possible?

Gaps

One branch of this theory says that texts are not really complete: they deliberately leave gaps or spaces for the reader to fill. In this way, instead of sitting back and letting the text take you over, you become a participant in making the text. In other words, the reader's role is active. But how can a text be incomplete? There are several senses in which this is true. Imagine a story that begins with a man walking down a road. If you were to make a film of that story you would have to choose a real road and a real person to fit the bill. That means that you would have to make all kinds of further decisions about the kind of man and the kind of road you wanted to present. The imagination works in a similar way – there is a tendency for us to complete mental images based on stereotypes in our heads. So:

- one meaning of 'gap' refers to visualisation of incomplete material in the story
- a second kind of gap might be when the reader has to assume a character's past, given a few brief hints at what it might have been
- a third, more significant kind, is when the writer gives information that does not seem to go together and the reader has to work to account for what has been read.

There are two important provisos to bear in mind here:

1 As a reader you have some freedom to fill in the gaps how you like, but assuming that Elizabeth Bennett from *Pride and Prejudice* is an alien will not get you very far
2 Gaps in texts are not just random. They are carefully constructed for you to fill in so that if, for example, a text describes a character in great detail it might not leave you much room for manoeuvre.

ACTIVITY 65

The second of the above points is followed up here. Read the following extract from Harold Pinter's play *The Caretaker* about a man, Aston, who invites Davies, who often sleeps rough, back to his home which is full of useless objects. The text contains carefully constructed gaps.

a Identify what you think are the gaps in the extract and the different ways that they are indicated.

b Say what you think might be the significance of these gaps in terms of the developing action of the play.

Key skills: Communication – reading

Davies: Nothing but wind then.
(Pause)
Aston: Yes, when the wind gets up it. . . .
(Pause)
Davies: Yes. . . .
Aston: Mmmmn. . . .
(Pause)
Davies: Gets very draughty
Aston: Ah.
Davies: Always have been.
(Pause)

         You got more rooms then, have you?
Aston: Where?
Davies: I mean, along the landing here . . . up the landing there.
Aston: They're out of commission.
Davies: Get away.
Aston: They need a lot of doing to.
(Slight pause)
Davies: What about downstairs?
Aston: That's closed up. Needs seeing to . . . The floors . . .
(Pause)
Davies: I was lucky you come into that caff. I might have done that Scotch git. I been left for dead more than once.

(Pause)

         I noticed that there was someone living in the house next door.
Aston: What?
Davies: (gesturing):   I noticed . . .
Aston: Yes. There's people living all along the road.
Davies: Yes, I noticed the curtains pulled down there next door as we come along.
Aston: They're neighbours.
(Pause)
Davies: This your house then, is it?
(Pause)
Aston: I'm in charge.
Davies: You the landlord, are you?
         (He puts a pipe in his mouth and puffs without lighting it.)
         Yes, I noticed them heavy curtains pulled across next door as we come along.

                                    [Activity adapted from Hayman, 1977]

COMMENTARY Pinter builds on western cultural conventions that dictate the 'rules' for natural conversation. That is, the reader (or audience) notices the pauses because they would not occur without having some extra significance beyond the surface level of the conversation. The pauses are signalled by dots, 'slight pause', 'pause', and the stage direction for Davies to put the pipe to his mouth. They are also indicated in more subtle ways such as the short replies, the absence of replies and the quickly changing topics. The pauses then suggest a more significant gap about the relationship between the two men and where it is leading. These gaps might be filled by suggesting that they are embarrassed, they are unable or unwilling to find a point of contact or they are both defensive. A final gap is that the conversation itself seems to be rather aimless. We expect conversations to lead somewhere, even when they are as mundane as this. Arguably, this opens up another gap which directs attention away from plot development and towards character development and style. Not all textual gaps are as blatantly signalled as these! For an indication of how a reader might respond to gaps in prose, see the responses to the beginning of the short story on page 71.

Focus on society 1: feminism

It is impossible not to make assumptions when you read. If the writer did not leave the reader to assume some things then he would have to explain everything – which would be impossible. This section looks at assumptions and how they can affect the way we read literature.

ACTIVITY 66

Read the following sonnet, then copy it and respond with your own comments in the margin. Concentrate on the kind of person portrayed by 'I' and the situation he is in. To get the most from this activity you will need to spend about half an hour making notes on the poem. Your response could be in the form suggested on page 86 or in any form you feel comfortable with. Note that 'fume' is excitement; 'blood' is associated with passion; 'to season' means to soften; 'propinquity' is nearness.

Sonnet XLI

I, being born a man and distressed
By all the needs and notions of my kind,
Am urged by your propinquity to find
Your person fair, and feel a certain zest
To bear your body's weight upon my breast:
So subtly is the fume of life designed,
To clarify the pulse and cloud the mind,
And leave me once again undone, possessed.
Think not for this, however, the poor treason
Of my stout blood against my staggering brain,
I shall remember you with love, or season
My scorn with pity, – let me make it plain:
I find this frenzy insufficient reason
For conversation when we meet again.

Here are one reader's responses to the poem. Compare your own with these and make further responses about anything you disagree with.

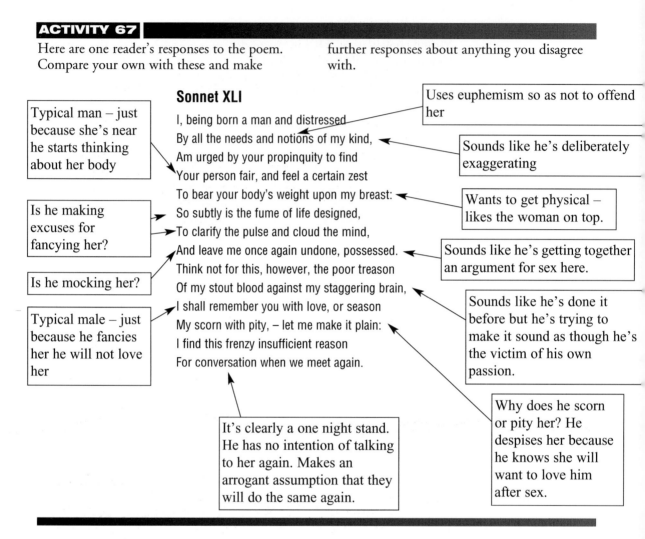

Sonnet XLI

I, being born a man and distressed
By all the needs and notions of my kind,
Am urged by your propinquity to find
Your person fair, and feel a certain zest
To bear your body's weight upon my breast:
So subtly is the fume of life designed,
To clarify the pulse and cloud the mind,
And leave me once again undone, possessed.
Think not for this, however, the poor treason
Of my stout blood against my staggering brain,
I shall remember you with love, or season
My scorn with pity, – let me make it plain:
I find this frenzy insufficient reason
For conversation when we meet again.

Typical man – just because she's near he starts thinking about her body

Is he making excuses for fancying her?

Is he mocking her?

Typical male – just because he fancies her he will not love her

Uses euphemism so as not to offend her

Sounds like he's deliberately exaggerating

Wants to get physical – likes the woman on top.

Sounds like he's getting together an argument for sex here.

Sounds like he's done it before but he's trying to make it sound as though he's the victim of his own passion.

Why does he scorn or pity her? He despises her because he knows she will want to love him after sex.

It's clearly a one night stand. He has no intention of talking to her again. Makes an arrogant assumption that they will do the same again.

Now do the same with what is the original version of the poem, noting the changes. How and why has your response changed?

Sonnet XLI

I, being born a woman and distressed
By all the needs and notions of my kind,
Am urged by your propinquity to find
Your person fair, and feel a certain zest
To bear your body's weight upon my breast:
So subtly is the fume of life designed,
To clarify the pulse and cloud the mind,
And leave me once again undone, possessed.
Think not for this, however, the poor treason
Of my stout blood against my staggering brain,

I shall remember you with love, or season
My scorn with pity, – let me make it plain:
I find this frenzy insufficient reason
For conversation when we meet again.

COMMENTARY   You should have found that reading 'man' or 'woman' in the first line made a big difference to the way in which you interpreted the poem. The man perhaps comes across as an arrogant predator who coldly explains what he is doing. The woman appears to be unusually frank about her feelings but she ultimately places herself above such passions. The vast majority of the words in the poem have stayed the same so the different readings must have come from assumptions made by the reader – in other words from the culture in which the reader lives. It is these assumptions that much feminist criticism seeks to challenge.

The poem is in fact itself a challenge to these assumptions. It was written by the American writer Edna St Vincent Millay in the early decades of the 20th century. Millay had the reputation as a 'new woman' of the 1920s, with liberated views to match.

The next section explores how feminism has tried to challenge these sexist assumptions.

Reading and writing as a woman

Reading as a woman may be just as difficult for women as for men. It requires reading with awareness of gender, even though that may not be the theme of the literature you are studying. This feminist position has arisen in the last few decades partly because many male critics have in the past assumed that readers are male.

Another way in which feminism has revealed itself is in feminist literature. This sets out to present the world from a woman's point of view or to highlight women's issues. Margaret Atwood's feminist dystopia, *The Handmaid's Tale*, (a nightmare vision of a future society) sees women as the victims of a fundamentalist backlash when human fertility is threatened. A variation on this is feminist re-interpretation of well-known genres and stories; for example; Angela Carter's book *The Bloody Chamber* re-interprets a number of traditional fairy tales.

ACTIVITY 69

Charlotte Brontë's novel *Jane Eyre* tells the story of the heroine's relationship with Mr Rochester. Rochester's wife, Bertha, is mad and kept in the attic of his house. The following two extracts from critical works both attempt to explain Bertha but in vastly different ways. Identify which of them is the feminist reading and state what kind of a reading the other is (use page 86 to help you with this). Write down your evidence for these opinions. There is a commentary at the end of the chapter.

Reading 1

The chilling image of mad Mrs Rochester locked in the attic of Thornfield Hall seems too horrific to be anything but the creation of Charlotte Brontë's imagination – yet it had a factual basis. When Charlotte was a governess, she visited Norton Conyers Hall near Ripon. The old house still stands today – an atmospheric place, strongly echoing Thornfield, and, tellingly, associated with an 18th century legend of a madwoman locked away upstairs. Moreover, in 1845, Charlotte went to North Lees Hall near Sheffield, an old farm belonging to a family called Eyre. Here too there was a legend of a madwoman (this one perished in a fire). In an age when asylums were few and far between, many caring families chose to keep their mad relatives at home.

Reading 2

… 'the Madwoman in the Attic,' the dark double who stands for the heroine's anger and desire, as well as for all the repressed creative anxiety of the nineteenth century woman writer. … Bertha not only acts *for* Jane in expressing her rage towards Rochester's mastery but also acts *like* her, paralleling Jane's childhood outbursts of violent rebellion against injustice and confinement … Jane … never sees her kinship with the confined and monstrous double, and … Brontë has no sympathy for her mad creature. Before Jane Eyre can reach her happy ending, the madwoman must be purged from the plot, and passion must be purged from Jane herself.

ACTIVITY 70

Thomas Hardy's novel *The Mayor of Casterbridge* is about an unemployed farm worker who sells his wife to a sailor at a fair whilst drunk.

If you don't know the story, think about how the story might continue and end using the following suggestions:

1 the man finds a better wife and successfully fights off her attempts at revenge.
2 the sailor abuses his new wife and eventually she returns to her first husband.
3 the man is eventually made to pay the price for what he has done.
4 the woman is happy with the sailor and the man happily remarries.

If one disapproves of the man's action and we expect the book to take a moral stance, then 3 is the only plot development that can be allowed.

Here is what one male critic has written about the beginning of the novel:

To shake loose from one's wife; to discard that drooping rag of a woman, with her mute complaints and maddening passivity; to escape not by slinking abandonment but through the public sale of her body to a stranger, as horses are sold at a fair; and thus to wrest, through sheer amoral wilfulness, a second chance out of life – it is with this stroke, so insidiously attractive to male fantasy, that *The Mayor of Casterbridge* begins. [Irving Howe]

This seems to assume that the reader is male and implies that male readers would sympathise with the man. But what about female readers? If the above represents a male perspective on the man's action, then what would a female perspective look like?

1 With a partner predict which aspects of the selling of the wife a feminist reading might focus on.

2 Read the following extract from the novel and write an assessment of Irving Howe's comment on the episode.

3 Write your own commentary with gender as the main issue. If you want to compare your commentary with ours, turn to page 95.

Key skills: Communication – writing

(Michael Henchard has just sold his wife Susan to a sailor for five guineas.)

The sailor looked at the woman and smiled. 'Come along!' he said kindly. 'This little one too – the more the merrier!' She paused for an instant, with a close glance at him. Then dropping her eyes again, and saying nothing, she took up the child and followed him as he made towards the door. On reaching it, she turned, and pulling off her wedding ring, flung it across the booth in the hay-trusser's [*Henchard's*] face.

'Mike,' she said, 'I've lived with thee a couple of years, and had nothing but temper! Now I'm no more to 'ee; I'll try my luck elsewhere. 'Twill be better for me and Elizabeth-Jane, both. So good-bye!'

Seizing the sailor's arm with her right hand, and mounting the little girl on her left, she went out of the tent sobbing bitterly.

A stolid look of concern filled the husband's face, as if, after all, he had not quite anticipated this ending; and some of the guests laughed.

'Is she gone?' he said.

'Faith, ay; she's gone clane enough,' said some rustics near the door.

He rose and walked to the entrance with the careful tread of one conscious of his alcoholic load. Some others followed, and they stood looking into the twilight. The difference between the peacefulness of inferior nature and the wilful hostilities of mankind was very apparent at this place. In contrast with the harshness of the act just ended within the tent was the sight of several horses crossing their necks and rubbing each other lovingly as they waited in patience to be harnessed for the homeward journey. Outside the fair, in the valleys and woods, all was quiet. The sun had recently set, and the west heaven was hung with rosy cloud, which seemed permanent, yet slowly changed. To watch it was like looking at some grand feat of stagery from a darkened auditorium. In presence of this scene after the other there was a natural instinct to abjure man as the blot on an otherwise kindly universe; till it was remembered that all terrestrial conditions were intermittent, and that mankind might some night be innocently sleeping when these quiet objects were raging loud.

Focus on society 2: Marxism

Marxist criticism stems from the thinking of Karl Marx (1818–1883) whose political theory led others to set up Communist states in countries such as Russia in the early decades of the 20th century. But Marx himself did not apply his theory to literature and those who have succeeded him have come up with many different ways of applying his ideas. In essence these ideas suggest that we should look at literature from the point of view of the class struggle. That is, how the different social classes regard each other or have done so at a particular point in history. Usually the focus is on how the more powerful people in society have taken advantage of those with less power.

In Shakespeare's time (end of the 16th century) there was no such thing as Marxist theory and as a literary theory it did not exist until the 20th century. This means that scholars in universities are now able to re-interpret Shakespeare's plays from the point of view of this new theory. Some people would say that that is what makes Shakespeare great – his plays can be read from a Marxist perspective, even though Shakespeare would not have been aware of the possibility.

So, what would a Marxist reading of Shakespeare actually be like? To some extent it is possible to guess at the kinds of things that would come into focus.

ACTIVITY 72

1 Write out a list of plays by Shakespeare that you (with a partner if you wish) know a little about.
2 Write out a list of the characters that you know.
3 Put the characters approximately into rank order from the person with the highest status to the person with the lowest status.
4 What happens to these characters and what is the relationship between their ranks? For example, the authority of those with high status in *Romeo and Juliet* (the prince, Capulet and Montague) is disregarded.
5 What does the text seem to be saying in these terms? Given the ending of *Romeo and Juliet*, we might say that those with power,

maintain it and those who struggled against it have got their just desserts. What about the part played by relatively lowly characters such as the Friar and the Nurse?

So, in interpreting Shakespeare from a Marxist perspective we would obviously have to consider the status of the characters and their role in the whole play. But the analysis would not get much further unless we discovered something about social class in Shakespeare's time. We would then be in a position to argue that a particular play was actually saying something about social class at the time that Shakespeare was writing. The critic Raman Selden gives the following example:

Most Marxist accounts of social and economic developments in the early seventeenth century ... perceive two main features of conflict underlying the political, ideological and cultural life of England:

1. The gradual rise of middle-class entrepreneurs and the steady decline of the older 'feudal' ruling class.
2. The growth of a dispossessed mass of day-labourers and able-bodied vagrants, accompanied by a steady increase in 'capitalist' agriculture and the 'enclosure of the common lands.'

If we look at *King Lear* (Shakespeare) in these terms, we see that the division between the main protagonists fits the first category of conflict: Lear, Gloucester, and Kent represent the old feudal order with its values of hospitality ... duty, social hierarchy and honour; the 'bad' characters, Goneril, Regan and Edmund, represent the rising new class of grasping and ruthless individualists and, by extension, the economic forces of capitalism.

Marxist critical theory is likely to be one of the most difficult you will encounter. But it applies well to novels where the social class of the characters is clearly defined. For example, it can be applied easily and with considerable reward to Emily Brontë's *Wuthering Heights* and to Daniel Defoe's *Robinson Crusoe*.

Focus on text 1: structuralism

The name suggests something to do with structures and that is indeed the emphasis that will be given here. This theory reached its height in the 1960s and is regarded by some as a little old-fashioned today. However, although this is true of its underlying philosophy, there are still elements of the theory that can be regarded as useful for the purpose of analysing literature. These can be regarded as tools that can be applied to the other theories presented here.

Structuralism was developed when some of the scientific rigour of linguistics (the scientific study of language) was applied to literature. The theory is vast and takes many forms, but only two or three elements of it will be explained here.

Story shapes

One of the real gains of structuralism was that it described ways in which plots develop, showing how the parts relate to each other.

One of the most basic story structures is 'placement' – 'displacement(s)' – 'replacement', a simple three part structure which is explained as follows:

Placement	A character is placed in a certain situation, usually with problems attached to it, e.g. a boy does not like being on holiday with his parents.
Displacement(s)	The situation changes in some way (there may be several of these), e.g. the boy's father dies.
Replacement	Some final change takes place that relates to the original placement, e.g. the boy changes his attitude (to the holiday and life).

ACTIVITY 73

Apply the three-part structure – placement, displacement, replacement – to the plot of Jane Austen's *Pride and Prejudice* (below). How satisfying do you find this?

1 Elizabeth and her sisters are unmarried women.
2 Elizabeth and Darcy meet.
3 He unknowingly insults her at a dance.
4 She dislikes him as a consequence.
5 He starts to find her attractive, but she finds him more disagreeable.
6 They meet again at his aunt's.
7 He proposes.
8 She refuses and tells him why.
9 He writes a letter defending himself.
10 Swayed by the letter, she begins to revise her impressions of him.
11 They meet yet again at his estate.
12 She realises she loves him.
13 He proves himself by helping the Bennett family in a time of trouble.
14 He proposes again.
15 She accepts.
16 They marry.
[Cohan and Shires, 1988]

COMMENTARY You probably found it easy to say that Elizabeth Bennett moves from an unmarried state to a married one. The middle section consists of various situations in which Elizabeth holds different views of Darcy. If you know the novel it is important to consider what other things are replaced at each stage. For example, the poverty of Elizabeth is seen as a potential problem for marrying well at the beginning of the novel. By the end this mere financial concern has been replaced by love. In the middle phase of the novel the state of being unmarried is replaced by several less satisfactory marriages than the one that ends the book.

ACTIVITY 74

1 Apply this structure to novels (or films) of different genres (science fiction, thriller, tragedy, parody, etc.) and assess the extent to which it can be applied. Don't forget to think in terms of ideas and not just events replacing each other.
2 If you have read a short story, apply this structure and compare it with its application to novels. You might like to try applying it to *Pattern* on page 71.
3 Apply the structure to any of the texts you are studying as part of your course.

Key skills: Communication – reading

Characters' roles

One of the great insights of structuralism was to see characters in terms of the parts they play in the whole story. This work was originally applied to fairy tales but it can be usefully adapted to novels and especially short stories. The fairy tale *Beauty and the Beast* is the story of a young woman who, to save her father's life, marries 'Beast' in spite of his ugliness and is rewarded when he turns into a handsome prince. The story can be analysed like this:

Subject (*the one who performs the main action*)	Beauty
Object (*the goal or destination of the action*)	Beast
Sender (*initiates or makes something happen*)	Witch
Receiver (*benefiting from the events*)	Beast's kingdom
Opponent (*opposes events or competes with subject*)	Beauty's jealous sisters
Helper (*helps the subject*)	Beauty's father

[based on Cohan and Shires, 1988]

In applying this you should bear in mind that each element can occur more than once and that a single character could fulfil more than one role. The system is useful because it can help to unearth common structures between stories, showing the extent to which novelists rely on existing myths for their inspiration.

ACTIVITY 75

1 Apply the above system to one of the following: *Pride and Prejudice* (you will need to know the whole story); a fairy tale; a short story you are studying.
2 How useful did you find it? Don't forget that if the system doesn't fit exactly, you will still learn something about the complexities of the text.

Binary oppositions

This idea is a useful tool for analysing all kinds of literature. It is based on the simple notion that we think by using ideas that are the opposite of each other and that literature uses these opposites to develop its themes. For example, in *Pride and Prejudice* 'getting married' and 'remaining single' together make a binary opposition that helps to structure the whole novel. Other binary oppositions that frequently occur in literature are: good/evil; home/away; male/female; strong/weak; and so forth.

ACTIVITY 76

Re-read the poem (*Sonnet XLI*) on page 86 and identify as many ideas as you can that appear to be opposites or near opposites; for example, several words and phrases suggest lust or passion ('zest', 'pulse', etc.) whereas others suggest reason or a lack of passion ('mind' and 'brain'). Set out these oppositions in two columns, trying to identify as many as you can, even when one of the opposites is not explicitly named. Take these ideas and try to explain what the poem seems to be saying about them.

The commentary on this activity can be found on page 95.

Focus on Text 2: stylistics

This takes linguistic methods of analysis and applies them to texts. See Chapter 6, page 97 for a detailed exploration. See also *Language and Literature*, by George Keith (Hodder & Stoughton, 1999), in the *Living Language* series.

Focus on text 3: deconstruction

Perhaps the best way to explain a small element of deconstruction is to demonstrate how it can grow out of a structuralist reading of the poem *Sonnet XLI* on page 86.

The poem seems to be about a woman (because it is written by a woman) who asserts her sexuality in spite of 'being born a woman' which traditionally means that she is not allowed to do this. 'Distressed' refers to the feelings she is supposed to have about her own sexual urges and there is a euphemistic coyness about 'needs' and 'notions', as if she is afraid of more direct expressions. She describes her feelings as so powerful that she cannot resist them and they seem to overwhelm her rational mind ('staggering brain'). Traditionally, sexual feelings had to be associated with love but she feels no such connection, indeed she feels quite the opposite ('scorn'). The poem ends powerfully with a statement of intent – she will take this no further and will go as far as to snub the man when she next sees him.

The above is a conventional way of reading the poem and it builds on the binary oppositions developed in the last section. It creates a snapshot of an

independent and out-spoken 'new woman' of the 1920s. A deconstructive
reading sets out to show that the text tends to work against this reading,
showing that the poem contains contradictions and begins to undo itself.

ACTIVITY 77

Before reading what follows, try to find ways in
which the above reading does not stand up.

Try, for example, to find ways in which the
woman is not as strong as she appears.

Deconstruction claims that without realising it, literature often contains
ideas that are the very opposite of the ones it intended. Here, for example,
the speaker asserts her strength but at the same time admits her weakness.
She claims to be direct ('let me make it plain') but has spent most of the
poem being rather indirect about her feelings. She hides her sexual feelings in
euphemisms ('stout blood', 'zest'). The word 'possessed' reminds us of what
men used to say about women who were too overtly sexual (that they were
mad), so here she is either allowing men their way of seeing her (using their
terms) or she is taunting her listener by using the word. She also hides behind
slightly archaic words like 'fair', unusual Latinate terms like 'propinquity'
and unusual usages ('fume' = excitement). We may accept that all of this was
necessary because the times in which she lived expected a certain restraint in
women in these matters. But she is only able to assert herself at the end by
being someone different from who she is. She admits to being 'possessed' and
that her mind is 'clouded', her brain 'staggering', so that we could claim that
these are the rantings of a woman who is mad. No sane woman would surely
make such outrageous statements in those times and then choose not to act
upon them. In seeking to assert herself, all she does is condemn herself.

Some critics regard deconstruction as negative because it sets out to destroy
satisfying readings, but there are a number of advantages from the point of
view of study at A level:

- it emphasises that there is no such thing as a correct reading so it should
give you the confidence to challenge
- it puts the emphasis on you (the reader) Texts cannot be pinned down
but you can!

ACTIVITY 78

Turn to the short story *Pattern* on page 71. If
you have already responded to this story,
attempt to deconstruct your reading using the

above method as a model. If you find one
reading difficult try another of the ones listed
on pages 81–82.

Drawing on the previous chapter, this chapter has concentrated on
introducing formal literary theories as examples of contexts of reading. The
opening table of the chapter shows that the theories have slightly different
areas of focus. Each theory is then applied to literary texts.

**COMMENTARY
ON ACTIVITY 69**

Instead of simply rejecting Bertha as a madwoman the second extract
shows how she symbolically contributes to Jane's development as a woman.
In claiming that Bertha represents the other side of Jane's personality it also
takes a psychological stance. A final feature that is typical of some feminist

writing is that feminist thinking can be applied to the position of the writer herself, in the society of her time. The first extract is from *Great Writers*, Marshall Cavendish, 1992, page 149. The second is from *The Female Malady*, Elaine Showalter, 1987, pages 68–69.

COMMENTARY ON ACTIVITY 71

It is not difficult to take the woman's part in this episode. Henchard has behaved foolishly in his drunkenness and there can be little sympathy for him. There is nothing to indicate that Susan has been a bad wife and Hardy gives us several reasons for thinking that she is the winner in the situation. The sailor is 'kindly' and would appear to be a better man than her husband. The gesture of throwing the wedding ring gives her the appearance of rejecting him for his vices ('nothing but temper') rather than vice-versa. Her final actions are also strong ones ('seizing', 'mounting') although clearly she is also upset. But one could argue that the purpose of all this is actually to let Henchard off the hook. Although he has made a mistake he has at least sent his wife to a good man and she has retained some dignity in the situation. He begins to realise his mistake ('a look of concern') and there is the implication that he had not fully intended all of this to happen ('he had not quite anticipated this ending').

In the paragraph that begins 'He rose and walked' there is a narrator intrusion. Here the narrator steps forward to comment upon the events of the story. He firstly condemns the man's actions by comparing his deed with horses rubbing each other's necks, but then he seems to prepare the reader for the excuses he is going to give Henchard. He seems to be saying that it is our natural instinct to condemn Henchard by comparison with the glory of the sunset, but then he introduces the concept of change, suggesting that on another occasion nature may not present itself well but humanity might.

From the feminist point of view, what is disconcerting is that Henchard's actions are allowed to stand for the whole of humanity. Hardy uses the word 'man' to refer to all people and, although that was acceptable in his time, it underlines, for the modern reader, that the narrator assumes his philosophical musings do not take account of the woman's experience in all of this. In short, the narrator fails to condemn Henchard's barbarous act by showing Susan to be a strong character, by hinting at the beginnings of remorse on Henchard's part and by excusing his behaviour as naturally changeable. It may be argued that Hardy needed to show some sympathy for Henchard because of how the plot develops but this simply underlines how women are asked to read like men. In order to 'go along with the plot' you have to read like a man.

COMMENTARY ON ACTIVITY 76

Your list may look something like this:

Man	Not man
Passion	Reason
Passion	Love
Scorn	Love
Straight talk	Beating about the bush
Not polite	Polite

Notice that 'love' is contrasted with both 'passion' and 'scorn' which raises questions about why 'passion' and 'scorn' seem to go together for the speaker. 'Straight talk' is suggested by 'let me make it plain' and its opposite is suggested by the first eight lines of the poem – which seem to beat about the bush in saying 'I fancy you'! The idea of oppositions helps us to identify these contrasts in the poem and so ask further questions. It could be, for example, that saying 'I fancy you' could not be said directly at that time and by that person. Note that such an analysis is only a starting point for a less rigid interpretation but it is a good way of getting a hold on the basic themes of a work.

Further reading

Texts and Contexts: Writing about Literature with Critical Theory by Steven Lynn (1994) Harper Collins.
An approachable text that tackles difficult issues with plenty of examples.

Studying Literature – Theory and Practice for Senior Students by Brian Moon (1990) Chalkface Press.
Contains a whole section on gender.

Working with Structuralism by David Lodge (1986) ARK Paperbacks.
A difficult book but there are some good examples of how to carry out a close reading using structuralist principles.

6 Stylistics – How Language Shapes Texts

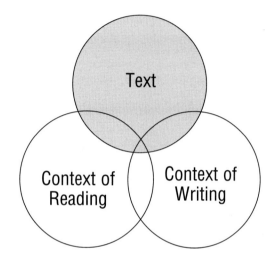

Text

Context of Reading

Context of Writing

ACTIVITY 79

Before starting on the central issues of this chapter, try creating a short poem/headline about sheep from the following words:

urine	and	they're	before	in	soaked
and	they're	in	garlic	excrement	rosemary
roasted					

The RSPCA used these words in an advertising campaign against the transportation of sheep. The advert can be found at the end of this chapter on page 113. If you trust your intuitions about language, try analysing the headline as if it were a poem. Ask yourself:

- What effect does it try to achieve and how does it do it?

- In what ways are the words connected in meaning?
- How do the ideas in the poem/headline develop?
- How are the words arranged on the page for maximum effect?

These kinds of questions will be addressed throughout this chapter.

Language selects, language patterns

Imagine the millions of things that happen to a sheep between birth and death: from struggling, messy birth, to grassy fields, the slaughter house, the supermarket and so on. The RSPCA advertising slogan picked out just two of such moments, so in an obvious way, language selects moments for our attention and ignores others. To put this another way, language firstly selects events; it cannot hope to cover everything that it wants to cover.

ACTIVITY 80

Look around you for a moment. Try to describe everything that is happening for one minute, writing as fast as you can.

COMMENTARY   You will soon have discovered the impossibility of doing this task. In fact the novelist Russell Hoban once described a story as what you have left when you miss out most of what happened. Because language is selective in this way, it leaves plenty of scope for the reader to re-create the big picture and to notice what is left out. This aspect of reading is covered in more detail on page 83.

The second thing that language does is create patterns and that is mostly what this chapter is concerned with. Patterns are essentially repeated similarities and differences. So far then:

language selects and language patterns

This could mean that the same grammatical pattern is repeated; that the same word is repeated; that an idea is repeated and it also contrasts with another idea in the text. For example, you should have found patterns in the sheep advertisement above. Here are two more examples:

'He kills – he killed – he will kill – he has killed – he had killed – he will have killed – he would have killed – he is killing – he was killing – he has been killing –he would have been killing – he will have been killing – he will be killing – he would be killing – he may kill.

We decided that none of these tenses or moods suited him.'

('The Verb to Kill' by Luisa Valenzuela)

'Today I am going to kill something. Anything.
I have had enough of being ignored and today
I am going to play God. It is an ordinary day,
a sort of grey with boredom stirring in the streets.'

('Education for Leisure' by Carol Ann Duffy)

Both of these texts, in their vastly different ways, select an idea for our attention and then create patterns by repeating words and ideas.

But before looking at this in more detail it is as well to clarify what is meant by stylistics.

What is stylistics?

Stylistics involves analysing the language of texts, but here particularly the focus is on literary texts. It uses the language of grammar and linguistics. Its particular power is that it allows you to look at a text in a great deal of detail and to describe it very precisely. It helps if you know about basic word classes such as noun, verb, adjective etc.

Essentially, stylistics moves between two kinds of response to literature, as shown in the diagram below.

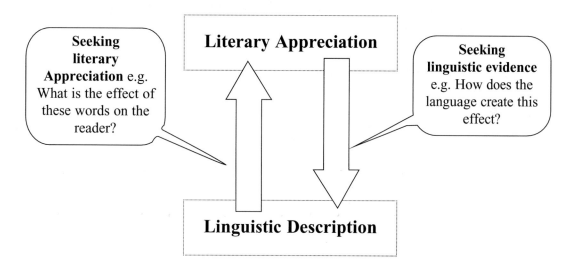

(Adapted from Leech and Short (1981) Longman).

Literary appreciation involves thoughts and feelings about the text you are studying. This might, for example, involve feelings about one of the characters, the theme or the plot. We study the language of a literary text to explain the connections between those thoughts and feelings and the text itself.

Notice that you can start either at the top or the bottom of the diagram. If you start at the top you will be using your intuitions about the text – the impressions you get from the text as you read. You will then need to seek linguistic evidence to support these responses. If you choose to start at the bottom, you are likely to piece together patterns of language and will then start to work out their effect on the reader. In practice, you are likely to work both from the top downwards and from the bottom upwards. The diagram shows how important it is to keep in mind both the language you are describing and the literary appreciation this helps to explain.

This chapter deals with aspects of stylistics that are applicable to any literary text. It does not deal with more specialised terms associated with genres such as poetry. These will be found in the genre-based chapters 9 to 11.

Where does this fit in?

Stylistics fulfils, in particular, Assessment Objective 3 which states:

'Students must 'show detailed understanding of the ways in which writers' choices of form, structure and language shape meaning'.

The key words as far as this chapter is concerned are 'language' and 'meaning'. Elsewhere in this book there is an emphasis on how the contexts of reading and writing help to shape meaning. In terms of the diagram in Chapter 1 (page 7) stylistic analysis will help you to focus on the top of the three inter-connecting circles. That is, it is an area of literary study in which the contexts of writing and reading are not especially important although they can never be completely excluded.

Stylistics is also relevant to Assessment Objective 2 which requires the use of appropriate terminology such as metaphor, connotation, semantic field, etc.

Both of these objectives apply equally to AS and A level.

Questions to ask when analysing the language of a literary text

1 Is anything repeated?

Repetition of some kind is essential to stylistic analysis because it suggests that whatever is happening in the language of the text is not just a chance occurrence. The classic example of a repeated word is 'fog' at the start of Dickens' *Bleak House* (see also the extract from *Bleak House* on page 200). But repetition does not mean that exact words have to be repeated. Several other kinds of repetition are possible:

> rhyme (repetition of the same vowel sound)
> alliteration (repetition of the same consonant sound)
> parallelism (repetition of the same grammatical construction)

The first two are covered on page 181.

Parallelism

ACTIVITY 81

Ask yourself what happens to the sheep in the RSPCA advert. Pinpoint the exact words. Then ask in what circumstances does this happen? Again pinpoint the exact words.

COMMENTARY The two questions can be answered like this

They're roasted

↓   ↓

They're soaked

In garlic and rosemary

↓   ↓

In urine and excrement

Both of the above are examples of parallel phrases. These phrases are grammatically equivalent and you can probably recognise this without knowing the grammatical terms. 'Roasted' and 'soaked' are both parts of a verb; 'garlic and rosemary' and 'urine and excrement' both contain two nouns linked by the word 'and'. Here the parallelism helps to emphasise the differences between the two sets of things that happen to the sheep. Those who eat mutton for Sunday lunch don't think about what has happened to the animals before they eat them, just as the parallelism lulls the reader, for a moment or two, into thinking that the urine and the excrement are just another aspect of the cooking procedure!

ACTIVITY 82

Find adverts in magazines and newspapers that use parallel phrases. Explain why you think they have been used.

ACTIVITY 83

Consider the role of repetition in the following poem.

■ What kind of repetition is used?

■ What is the effect of the repetition on the reader/listener?

Key skills: Communication – reading

Your Dad Did What?

Where they have been, if they have been away,
Or what they've done at home, if they have not –
You make them write about the holiday.
One writes *My Dad did*. What? Your Dad did what?

That's not a sentence. Never mind the bell.
We stay behind until the work is done.
You count their words (you who can count and spell);
All the assignments are complete bar one

And though this boy seems bright, that one is his.
He says he's finished, doesn't want to add
Anything, hands it in just as it is.
No change. *My Dad did*. What? What did his Dad?

You find the 'E' you gave him as you sort
Through reams of what this girl did, what that lad did,
And read the line again, just one 'e' short:
This holiday was horrible. My Dad did.

Sophie Hannah

COMMENTARY The poet repeats the words 'My Dad did' as the teacher repeatedly considers the words the boy has written. The variations represent the teacher's frustrations at not being able to understand what they mean. In the last stanza there is parallelism in: 'what this girl did, what that lad did' suggesting that the teacher is going through the motions, perhaps bored by the mundaneness of the task set. This adds poignancy to the dramatic reversal in the last line. The reader feels the pain of the gap between the teacher's understanding and that of her pupil. At the same time, in a more distanced sense, the reader feels the satisfaction of understanding what the teacher has implied in the last line and what has been implied earlier in the poem.

2 What kind of vocabulary does the writer use?

It is very common for students to say things like, 'It's just ordinary or normal language.' But if you put language under a microscope, you will often see that there is a great deal to observe. You can achieve a lot simply by asking a series of sub-questions such as:

- Is the vocabulary formal or informal? The use of 'piss' and 'shit' instead of urine and excrement in the advert on page 113 would destroy some of the subtlety of the advert because of the informality of these words.
- Is the language archaic (e.g. thine, thou) or modern?
- Which semantic fields are mentioned in the text? This is explained below.
- Is the vocabulary literary (in the sense that no one would ever speak like this) or the spoken language of everyday life? Note that the distinction does not always hold up as some literature imitates spoken language, especially in dialogue.
- Is the vocabulary simple or complex? For example, does it contain medical terms like 'clavicle' or just 'collar bone'?
- Does the text contain proper nouns, common nouns or both? Proper nouns are, for example, names of people, places and companies, and begin with a capital letter.
- Are the nouns concrete or abstract? Abstract words tend to emphasise ideas without creating vivid images in our heads (e.g. subservience, ability). Concrete words tend to emphasise objects (table, ferret).
- Is the language referential or emotive? That is, does it simply name objects in a neutral way or does it attempt to arouse emotions? e.g. 'He entered the room quickly' is not emotive whereas 'He stormed into the room' is.

These questions can be applied to any of the texts in this chapter. Only some of them will be addressed here.

Semantic fields: The shock of what happens to the sheep in the advert is increased by manipulation of the semantic field. A semantic field is, roughly speaking, the language of a particular subject area; for example, 'saw', 'hammer', 'chisel' are all in the semantic field of tools.

ACTIVITY 84

Take the key words in the text and decide what semantic fields you would divide them into:

roasted, garlic, rosemary, soaked, urine, excrement.

COMMENTARY

Here 'soaked' takes on two semantic fields at the same time: cookery and the less specialised usage that deliberately exaggerates, as when we say, 'I was soaked to the skin'. The shocking effect of this word is that it can have two such contrasting meanings at the same time.

Follow up activities to this can be found on pages 105 and 111.

Metaphor: Metaphor is probably the most powerful tool in literature and in language. Its power lies in the ability of literature to connect words and ideas that would otherwise remain separate. Essentially metaphoric language involves meanings that cannot be literally true, as in: 'the words gushed out of his mouth.' Here 'gushed' at once suggests water, speed, a sudden release, etc. – showing how metaphor is an incredibly economical way of using language.

When metaphors are combined, texts build themes. That is, writers often use a variety of metaphors that say roughly the same thing so that the text develops ideas on one theme. Often a concrete image described in a number of ways stands for an underlying set of ideas. The following activity will clarify this.

ACTIVITY 85

Each stanza in the following poem contains at least one metaphor but there is some variation in what they stand for. By considering the title, piece together the examples of metaphor and work out what the poem as a whole is saying.

Writing Block

When the rowing boat comes in over grey stones
and clear water, no need for a touch
on the oars,

when the bird on the summer bough drowses,
his song bubbling to nothing
between the leaves,

when memory runs clear as water
over its words, no need for a touch
on pen or printer,

when thick leaves shelter
what will be stripped in winter
and forced to sing.

Helen Dunmore (from *Bestiary*)

COMMENTARY The key to unlock the metaphor in this poem is the title. When a writer has a writing block, nothing flows; when there is no block the ideas flow smoothly. Each stanza seems to have something to say about one of these two alternatives. The first stanza suggests clarity and movement – the boat is moving of its own accord and the water is clear. In the second stanza the writer picks up the semantic field of liquid ('bubbles') but this time to show the opposite as the bird drowses. The third stanza again describes ideas flowing freely (notice how ordinary language picks up the liquid metaphor) and for a moment it steps out of the metaphorical by mentioning 'pen or printer'. The last stanza suggests a more severe block, perhaps implied by the stronger verbs 'stripped' and 'forced'. It also hints at the deception of the leaves because they are hiding the block that is to come in the winter when the writer will force herself to write.

ACTIVITY 86

Arguably, Seamus Heaney's poem *The Rain Stick* can be interpreted metaphorically.

1 Decide which of the interpretations that follow is metaphorical and which is literal.
2 Decide which of the statements below best describes the poem. With a partner, rank order the statements from best to worst as explanations of the poem. Note that a rain stick is a hollow piece of wood containing dried seed that makes a soothing sound when up-ended.

Key skills: Communication – reading

The Rain Stick

Upend the rain stick and what happens next
Is a music that you never would have known
To listen for. In a cactus stalk

Downpour, sluice-rush, spillage and backwash
Come flowing through. You stand there like a pipe
Being played by water, you shake it again lightly

And diminuendo runs through all its scales
Like a gutter stopping trickling. And now here comes
A sprinkle of drops out of the freshened leaves,

The subtle little wets off grass and daisies;
Then glitter-drizzle, almost breaths of air.
Upend the stick again. What happens next

Is undiminished for having happened once,
Twice, ten, a thousand times before.
Who cares if all the music that transpires

Is the fall of grit or dry seeds through a cactus?
You are like a rich man entering heaven
Through the ear of a raindrop. Listen now again.

This poem expresses:

a The poet's experiences with a rain stick. It simply re-counts the pleasure that the poet gets from using the rain stick with particular emphasis on the sounds it makes and its simplicity.

b A male individual fantasy in socially acceptable form. The rain stick is obviously a phallic symbol. The poet is celebrating his own selfish sexuality; he needs no one else, the effect is like music to him and he clearly feels no guilt.

c The poet's fascination with the variety of sounds that can be produced by the rain stick. It is simply produced, repetitive, yet such an unexpected pleasure that the user feels privileged to experience it.

d The poet's instructions to a young child in how to use a rain stick. He describes what the child is supposed to listen out for, emphasising discipline yet enjoyment and urging the child to give no attention to what is ultimately causing the sounds heard.

e The poet's belief in the need to live for the moment. He believes that pleasure, although based on simple repetition, should be experienced to the full. It is only destructive to think about the causes of things.

f The poet's belief that first-hand experience is preferable to received wisdom – second-hand ideas picked up from others. We should not be dominated by wise sayings passed down from ancient texts; our own experiences will often prove them wrong.

Connotations: The connotations of a particular word are its associations. The word 'jaguar' refers to (denotes) a member of the cat family but it has connotations of speed, grace and power. This is why it has been used as the name of a car. In the sheep transportation advert the connotations of garlic and rosemary are distinctly French (and French cuisine is world famous) – because it was the French who were accused of mistreating sheep in transit.

An important aspect of connotation is that you may have to learn the meaning of a word in a different period or in a different culture. The word 'gay' is an obvious case in point, but try looking up the words 'buxom' and 'silly' in the Oxford English Dictionary.

Modifiers: These are descriptive words that go before nouns. E.g. The *big* plate; the *open* sky. They obviously provide the descriptive meat in the textual sandwich. Identifying what the modifiers have in common and then working out the flavour that they give the text can be a useful exercise.

ACTIVITY 87

In the following text from *The Mill on the Floss*, 42 modifiers have been deleted and are listed at the bottom of the passage. The first sentence has been completed.

1 Put the modifiers in the correct places.
2 What are the connotations, on the whole, of these modifiers?

3 What is the effect of the modifiers on the text and what would it be like without them?
4 Divide the modifiers into semantic fields (including the first sentence) and discuss why they have been used.

A *wide* plain, where the *broadening* Floss hurries on between its *green* banks to the sea, and the *loving* tide, rushing to meet it, checks its passage in an *impetuous* embrace. On this _____ tide the _____ ships laden with the _____ – _____ fir-planks, with _____ sacks of _____ – _____ seed, or with the _____ glitter of coal – are borne along to the town of St Oggs, which shows its _____, _____ _____ roofs and the _____ gables of its wharves between the _____ _____ _____ hill and the river-brink, tinging the water with a _____ _____ hue under the _____ glance of this _____ sun. Far away on each hand stretch the _____ pastures, and the patches of _____ earth, made ready for the seed of _____ – _____ _____ crops, or touched already with the tint of the _____ _____ _____ – _____ corn. There is a remnant still of _____ _____ _____ clusters of _____ ricks rising at intervals beyond the hedgerows; and everywhere the hedgerows are studded with trees: the _____ ships seem to be lifting their masts and stretching their _____ _____ sails close among the branches of the _____ ash. Just by the _____ – _____ town the _____ Ripple flows with a _____ current into the Floss. How lovely the _____ river is, with its _____ _____ wavelets! It seems to me like a _____ companion while I wander along the bank and listen to its _____ _____ voice as the voice of one who is deaf and loving. I remember those _____ _____ willows. I remember the _____ bridge.

The modifiers: mighty, black, brown, fresh-scented, rounded, dark, aged, red, low, wooded, transient, lively, soft, purple, February, broad-leaved, autumn-sown, fluted, last year's, golden, beehive, distant, spreading, red-roofed, tributary, dark, green, little, dark, changing, living, low, placid, large, dipping, stone, broad, tender, bladed, rich, oil-bearing, red.

ACTIVITY 88

Find a summary of *The Mill on the Floss*. How do the modifiers and their semantic fields connect with the events that happen later in the story?

ACTIVITY 89

The following extract is taken from the beginning of a science fiction novel, *The Left Hand of Darkness* by Ursula Le Guin. What expectations does the writer create in the reader for the rest of the novel? Give your answer with reference to the vocabulary of this extract. There is a commentary at the end of the chapter.

A Parade in Erhenrang

From the Archives of Hain. Transcript of Ansible Document 01–01101–934–2–Gethen: To the Stabile on Ollul: Report from Genly Ai, First Mobile on Gethen/Winter, Hainish Cycle 93 Ekumenical Year 1490–97.

I'll make my report as if I told a story, for I was taught as a child on my homeworld that Truth is a matter of the imagination. The soundest fact may fail or prevail in the style of its telling: like that singular organic jewel of our seas, which grows brighter as one woman wears it and, worn by another, dulls and goes to dust. Facts are no more solid, coherent, round, and real than pearls are. But both are sensitive.

The story is not all mine, nor told by me alone. Indeed I am not sure whose story it is; you can judge better. But it is all one, and if at moments the facts seem to alter with an altered voice, why then you can choose the fact you like best; yet none of them are false, and it is all one story.

Naming

An important aspect of literary stylistics is how people and objects are referred to. For example, is a character always referred to by his/her full name or by a less formal alternative? By changing the vocabulary the writer can suggest a variety of views of that object or person. Is a character, for example, called 'the man', 'Peter Denby', 'Petey', 'D', etc?

ACTIVITY 90

Look again at *The Rain Stick* on page 104. In
how many ways is the rain stick referred to?
What is the poet's purpose in doing this?

3 Is there anything unusual about the grammar?

For many students the mere mention of the word grammar sends them
running for cover. But in fact, getting a few basic principles under your belt
can be an immense help in understanding the way in which a text works.
These principles can raise your thinking above the impressionistic and give
you some real, concrete evidence for your feelings about a piece of literature.

There is only room here for a brief coverage of one aspect of grammar. For
a broader perspective see: *Language and Literature* – George Keith (1999);
and *Grammar* – Michael Jago (2000), both published by Hodder and
Stoughton.

One of the most useful grammatical systems involves what are called clause
elements. These are best explained using an example:

Sentences revolve around the part of the sentence that creates action – the
verb (to love, to hate, to explode etc.). Once you have found the verb the
other elements are relatively easy to find. The following diagram will help
to find the subject, the object and the adverbial. It uses the example
sentence 'She kicked the ball hard.'

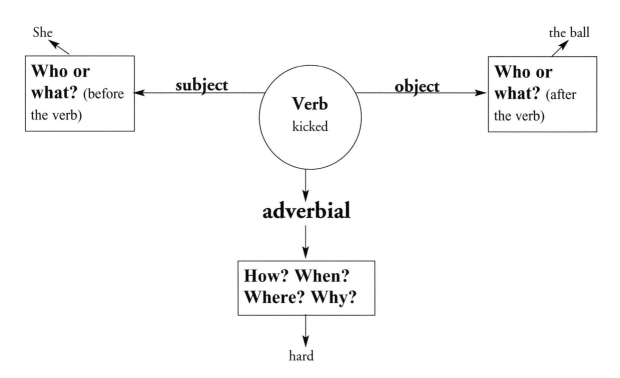

This system can be applied to poetry and prose, as in the following examples:

Subject	Verb	Object	Adverbial	
You	can take	a length of steel		(*Five Ways to Kill a Man*, page 14)
A haunted apparatus	sleeps		In homes,	(*A Martian Sends a Postcard Home* page 13)
The broadening Floss	hurries on		between its green banks	(*The Mill on the Floss* page 105)

Seamus Heaney's poem *The Rain Stick* shows how grammar can be employed to particular effect in a poem. One personal response to part of the poem might be that there is a sense of surprise when the rain stick is first turned up. This is what is meant by 'literary appreciation' in the diagram on page 110 – there is an effect in the reader. So the reader tries to work out how this is happening and an analysis of clause elements seems to help here. The next activity will clarify this.

ACTIVITY 91

Analyse the lines '... in a cactus stalk/Downpour, sluice-rush, spillage and backwash/Come flowing through', for its clause elements. Ask yourself what the clause element order is and why this has been used. Which clause element dominates? How do the clause elements compare with the poet's lineation (the way the lines are set out)?

COMMENTARY

At the end of the first stanza, the poet writes:

In a cactus stalk

This is an adverbial element of place (it is telling you where something happens). What follows is the subject of the sentence, followed by the verb and another adverbial, so that the final analysis of this sequence might look like this:

Subject	Verb	Object	Adverbial
			In a cactus stalk
Downpour, sluice-rush, spillage and backwash			
	Come flowing		through.

It might be argued that the surprise is created in a number of ways. Firstly, by beginning the sentence at the end of the stanza and using a run-on line (it continues into the next line), a sense of expectation in the reader is created. Then, when the action does arrive it gushes out in a series of nouns, each with the stress on the first syllable. This creates a sense of repetition which prolongs the gushing. But we still haven't reached the verb in this sentence (as readers we have learned to expect a verb) and so the effect is that it makes the reader wait whilst the gushing is taking place.

Whilst it is unusual to disagree with the grammatical analysis, it is possible to disagree about the *effect* of the grammatical arrangement, so grammatical analysis still leaves room for individual interpretation. It does not relieve you of the need to feel and think about what you are reading.

Here are some basic tips about doing this kind of analysis:

1 The usual order of clause elements in English is: SVOA, that is – Subject, Verb, Object, Adverbial. If the writer deviates from this it is for a purpose. So, for example, if the object or the adverbial is brought to the beginning of the sentence, known as foregrounding, it is usually because these elements need to be emphasised.

2 All sentences contain a verb. This comes in the first half of most sentences. If the verb is missed out or appears late there is usually a reason for it.

3 If one of the clause elements is much longer than the others, there is usually a literary reason for it.

For some quick practice, analyse this from the marriage service:

'With this ring I thee wed.'

Use the above diagram to help you identify the clause elements.

ACTIVITY 92

Look again at the poem *Writing Block* on page 103. Stanzas one and three represented the flowing of ideas, and stanzas two and four represented some kind of writing block. By carrying out a clause analysis, show how the grammatical structure of these stanzas reinforces the ideas expressed. You are advised to carry out an approximate analysis following this model:

Adverbial	Implied subject and verb	Object*
When the rowing boat comes in over grey stones and clear water,	(there is)	no need for a touch on the oars,

*Technically, this is a complement – for more on this see *Grammar* by Michael Jago, Hodder & Stoughton (2000).

COMMENTARY

The most interesting thing about the grammatical construction of this poem is that its subject matter is very clearly reflected in its grammar. Verses two and four express the writing block and it is these two verses that fail to get beyond their opening adverbial. It is as if these adverbials fail to come to fruition – they do not progress to the main verb of the sentence and so remain blocked, just like the writer.

ACTIVITY 93

The extract below uses an unusual (marked) word order. The main verbs in the first two sentences are in bold. Identify the clause elements in terms of SVOA and:

1 suggest why the writer has used this unusual order.
2 comment on how the length of each element helps to contribute to the writer's purpose.

> During the whole of a dull, dark, and soundless day in the autumn of the year, when the clouds hung oppressively low in the heavens, I **had been passing** alone, on horseback, through a singularly dreary track of country; and at length **found** myself, as the shades of the evening drew on, within view of the melancholy House of Usher.'
> [Edgar Allan Poe – *The Fall of the House of Usher*]

We are now in a position to fill the diagram presented on page 99, with the kinds of statements you could make about the language of a text and in literary appreciation.

The examples are all taken from the passages studied in this chapter.

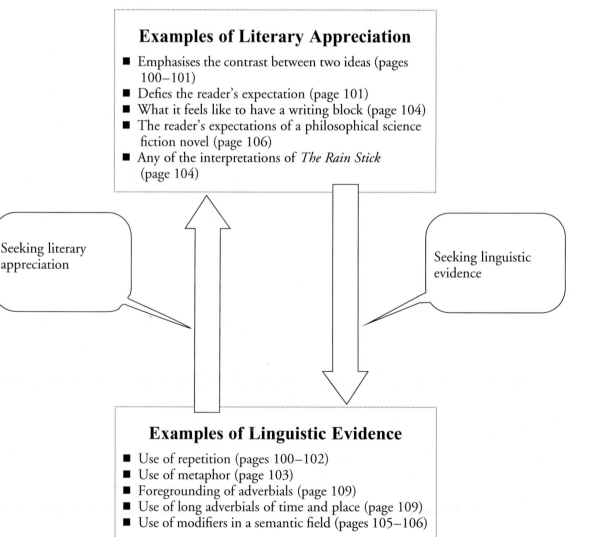

Examples of Literary Appreciation

- Emphasises the contrast between two ideas (pages 100–101)
- Defies the reader's expectation (page 101)
- What it feels like to have a writing block (page 104)
- The reader's expectations of a philosophical science fiction novel (page 106)
- Any of the interpretations of *The Rain Stick* (page 104)

Seeking literary appreciation

Seeking linguistic evidence

Examples of Linguistic Evidence

- Use of repetition (pages 100–102)
- Use of metaphor (page 103)
- Foregrounding of adverbials (page 109)
- Use of long adverbials of time and place (page 109)
- Use of modifiers in a semantic field (pages 105–106)

How not to do stylistics

It is possible to describe a text linguistically but say nothing interesting about it. There are two ways of making this mistake:

1 By describing at a level which is too general. All of your facts may be true but you may be missing the point of how this particular text creates meaning.
2 By failing to link linguistic description with literary appreciation. If this is happening you are not making full use of the diagram on page 110.

ACTIVITY 94

Which of the following examples of writing about *Writing Block* is making mistake number 1, and which mistake number 2?

Text A: 'The poem uses lots of metaphor, which is when something is compared with something else to achieve a particular effect. This makes the poem less boring and more interesting to read instead of just saying 'I've got a writing block'. There are modifiers such as 'clear' and 'grey'. These modifiers are words that appear in front of nouns to help make the poem more descriptive.'

Text B: '*Writing Block* uses a series of metaphors to express the writer's feelings. It also repeats the same pattern over and over at the beginning of each stanza. But each stanza ends in a different way, the second and fourth appearing not to end the sentence that they have started.'

Further tips

1 When writing, don't point out to the examiner that you know what a metaphor is. That is, don't say: 'This is an example of metaphor.' Put something like: 'This example of metaphor shows that . . .'. In other words, your knowledge of linguistic (or literary) terms should slip into your analysis almost unnoticed.
2 Don't organise your response around the text's linguistic features. Linguistic features should *support* what you have to say about the themes of the text and (if necessary) its contexts of reading and writing.
3 Don't feel that you have to mention a particular kind of feature. It's no use pointing out, for example, that the grammar and pronouns are entirely in the unmarked order. If there is nothing to report, then don't!

ACTIVITY 95

Carry out a full analysis of *The Rain Stick* using as many of the features mentioned in this chapter as possible. Work methodically through each feature. Try to decide, and then emphasise, the ones which are most helpful, ignoring those that seem to be leading nowhere. Explain how Heaney: creates surprise; creates a sense of wonder; uses a variety of semantic fields; uses metaphor and simile; and uses vocabulary with certain connotations (look up the origins of the word 'transpire'). To supplement this analysis you may also wish to use ideas from Chapter 9.

Key skills: Communication – presentation

ACTIVITY 96

Compare the following two extracts. One is taken from a well-known 19th century novel. The other is a paraphrase of the same novel. Decide which version is which and then analyse the passages stylistically using the features mentioned in this chapter.

Hints: which one is more consistent in its use of language? Which one sounds more like a 19th century novel?

a In front of me is this tract of flat country where the river Floss, getting wider all the time, rolls seaward between its green banks, and where the tide comes up to meet it with all the impetuosity of a lover hastening to a tryst. That powerful tidal insurge carries along to St Ogg's the black ships laden with timber, linseed, and coal. St Ogg's is here in the foreground; we see its fluted red roofs and the broad gables of its wharves, with the river on one hand, and on the other, behind the town, the low wooded hill. Caught in the light of the February sun, the little town makes colourful reflection in the water.

On either side, as far as the eye can see, stretch the farmlands, some of them newly ploughed, others just showing the first shoots of spring corn. We can see the remains of the haystacks made last autumn, and everywhere, all along the hedges, we see trees – why, even the masts and sails of distant ships seem to merge into the branches and foliage! Not far from the town, with its red roofs, is the swift-flowing river Ripple, a tributary of the Floss and a most attractive watercourse. For me its sound is like the voice of a real person, a companion in my rambles round charming old-world St Ogg's. Everywhere I turn I meet well-remembered topographical features – those willows, for example, and the stone bridge.

b A wide plain, where the broadening Floss hurries on between its green banks to the sea, and the loving tide, rushing to meet it, checks its passage in an impetuous embrace. On this mighty tide the black ships laden with the fresh-scented fir-planks, with rounded sacks of oil-bearing seed, or with the dark glitter of coal – are borne along to the town of St Oggs, which shows its aged, fluted red roofs and the broad gables of its wharves between the low wooded hill and the river-brink, tinging the water with a soft purple hue under the transient glance of this February sun. Far away on each hand stretch the rich pastures, and the patches of dark earth, made ready for the seed of broad-leaved green crops, or touched already with the tint of the tender bladed autumn-sown corn. There is a remnant still of last year's golden clusters of beehive ricks rising at intervals beyond the hedgerows; and everywhere the hedgerows are studded with trees: the distant ships seem to be lifting their masts and stretching their brown sails close among the branches of the spreading ash. Just by the re-roofed town the tributary Ripple flows with a lively current into the Floss. How lovely the little river is, with its dark changing wavelets! It seems to me like a living companion while I wander along the bank and listen to its low placid voice as the voice of one who is deaf and loving. I remember those large dipping willows. I remember the stone bridge.

Health Warning!

Analysis of language should not stand on its own. You should always connect language with an effect in the reader.

The chapter began by showing that language selects things and then puts them into patterns. The reader's job is to match this linguistic evidence and literary appreciation by asking questions about repetition, vocabulary and grammar. The chapter provides the basic tools for examining such features.

Answer to Activity 79:

> Before they're roasted
> in garlic and rosemary
> they're soaked
> in urine and excrement

COMMENTARY ON ACTIVITY 89

The pre-dominance of proper nouns (invented names of places and people such as 'Erhenrang', 'Hain' and 'Genly Ai') immediately suggests the science fiction genre and all that is implied by this. The invented but instantly recognisable word 'homeworld' (which doesn't exist yet but might do in the future) reinforces this. The technical vocabulary of an official report such as 'transcript', 'document', 'report', 'archives' suggests a military or institutional context, which is not surprising, given the science fiction genre. It is highly likely that the writer of the report is a member of some organisation. The word 'report' leads us into a slightly different semantic field associated with storytelling of a more imaginative kind. Thus there is: report, story, imagination, fact, style, telling, told, voice. The report is dominated by abstract ideas such as truth, imagination and fact which is a little unexpected for science fiction. Nothing of any concrete nature has actually happened in this created world and instead the narrator is speculating on the nature of his own story. This is surprisingly self-conscious, suggesting that this science fiction novel will be more philosophical than packed with laser sword fights. Three concrete nouns stand out: 'jewel', 'dust' and 'pearl'. All of these are used for metaphorical or comparative purposes and to shed light on the nature of facts. The novel is intriguing because it sets up a futuristic world using conventional sci-fi techniques but then defies expectation by following with a highly reflective passage.

Further reading

Style in Fiction by Leech, G. and Short, M. (1981) Longman.
An excellent text containing the analysis of many examples.

A Linguistic Guide to English Poetry by Leech, G. (1969) Longman.
Highly technical. Better for teachers than students.

The Art of Fiction by Lodge, D. (1992) Penguin.
A series of articles originally published in a daily newspaper. More literary than strictly linguistic.

Considering Prose by Mayne, A. and Shuttleworth, J. (1984) Hodder & Stoughton.
A more basic and approachable text.

7 Studying Shakespeare

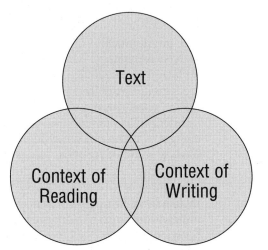

Shakespeare – over four hundred years old and still topical

Health Warning!

In 1999 listeners to Radio 4 voted William Shakespeare (1564–1616) the British person of the millennium. The criteria were not crystal clear but listeners were asked to vote for the British person who had most influenced the world over the previous thousand years. William Shakespeare may seem a surprising choice and we could all think of people who may have been more obviously influential. However, the fact remains that all over the world the plays of Shakespeare are performed, adapted and studied. It is also true that the more you read Shakespeare the more you want to read, and the more you know the more you want to know! Be prepared for finding Shakespeare's words and works cropping up in the most unexpected places!

Where does this fit in?

Whatever specification you are following, study of Shakespeare is compulsory and it is highly likely that the study of a Shakespeare play will be the basis of one whole module at AS which will be assessed either through coursework or examination. All Assessment Objectives are covered but AO3, AO4 and AO5(i) are the key ones.

In this chapter you will check how much you already know about Shakespeare and then look in detail at how three aspects of his plays have changed through time. There will be reference in particular to *The Merchant of Venice*, *Measure for Measure* and *King Lear* and you will examine the portrayal of character, a moral issue and a change in the story line. At the end of the chapter there are some activities which can be used to deepen your understanding of a Shakespeare play you are studying.

William Shakespeare

What do you know?

1

  a On your own, write down all the titles of plays by Shakespeare that you can remember.

  b In groups of four compile one list and try to put the plays into categories. You could link them by subject matter or genre, for example you could put the comedies together. Check your lists with other groups. When you have done this, check at the end of the chapter for the broad classifications.

Key skills: Communication – discussion

2 Pool your knowledge of the Elizabethan theatre and then do some research to find out more. Look at the buildings, the types of plays and the places where they were performed. What was the stage like? What were the actors like? It is fairly easy to find this information. The new *Globe* theatre in London and the film *Shakespeare in Love* also provide information. Write a short pamphlet introducing the features of the Elizabethan stage to a visitor to the *Globe*.

Key skills: Communication – reading

3 Find out on which plays by Shakespeare these adaptations are based.
  a *Kiss me Kate*
  b *Return to the Forbidden Planet*
  c *West Side Story*
  d *A Thousand Acres*
  e *The Boys from Syracuse*

Answers at the end of the chapter.

Plays like *Rosencrantz and Guildenstern are Dead* by Tom Stoppard (1966) and *The Merchant* by Arnold Wesker (1976) are spin offs from Shakespeare's plays. There are also opera and ballet versions of *Othello, A Midsummer-Night's Dream,* and *Romeo and Juliet.* There are famous film versions of *Much Ado About Nothing* and *Romeo and Juliet.* Since 1909 when a black and white silent version of *King Lear* was made, it has been produced six times for television and eight times for the cinema, one of which is in Russian and one is Yiddish. There is also the play *Lear* by Edward Bond written in 1972.

Shakespeare for the young!

In 1807 Charles and Mary Lamb produced their *Tales from Shakespeare* addressed to 'the young reader as an introduction to the study of Shakespeare'. The following section from the preface is entertaining for the modern reader. It contains a very long sentence but it is well worth reading!

It was no easy matter to give the histories of men and women in terms familiar to the apprehension of a very young mind. For young ladies, too, it has been the intention chiefly to write; because boys being generally permitted the use of their fathers' libraries at a much earlier age than girls are, they frequently have the best scenes of Shakespeare by heart, before their sisters are permitted to look in this manly book; and, therefore, instead of recommending these Tales to the perusal of young gentlemen who can read them so much better in the originals, their kind assistance is rather requested in explaining to their sisters such parts as are hardest for them to understand: and when they have helped them to get over their difficulties, then perhaps, they will read to them (carefully selecting what is proper for a young sister's ear) some passage which has pleased them in one of these stories, in the very words of the scene from which it is taken.

How things have changed! It is unlikely that you were treated differently from your siblings on the basis of gender and also it is fairly unlikely that your father has a 'library' for himself alone. When you think about reading Shakespeare's plays today it probably does not occur to you that they should be censored for female readers. The stories are not really considered specifically 'manly'!

Almost four hundred years after the first *Globe* theatre was established in London, it has been recreated in the same position on London's South Bank. A visit here will transport you back to the theatrical experience of Elizabethan audiences. Groundlings stand for hours at a time and the audience is exposed to the open air. Many productions are in Elizabethan dress and there are some all male productions. The sound effects such as wind machines and lightning are probably as good as those in Shakespeare's day! At the same time the relevance of the plays to today's society is quite obvious. It's a very interesting experience and cheap if you are prepared to stand! Hopefully with modern safety precautions the present theatre will not suffer the fate of its predecessor. The original *Globe* was burnt to the ground in 1613 when a piece of wadding from a stage canon set the thatched roof on fire during a production of *Henry VIII*! Although the theatre was rebuilt, it was demolished in 1644 when all of London's theatres were closed by the Puritans. The theatre was identified with the court and as the writers were considered Royalists it was inevitable that after the Civil War broke out between the king and Parliament in 1642 the theatres were closed. They were considered to be both immoral and supportive of the monarchy.

For the purposes of study, this chapter will discuss Shakespeare's work in the context of his time and also look at some interpretations and adaptations since then. You will also find more discussion of the different interpretations of 'context' in Chapters 3 and 4. It will also look at some of Shakespeare's sources and his use of them. More traditional methods of study will be discussed at the end of the chapter where activities are suggested.

Theatre is alive and kicking. Productions change in the light of current social and political values. Sometimes plays are changed in major ways to accommodate current thinking, sometimes only minor changes in intonation or gesture will suffice to indicate a different interpretation to update a production. Plays are often given a different perspective by critics and directors in the light of social and cultural values. Three plays will be discussed here concerning

a the portrayal of character
b the interpretation of a moral issue and
c the change of the actual story line to make the play more acceptable to the audience.

Shylock, 'a fully rounded human being' or a 'cut-throat dog'?

You may already be familiar with *The Merchant of Venice*. It has always been popular as a play for GCSE study. Here is an outline of Shakespeare's story. You could tell each other the story or write it down, perhaps in the form of a diagram, if you are already familiar with it!

The plot

As with any good play it is difficult to do it justice when you try to retell it and simplify it. There are two main plots in this play. The first concerns Shylock and his agreement with Antonio and this is the one we are going to concentrate on. The second main plot concerns the love story of Bassanio and Portia and how their marriage comes about. There is also a subplot concerning Shylock's daughter and a subplot which connects the marriage of Portia and Bassanio with the main plot!

The plot which concerns us begins with Bassanio asking to borrow money from Antonio who is *The Merchant of Venice*. He needs the money to go to Belmont to try to win Portia. Antonio does not have the money but is willing to borrow it for a short while as when his ships return from sea he will be a wealthy man. Shylock, a Jewish money lender is approached to lend the money. Antonio does not hide his hatred of Shylock and the feeling is mutual. Although they hate each other, a deal is struck. Shylock agrees to lend the money but they agree that if the debt is not paid by a certain date Shylock will be entitled to a pound of Antonio's flesh.

You can guess that the money is not paid and Shylock demands his pound of flesh. This, of course, is the origin of the expression to demand your pound of flesh! It looks as if Shylock will be able to take revenge on Antonio in this way. He resists all attempts to persuade him to be merciful.

However, a clever lawyer (who is in fact Portia in disguise!) states that if one drop of blood is spilt or if even a touch over one pound is taken, then Shylock's goods are forfeit. Shylock eventually agrees to accept the money but the court says it is too late. Also Shylock is accused of plotting against the life of a Venetian. His life is only saved if he gives up his fortune and also becomes a Christian. He leaves the court a broken man.

It is the portrayal of Shylock that we'll be studying in this section. *The Merchant of Venice* has a chequered history. At times it has been considered unsuitable for study because of its anti-Semitic content. In this section we are going to consider the way the character of Shylock has been interpreted since Elizabethan times.

The Jews first entered England around 1066 but by 1290 they had for the most part been expelled. For three hundred and fifty years Jews were exiled from England unless they pretended not to be Jewish at all. Elizabethans were suspicious of Jewish people more so because they lived in foreign lands and were thought of as both exotic and monstrous. In 1589 Christopher Marlowe's play *The Jew of Malta* portrayed a villainous Jew, Barabas. Shakespeare's play was produced in 1605 and then no other performance of it is recorded until 1741, when it was again seen on the stage.

Shylock through time

There was no doubt hostility to Jewish people in Elizabethan England and Shakespeare's play reflects this. He could have been agreeing with this view, trying to question it or simply representing what his audience wanted to see and were familiar with.

Here is a summary of how the character has been interpreted.

1 Richard Burbage and Will Kemp were actors who were contemporaries of Shakespeare. The only thing known about their portrayal is that Shylock had a red beard and a false nose. This follows the tradition of presenting Judas with a red beard. These were not sympathetic portrayals and were probably comical.
2 Charles Macklin in 1741 played a Shylock who had a malicious streak – evil but not outrageous. It seems that Macklin himself was quite vicious. He is said to have killed a fellow actor over a beard!
3 In 1814 Edmund Kean's Shylock was more palatable for his audience, presenting him as a man with some humanity and a black wig and beard who arouses the sympathy of the audience.
4 A more aristocratic Shylock was portrayed in 1840 by William Charles Macready. This Shylock is dignified and restrained.
5 A female actress (Catherine Macready) played Shylock, in 1850.
6 In 1861 Edwin Booth's Shylock was a character who could hardly express his feelings. He was a kind of emotional cripple.
7 Henry Irving's Shylock (1880) was a noble and well-read man.
8 Shylock becomes a devilish malignant force of Judaism in the 1920s German Expressionist versions of the play.
9 More recently, in 1997, Philip Voss sees Shylock differently again. He sees Shylock as initially very funny but he also portrays him as a 'nice human being' who has an obsessive hatred. He has a genuine love for his daughter but is unable to show it. His Shylock is not cringing and browbeaten but he is a fully rounded and understandable human being.

Comments by Gregory Doran, the Director of a production by the Royal Shakespeare Company in 1997, suggest that, although the play has been seen as about racial prejudice particularly since the Holocaust, he feels it is about 'value, the true value we place upon things and the value at which we set human life'. (From an interview on the website of the Royal Shakespeare Company.)

The website of *The National Theatre* (www.rsc.org.uk/education/) states this about the summer 1999 production:

One of Shakespeare's most grippingly dramatic plays, addressing the universally absorbing themes of love, money and prejudice. The story centres on Shylock, a Jewish money lender, and the young heiress Portia, who finds herself in a life or death confrontation with him in a climactic courtroom trial. The attitudes thus revealed have reverberated through the succeeding centuries, and most disturbingly our own.

The setting for this production was Venice in the early 1930s with Shylock as an enigmatic character considered by John Peter of the *Sunday Times* (June 1999) as 'weary and wary, hard and vulnerable, embattled and defensive. His body, vigorous but slightly bent, speaks of humiliations and belligerent endurance'. He describes the trial scene as morally harrowing. If you know the play well you will be surprised by the idea that the final scene is considered to be 'moving and darkly ambiguous' with all the characters feeling devalued and troubled.

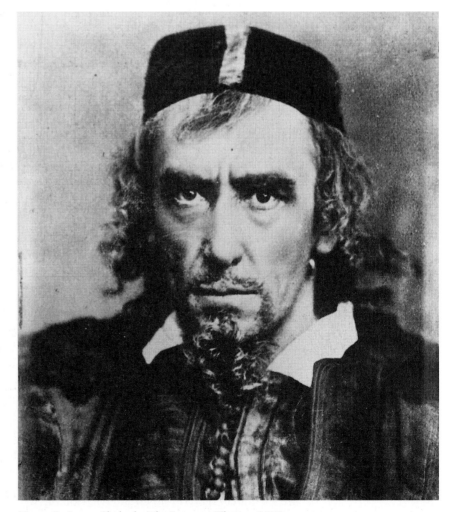

Henry Irving as Shylock. The Lyceum Theatre 1879

ACTIVITY 98

This activity could be the basis for an individual research task and presentation. How do you think Shylock should be interpreted today in the theatre? Consider how a modern audience reacts to Jewish people. Would your Shylock be a simple villain or a Jew first and foremost? If you were producing the play, what stance would you take and why? You might like to consider psychological as well as physical attributes. Try to develop a list of adjectives – for example shifty, clever, pathetic. You may be able to find some illustrations of different actors portraying Shylock. Here are two speeches from Act Three which will give you some more information.

Shylock explains his feelings about Antonio in this way:

He hath disgraced me, and hindered me half a million – laughed at my losses, mocked at my gains, scorned my nation, thwarted my bargains, cooled my friends, heated mine enemies – and what's his reason? I am a Jew. Hath not a Jew eyes? Hath not a Jew hands, organs, dimensions, senses, affections, passions? Fed with the same food, hurt with the same weapons, subject to the same diseases, healed by the same means, warmed and cooled by the same winter and summer as a Christian is? If you prick us do we not bleed? If you tickle us do you not laugh? If you poison us do we not die? – And if you wrong us, shall we not revenge?

On hearing of his daughter's elopement this is his response:

A diamond gone cost me two thousand ducats in Frankfurt – the curse never fell upon our nation till now, I never felt it till now – two thousand ducats in that and other precious, precious jewels. I would my daughter were dead at my foot, and the jewels in her ear; would she were hearsed at my foot, and the ducats in her coffin.

Key skills: Communication – presentation

ACTIVITY 99

Obtain copies of the play and, taking an act each, divide the play between the group. Find all the references to Shylock. Make a chart to show the times where he is portrayed in a sympathetic light and where he is not. Look at the final act to see how he is manipulated by Portia. You could do this as a word search on an electronic version of the text.

From this research, suggest what attitude you think Shakespeare has to the character.

Key skills: Information Technology – different sources

ACTIVITY 100

Arnold Wesker's play *The Merchant* was performed in Scandinavia in 1976 and in New York in 1977 (where it was a disaster!) but not in London because of its large cast. In this play Shylock and Antonio are good friends. The loan is agreed but as the law insists that a loan between a Jew and a Gentile must be made formally, they agree to the pound of flesh bond to mock the law which denies friendship between Jew and Gentile. As the bond needs to be met they agree to be martyrs. However, Antonio is saved and Shylock remains bitter and isolated as all his goods are confiscated. The friends had believed that the laws of Venice would treat them equally.

Consider if you think this is a more appropriate version of the story for a modern audience.

Key skills: Communication – discussion

ACTIVITY 101

Research into the portrayal of one of the main characters in a play by Shakespeare you are studying. Use the Internet and versions of the text with good introductory notes. Try to see if the character has been portrayed differently throughout time. Suggest how you might portray the character if you were an actor.

Key skills: Communication – reading

Isabella – sex or soul-saving?

In June 1999 Peter Hall produced *Measure for Measure* with an all American cast in Los Angeles. John Peter comments (*Sunday Times* June 1999) 'Shakespeare's famous universality has a practical aspect; like mythology it can be at home almost anywhere'. This production was set in late 18th century America. The British producer, Peter Hall, concentrated on the clarity of verse speaking so that the audience, who may well not have known the play at all, understood the action and characters and responded with a freshness that is reminiscent of the *Globe* in London. *Measure for Measure* is doubtless a controversial play. Its appeal to audiences all over the world even in modern times demonstrates this.

In this section the interpretation of a moral issue will be discussed. Here is a brief summary of *Measure for Measure*.

The plot

Act One. The Duke of Vienna decides to leave the city for a while in the hands of his deputy, Angelo. The city is in a state of moral decay and the Duke to some extent is trying to leave the problem for Angelo to sort out. However, rather than leave the city, the Duke is actually going to disguise himself as a friar to monitor what happens. The first action Angelo performs is to arrest a young man, Claudio, for getting his girlfriend pregnant. Angelo is resurrecting an old law which gives the death penalty for this crime. Claudio's sister, Isabella, is persuaded by a friend of Claudio to go to Angelo to plead for her brother's life. Although Isabella is about to enter a convent as a nun, she agrees to this. There is a subplot with minor characters frequenting a brothel.

Act Two. Angelo's deputy, Escalus pleads unsuccessfully to Angelo for the life of Claudio. Isabella enters and, although she accepts that Claudio committed the crime, she pleads for mercy for her brother. Angelo becomes attracted to Isabella and asks her to return the next day. Angelo, although anguished by his feelings for Isabella, offers to reprieve Claudio if Isabella will sleep with him. Isabella refuses on the grounds that this will mean the loss of her immortal soul and it would be better for Claudio to die.

Act Three. Isabella visits Claudio in prison and tells Claudio of Angelo's plan and she expects that he will agree with her. When he shows he is afraid to die, Isabella rejects him and accuses him of weakness and cowardice. The Duke, now watching the events disguised as a friar, overhears the conversation between Isabella and Claudio. He meets Isabella and puts a plan to her. We learn that Angelo had a girlfriend called Mariana whom he treated badly. The Duke suggests that Isabella agrees to Angelo's plan and that Mariana is substituted for Isabella without Angelo's knowledge. Both Isabella and Mariana agree.

Act Four. The bed trick is arranged and done. Angelo, however, in spite of his agreement, orders the execution of Claudio and insists that Claudio's head is sent to him as proof.

ACTIVITY 102

Acts Four and Five. D.I.Y.

(If you know the ending of the play you need only complete one of these activities!) You will need to refer to the definitions of Tragedy and Comedy in Chapter 11 (Studying Plays) and Chapter 8 (Studying Older Texts).

1 Assume that this play is classed as a tragedy and complete the summary of the rest of Act Four and then Act Five.

2 Assume that this play is classed as a comedy – in the Shakespearean sense – and complete the summary of the rest of Act Four and Act Five.
Justify your ending by referring to the features of either tragedy or comedy.

See the end of the chapter for Shakespeare's original ending.

ACTIVITY 103

If you have studied this play discuss what has been left out of this summary!

ACTIVITY 104

This play is sometimes called a problem play. Looking back at the plot summary can you suggest why?

COMMENTARY

There are several 'problems' with this play. Here are some of them:

1 Some of the problems surround the story itself. It seems as if the Duke knew the real nature of Angelo, so why did he leave Vienna under his power? Why did the Duke make the plan about leaving but then not leave?
2 Is the subject matter appropriate to a comedy? It is certainly a dark play. How can it be appropriate to give it such a happy ending?
3 The character of Isabella is always a matter for debate. How can she condone the bed trick? How can she be manipulated in the final act to lie about whether she slept with Angelo or not? Should she and does she accept the Duke as her husband?

ACTIVITY 105

Write a speech justifying or criticising Isabella's actions. You should look at the dilemmas she faces and identify the turning points in her life. You could do this on a flip chart.

Key skills: Communication – presentation

Isabella's dilemmas

- She wants to save her brother but she agrees he has broken the law.
- She is unable to save him by the only avenue available to her which is yielding to Angelo.
- She says she would give up her life for her brother but not her virginity.
- Although about to become a nun, she agrees to the deception of the bed trick and later to lying about it.
- She agrees to beg for mercy for Angelo in spite of his behaviour.
- She appears to agree to marry the Duke and renounce her vocation as a nun.

Isabella certainly poses some problems for us. It is interesting to note that Shakespeare's sources all have the Isabella character yielding to the corrupt judge. It is only in Shakespeare's version that Isabella refuses to submit to the ruler. It is only in Shakespeare that the bed trick is arranged.

A good account of reactions to this problem is in the Casebook series, *Measure for Measure* edited by C.K. Stead (Macmillan). Isabella has been variously described as 'an angel of light', 'unamiable'. Coleridge found the whole play 'hateful'. More recently it has been seen as 'a dramatic parable, embodying some of the noblest precepts of the Christian religion' (*The Signet Classic Shakespeare* – Introduction).

Strict theologians see her plan to put her soul above her brother's life as correct. Liberal humanists see her as heartless and inhuman. On stage an audience may be more sympathetic to her as a young woman placed in an impossible situation with whom we should sympathise. A modern audience or reader may just wonder what all the fuss is about! In the past the play may have been interpreted as about chastity. Perhaps today it may be seen to be about sex, private and public morality and forgiveness!

A feminist response

A feminist perspective would comment that women are seen as sex objects in the play and would look at the subplot of the brothel as a subject for discussion. In Act Two Scene Four Angelo, confronted by the refusal of Isabella to agree to his proposition says:

> Be that you are,
> That is, a woman; If you be more you're none.
> If you be one, as you are well expressed
> By all external warrants, show it now,
> By putting on the destined livery.

By 'destined livery' he means the usual submissive behaviour of women. He sees her as rejecting the traditional female role. Isabella has already agreed with the traditional female role in her comment earlier in the scene:

> Nay call us ten times frail,
> For we are soft as our complexions are
> And credulous to false prints.

Here she is agreeing that women are weak, easily suppressed and manipulated. Isabella is assertive in her treatment of her brother but she is easily manipulated by the Duke and agrees to the bed trick and to tell lies at the end of the play. It is hardly acceptable that she should submit easily to the Duke's offer of marriage. In a feminist reading her actual silence on this point would be read as refusal. Marriage to the Duke would not be seen as a reward for her behaviour or suffering.

For more discussion on feminist readings see Chapter 5 (Methodologies).

ACTIVITY 106

Discuss how you would make the feminist aspect of the play interesting and acceptable to a modern audience. Think about Isabella's refusal to sleep with Angelo and her marriage to the Duke; how would you respond to them? Are there any other plays by Shakespeare which would be equally as intriguing if looked at from a feminist perspective?

Key skills: Communication – discussion

A recent production

In 1998 the Royal Shakespeare Company performed *Measure for Measure*. Clare Holman played Isabella. In an interview summarised on the RSC webpage, Clare sees Isabella's change during the play as a key aspect for the actress.

The play is a story of two halves – not that she loses her faith but that the strictness, the fundamentalism, is what collapses in the second half and a softer more approachable woman emerges. I think there is a great journey from youthful confidence, which is taken advantage of, to a doubt in humanity. Finally she grows up into a woman who makes a decision on her own terms.

Isabella fleshes out forgiveness. What she does, for the Duke, is represent in literal flesh and blood, the symbol of forgiveness. He pushes her to the point where she has to make a huge self-sacrifice and unless she does, the New World can't happen. . . .

I wasn't sure how to end the play when we started; I didn't know what Isabella would want. Because of the way the production has gone there is a decision to be with the Duke, which feels right. It feels for this Isabella like a very important lesson. Her strict, purist religious belief has taken a battering and I think she emerges as a better person. It's almost like she's seeing reality, living in the world as opposed to running away from it

I think it is a great play for women. Sometimes Isabella is seen as such a difficult character but most women I've spoken to have found her forgiveness and her decision to be with the duke really moving. In a post-feminist world a lot of people might say, "we don't want her to be with a man – she's been treated badly so we don't want her to be with the Duke". But in our production I think it's sense that for all of us, men and women, we're all fallible, none of us are better or worse, and I've based the performance on that.

ACTIVITY 107

Consider a play you know well. Look at the role and function of one of the women characters. Suggest how the character could be played from a feminist perspective. See Chapter 4 for more discussion on this. Plot summaries of *The Taming of the Shrew*, *Macbeth*, *King Lear* and critical works will help if you do not already know appropriate plays. Write an article suitable for the programme notes of a production of one of these plays, looking at it from a feminist perspective.

Key skills: Communication – reading/ writing

ACTIVITY 108

Below is an extract from Act Three of the play. It is the section where Isabella tells her brother Claudio of Angelo's proposition. In an earlier comment she tells Claudio to prepare himself to be Angelo's messenger to heaven because he has been condemned to death with no chance of reprieve. You might like to role play the situation first to get a feeling for the sensitivity of the issues. Now study the extract and consider the questions below.

CLAUDIO	Is there no remedy?	1
ISABELLA	None but such remedy as, to save a head,	
	To cleave a heart in twain.	
CLAUDIO	But is there any?	
ISABELLA	Yes, brother, you may live;	5
	There is a devilish mercy in the judge,	
	If you'll implore it, that will free your life,	
	But fetter you till death.	
CLAUDIO	Perpetual durance?	
ISABELLA	Ay, just. Perpetual durance, a restraint,	10
	Though all the world's vastidity you had,	
	To a determined scope.	
CLAUDIO	But in what nature?	
ISABELLA	In such a one as, you consenting to't	
	Would bark your honour from that trunk you bear,	15
	And leave you naked.	
CLAUDIO	Let me know the point.	
ISABELLA	O, I do fear thee. Claudio, and I quake	
	Lest thou a feverous life shouldst entertain,	
	And six or seven winters more respect	20
	Than a perpetual honour. Dar'st thou die?	
	The sense of death is most in apprehension,	
	And the poor beetle that we tread upon	
	In corporal sufferance finds a pang as great	

	As when a giant dies.	25
CLAUDIO	Why give me this shame?	
	Think you I can a resolution fetch	
	From flowery tenderness? If I must die,	
	I will encounter darkness as bride,	
	And hug it in mine arms.	30
ISABELLA	There spake my brother. There my father's grave	
	Did utter forth a voice. Yes, thou must die.	
	Thou art too noble to conserve a life	
	In base appliances. This outward-sainted deputy,	
	Whose settled visage and deliberate word	35
	Nips youth i'th'head, and follies doth enew	
	As falcon doth the fowl, is yet a devil.	
	His filth within being cast, he would appear	
	A pond as deep as hell.	
CLAUDIO	The precise Angelo?	40
ISABELLA	O, 'tis the very cunning livery of hell,	
	The damned'st body to invest and cover	
	In precious guards. Dost thou think, Claudio,	
	If I would yield to him my virginity,	
	Thou might'st be freed?	45
CLAUDIO	O heavens, it cannot be.	
ISABELLA	Yes, he would give't thee, from this rank offence,	
	So to offend him still. This night's the time	
	That I should do what I abhor to name,	
	Or else thou diest tomorrow.	50
CLAUDIO	Thou shalt not do't.	
ISABELLA	O, were it but my life,	
	I'd throw it down for your deliverance	
	As frankly as a pin.	
CLAUDIO	Thanks, dear Isabel.	55
ISABELLA	Be ready, Claudio, for your death tomorrow.	
CLAUDIO	Yes. Has he affections in him	
	That thus can make him bite the law by th'nose,	
	When he would force it? Sure it is no sin,	
	Or of the deadly seven it is the least.	60
ISABELLA	Which is the least?	
CLAUDIO	If it were damnable, he being so wise,	
	Why would he for the momentary trick	
	Be perdurably fined? O Isabel.	
ISABELLA	What says my brother?	65
CLAUDIO	Death is a fearful thing.	

Claudio goes on to show his fear of death and finally entreats Isabella to save him.

Look at how Shakespeare has made Claudio respond to Isabella here. Do you notice anything about the nature of Claudio's input? What does this tell you about his state of mind and Isabella's sensitivity to it?

Can you find any evidence of Isabella as manipulative here?

Can you suggest where, in Claudio's responses, the actor should pause before continuing?

What is the overall impression you get of Isabella here?

There is a commentary on this activity at the end of the chapter.

ACTIVITY 109

After the above section Claudio finally asks
Isabella to save him because he is afraid to die.

This is her response.

> O you beast!
> O faithless coward! O dishonest wretch!
> Wilt thou be made a man out of my vice?
> Is't not a kind of incest to take life
> From thine own sister's shame? What should I think?
> Heaven shield my mother played my father fair,
> For such a warped slip of wilderness
> Ne'er issued from his blood. Take my defiance,
> Die, perish. Might but my bending down
> Reprieve thee from thy fate, it should proceed.
> No word to save thee.

Here she makes her position quite clear. Now
she would not do anything to save him. What
do you think of her now? If you were acting or
directing this section for a modern audience
would you portray her as a frightened isolated
girl or a strong religious character or even a self-
centred child?

ACTIVITY 110

It is difficult for a modern audience to appreciate the religious fervour of
Isabella who lives in a strong Roman Catholic environment. The director
has the option of staging the play with its original emphasis on chastity –
although this is not the only theme – or playing up the forgiveness issue
which comes to the fore at the end of the play. Isabella is loved or hated for
her behaviour!

Referring to a play by Shakespeare that you
know well, write down the issues which are
highlighted – for example, kingship, loyalty,
justice, family relationships. Divide the issues
between the group and do some research on the
significance of these issues to an Elizabethan
audience. Introductions to the texts or a book
on Elizabethan England will help. Find out how
an Elizabethan audience would react to these
issues. Present your findings to the group and
then discuss if the reaction of a modern
audience would be the same. Do you think a
modern audience has the same values and
would react in the same way?

Key skills: Communication – reading

ACTIVITY 111

In 1998 the Royal Shakespeare company
production of *Measure for Measure* was designed
by Tom Piper. In an interview he said this:

> The starting point for this production was imagining a sort of late 19th century
> world, probably somewhere akin to the Balkans. It's a place where there's still a
> chance of major political unrest, so that the Duke going off has political implications
> rather than just moral ones.... We've gone for a staircase that dominates the set,

to give the impression that you can either be coming down into a pit or going up into the skies. It is used for Isabella's entrance to see Angelo: she comes down the staircase dressed as the bride of Christ in a long sweeping bridal entrance into the scene, a merging of a secular and religious image.... At the end when Isabella forgives Angelo we'll have two things happening – one is we'll release all the prisoners almost like a Day of Judgement. The other thing is to open up all the narrow windows that you haven't been aware of in the wall. And through them shines real daylight.

Bearing in mind the ideas outlined above about the significance of design to reinforce the themes of the play, produce a set of notes to show how you think a play by Shakespeare, that you know well, should be staged. Describe how you would want the characters to be dressed, what the set would be like, what postures the characters might adopt and if there are any symbolic elements you could portray in the staging of the play. You could confine your response to one particular scene and this may be a suitable coursework task.

This could also be a presentation activity.

Key skills: Communication – presentation

Should Cordelia die?

A.C. Bradley (1851–1935) gave a series of lectures on Shakespeare which were published in 1904 under the title *Shakespearean Tragedy*. His work is highly respected and studied by all students of Shakespeare. One of his comments on *King Lear* in *Shakespearean Tragedy* is that *King Lear* is Shakespeare's greatest achievement but **not** his best play. In fact although it is one of the four great tragedies it is the least often presented in the theatre, probably because it is the most difficult to stage. One character is blinded on stage and there are violent storm scenes to simulate. Joseph Wharton said in 1753 that the play had 'considerable imperfections'. It was first performed in 1605 and again between 1609 and 1610. After 1681 an adaptation by Nahum Tate became popular and for 150 years the story was changed to give it a happy ending. The play was restored to its original form in 1838. Apart from many modern stage versions, a modern film, based on the story, called *A Thousand Acres* has been made. The film is based on the novel which is an updating of the story and is set in the mid-west of the United States.

The plot

What, then, is *King Lear* all about?

King Lear is an old king who decides to divide up his kingdom before his death and relinquish his responsibility. He asks his three daughters to say in turn how much they love him and he intends to reward them accordingly. Two daughters (Regan and Goneril) flatter him but the third and youngest (Cordelia) refuses to join in the deception. Lear, showing his rashness, banishes her. He intends to spend the rest of his life being looked after by his daughters. They resent this. Eventually after he is treated badly by them, Lear leaves them and goes mad out on the heath when he realises his mistake of banishing Cordelia, the daughter who in fact did love him.

Cordelia is the innocent daughter of Lear who refuses to flatter him. She is banished but is accepted as a bride by the King of France. She eventually rescues Lear from the harshness of the heath and tries to restore his sanity.

Goneril is Lear's daughter. She is married to Albany who is rather weak at the beginning of the play. She flatters Lear and then rejects him.

Regan is Lear's other daughter and she treats her father badly also. She is married to Cornwall who is as wicked as she is. They are responsible for the blinding of Gloucester whose only crime was to try to help Lear.

Gloucester is a supporter of Lear but is too weak to really help him. He is blinded for trying to help Lear when he is exposed to the elements on the heath. He has two sons, Edgar and Edmund.

Edgar is Gloucester's legitimate son. He is gullible and is tricked into leaving his home, on suspicion of being a traitor, by his wicked half brother Edmund.

Edmund is Gloucester's illegitimate son who is jealous of Edgar and eventually supplants him in his father's favour by trickery.

Here are two family trees to help you sort this out!

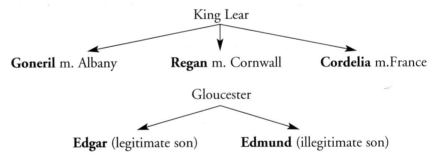

King Lear

Goneril m. Albany   **Regan** m. Cornwall   **Cordelia** m. France

Gloucester

Edgar (legitimate son)   **Edmund** (illegitimate son)

As the play progresses Lear is rejected by Regan and Goneril and eventually goes mad. He is rescued by Cordelia. These two (Lear and Cordelia) are caught by Edmund and they are sent away to their deaths.

Edmund is challenged by his good brother Edgar and is killed in a duel.

Regan and Goneril both die. They both loved Edmund and Goneril poisons Regan and then kills herself when this is discovered by her husband.

Any suggestions as to how the rest of the play could be made less depressing or even romantic?

In fact Cordelia is murdered as Edmund planned but King Lear tries to save her and then dies with her in his arms. Some people think he dies of joy because he thinks she is alive. Others think he dies of a broken heart and others think he is happy to die to join her in heaven.

An alternative ending

Nahum Tate's ending, favoured during the 18th century, had Cordelia and Edgar as lovers and Cordelia being saved so that they could marry. Cordelia is rewarded for her honesty and integrity with the hand of the honest and faithful Edgar! A real fairy tale ending!

What is your opinion of the two endings? It is usually considered that in this play people get what they deserve except for Cordelia who is considered pure and innocent. Early audiences found her death intolerable. Samuel Johnson wrote in 1765 'I might relate, that I was many years ago so shocked by Cordelia's death, that I know not whether I ever endured to read again the last scenes of the play till I undertook to revise them as an editor' – taken from the programme notes of the RSC production of 1993. Shakespeare's source *The true Chronicle of King Leir* with which Shakespeare's audience would be familiar, ended with Lear restored to his throne and Cordelia's forces victorious against her sisters.

ACTIVITY 112

Consider these speeches by Cordelia at the beginning of the play. She finds that her sisters protest their love to her father whilst she is more honest and restrained. Using these quotations prove that she is:

a honest and shy

and /or

b strongwilled and headstrong like her father!

Key skills: Communication – discussion

All these extracts are from Act One, Scene One.

> Good my Lord,
> You have begot me, bred me, lov'd me: I
> Return those duties back as are right fit,
> Obey you, love you, and most honour you.
> Why have my sisters husbands if they say
> They love you all? Happily, when I shall wed,
> That lord whose hand must take my plight shall carry
> Half my love with him, half my care and duty:
> Sure I shall never marry like my sisters
> To love my father all.

In this extract she wants Lear to make his reasons for banishing her clear to all:

> I yet beseech your majesty,
> (If for I want that glib and oily art
> To speak and purpose not, since what I well intend,
> I'll do't before I speak), that you make known
> It is no vicious plot, murther or foulness,
> No unchaste action, or dishonour'd step,
> That hath depriv'd me of your grace and favour,
> But even for want of that for which I am the richer,
> A still-soliciting eye, and such a tongue
> That I am glad I have not, though not to have it
> Hath lost me in your liking.

When a suitor refuses to take her without a dowry she says:

Since that respects and fortunes are his love,
I shall not be his wife.

On leaving her sisters this is what she says:

The jewels of our father, with wash'd eyes
Cordelia leaves you: I know what you are;
And like a sister am most loth to call
Your faults as they are named. Love well our father:
To your professed bosoms I commit him:
But yet, alas! stood I within his grace,
I would prefer him to a better place.

COMMENTARY You have probably found evidence for both of the views! If some of these words are spoken sarcastically, Cordelia is as vicious as her sisters. For example she calls her sisters the 'jewels of our father' and comments that she will never marry as her sisters have done and still love her father 'all'. She questions how her sisters could marry at all if they love their father as much as they have declared. She is also assertive here and even from a weak position she retains her dignity and strength. She asks her father to let it be known why she has been banished. In fact it is for something she is glad that she does not have 'a still-soliciting eye' and clever speech. She makes her feelings for her sisters quite clear for all to hear but at the same time her comments could be considered as snide and unpleasant. The two 'wicked' sisters in this part of the play simply tell their father what he wants to hear and we have all done that!

In order to heighten the tragedy Cordelia is usually portrayed as honest and innocent and this makes her death all the more tragic. Surely Shakespeare was telling us something very true about life? Things are often not fair or just. Human beings are cruel and selfish and innocent people do suffer! A fairy tale ending with Lear restored to power and a happy marriage for Cordelia with Edgar seems a little too trite for the modern audience, don't you think?

Let Harley Granville Barker have the last word – 'In general, however, better play the plays as we find them. The blue pencil is a dangerous weapon and its use grows on a man, for it solves too many little difficulties far too easily'. *Prefaces to Shakespeare* (1945)

General activities

Here are some activities which will develop your understanding of Shakespeare's plays. Some of these may be used for coursework activities.

ACTIVITY 113

Identify two themes from a play by Shakespeare that you know well and apply them to modern society. (You might like to look at justice, loyalty, marriage, kingship or religion). Suggest how the issues and reactions to them have changed since Elizabethan times. You will find that Shakespeare explores many issues that are still applicable to today's world but perhaps our interpretation 400 years later is different.

Here are some suggestions: (i) There have been cases recently where babies are alleged to have been killed by their nannies and there have been long debates about punishment for this. (ii) There have also been several cases of miscarriage of justice. (iii) In recent years revelations about people who have betrayed their country through spying have provoked a lot of discussion. (iv) There has been much publicity about the personal and public role of the heir to the throne.

ACTIVITY 114

Hot seating. Divide into groups of three. Each group should choose a main character from a Shakespeare play you are studying. Prepare one member of the group to be in the 'hot seat' and justify their actions in the play. In the same group prepare questions to ask of the characters chosen by other groups. In turn, put each character in the 'hot seat' and explore motivation and attitudes in the form of questions from the other groups.

ACTIVITY 115

Look at the sources of a Shakespeare play you know well. You should be able to find these in any good edition of the play. The *Arden Shakespeare* is particularly good. Sort out what action Shakespeare has added or omitted.

Suggest why this has been done and what its significance is.

Key skills: Communication – discussion/presentation/reading

ACTIVITY 116

Find out if the play you are studying has had alternative endings and what they were. Discuss the significance of this.

Key skills: Communication – reading/discussion

ACTIVITY 117

Design two posters. One is for the performance of a play you know well, advertising the production for an Elizabethan audience. The other is for a modern audience. Try to demonstrate how the emphasis might have changed. Use words as well as pictures! Write a commentary explaining your approach.

Key skills: Communication – writing

ACTIVITY 118

The storm scenes in *King Lear* are played in many different ways. On stage there can be an attempt to create wind and rain with sound effects. A film version may have more realistic scenes. These scenes have been played on a virtually empty set with a naked actor and the words themselves set the scene. How do you think 'difficult' scenes should be played in the theatre? What about scenes of torture, crowd scenes, battle scenes, scenes on islands or on ships that are about to be wrecked? Think about a specific scene from a play and decide how it could be staged (a) in the theatre and (b) on film.

ACTIVITY 119

Try to find two different film versions of a play, for example *Henry V* with Branagh or Olivier. Study the portrayal of one particular character and see how it is different. Suggest which is most justifiable from the text. Try to identify what the exact differences are. Compare also the costumes and scenery.

ACTIVITY 120

This is an extension of Activity 50 in Chapter 4 (Contexts of Reading). Find as many different editions of single Shakespeare plays as you can. Look at them and make notes on how they are presented. Notice where the textual notes are and what is included in the introduction and at the back. Look at any critical commentary and see what this is. Is it extracts from famous critics or simply notes that A level students can 'learn'?

Draw up a detailed plan for an edition of the play you are studying. Suggest the layout of the text which is most useful for A level students. If you can do some research, provide some critical reaction to the play. Suggest what information would be most useful to have all in one place for A level students.

Key skills: Communication – reading/ writing

ACTIVITY 121

Write programme notes for a theatre production of a play you know well. Try to model this on the programme from a production which you may have seen. Think what information a modern audience needs to know to enable them to get the most out of a visit to the theatre to see the play you have chosen.

ACTIVITY 122

Retell the story of a play you know well as if it were a story for children. You will need to decide how to simplify the story itself as well as how to write for children.

ACTIVITY 123

Choose a specific moment in a play e.g. the end of an act. Draw a diagram to show the relationship of the characters at this time. If the characters are near to each other (i.e. in love or in each other's confidence!) put the names close together. If they are in conflict indicate this by distance. Use keywords to explain why you have put characters where you have. You could then choose a later moment in the play and show how the relationships have changed.

Key skills: Communication – presentation

Answers to Activity 97

1 **b** You have probably categorised the plays into 'tragedies', 'comedies' and 'histories'. However there is also a group of 'Roman plays' 'problem plays' and 'late plays'. The four great tragedies *King Lear*, *Macbeth*, *Hamlet* and *Othello* are also often separated for special study.

3 **a** *The Taming of the Shrew*
  b *The Tempest*
  c *Romeo and Juliet*
  d *King Lear*
  e *The Comedy of Errors*

Answers to Activity 102
Shakespeare's original ending

The actual story continues like this: The head of a prisoner who has already died naturally is substituted for the head of Claudio who is kept alive secretly. The Duke lets it be known that he is going to return. It is arranged that Isabella confronts Angelo in front of the Duke.

Act Five. The ending is complicated. Isabella has agreed to lie and pretend **she** went to Angelo and not Mariana. Angelo is eventually revealed as a villain and is forced to marry Mariana. His life is forfeit but because of the intervention by Isabella, who does so at the request of Mariana, he is saved. Isabella still believes her brother is dead. A prisoner is brought in and he is revealed as Claudio. In the final moments of the play the Duke asks Isabella to marry him and it is usually assumed that she does so.

COMMENTARY TO ACTIVITY 108

Notice how Claudio is forced to keep asking Isabella questions to gain any information. She is not telling him all the facts. She forces him to accept death before he knows the conditions. She seems oblivious to his anxious state.

Isabella is almost teasing Claudio by telling him there is one method by which he may be reprieved but without giving details. She forces him to confirm his willingness to die by suggesting she does not trust him to accept his death. She almost accuses him of being a coward, so he has to defend himself. She then flatters him.

By line 57 Claudio is gradually formulating a response about Angelo's action. He suggests that it cannot be a sin or Angelo himself would not contemplate it. This is where an actor would pause to show he is trying to see his way forward. He would be choosing his words carefully. Before the words 'O, Isabel' (line 64) the actor might pause as he is about to implore her to save him.

You might consider Isabella cruel, selfish and teasing here. Or you might think she is making light of death to make it easier for Claudio. She certainly appears rather nervous about what she has to say.

Further reading

Many plays by Shakespeare are examined in the useful *Casebook* series (Macmillan), general editor A.E. Dyson. For example *Measure for Measure*, edited by C.K. Stead, 1st printed 1971, 5th reprint 1993.

Macmillan Master Guides are also at an appropriate level and easily accessible.

The Genius of Shakespeare by Jonathan Bate (1997) Picador. This is an entertaining book which justifies Shakespeare's reputation as a 'genius'.

8 Studying Older Texts

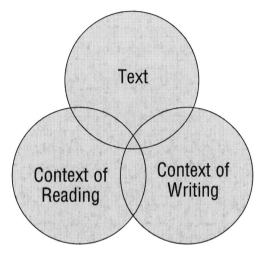

Where does this fit in?

This chapter does cover all the Assessment Objectives to some extent. However, 2(i) and 5(i) and (ii) are the key ones. Remember that you have to study at least one pre-1900 text for AS and a pre-1900 and a pre-1770 text for A2.

Studying extracts from texts you do not study in detail will also help with the synoptic aspect of the course.

In this chapter texts written before the 20th century will be discussed. Some of the major authors will be looked at in chronological order. The novel is dealt with in more detail in Chapter 10 and you should also look at the poetry chapter (Chapter 9). Here there will be a brief look at Chaucer, John Donne, Restoration Comedy, John Milton and the 'Romantic' poets (Wordsworth, Coleridge and Keats). Shakespeare has had a chapter all to himself.

At the end of the chapter there is a 'quiz' which encourages you to find out more about the periods in which these writers were writing.

This chapter can only dip into the mass of literature which may be studied but it should give you an insight into the contexts in which literature was written and suggest ways in which readers today can appreciate and interpret texts for themselves.

Health Warning!

Reading texts written before the 20th century does pose problems for the modern reader. Poetic, theatrical and literary conventions have to be put into context and understood. Words may have changed in meaning or spelling. Contemporary references are often difficult to appreciate. Somehow when you read comedies from before 1900 they just don't seem funny. In the theatre, this can be solved by adding stage business, making the references topical and dress or settings modern. However, when it comes to poetry and prose, it is often difficult to appreciate how the original readers understood the complicated thoughts and language of some of our greatest writers.

'The father of English poetry'

The most well-known early poetry is the epic *Beowulf* which was written in Anglo-Saxon in 800. However, the poet Geoffrey Chaucer is the first major poet whose language is really accessible to us today.

John Dryden, writing around 1700, described Geoffrey Chaucer, the author of the famous *Canterbury Tales*, as the father of English poetry. Chaucer lived in the second half of the 14th century and his *Tales* were written from about 1386. The details of Chaucer's life are quite well documented as he was a courtier, civil servant and politician.

The Tales is a collection of stories told by different narrators in the framework of a pilgrimage to the shrine of Thomas à Becket in Canterbury Cathedral. This idea was not particularly new to Chaucer's contemporaries. They would be familiar with collections of tales. It is possible that Chaucer added the idea of a common purpose and framework. The journey to

Geoffrey Chaucer

Canterbury starts at the Tabard Inn in Southwark, London. The pilgrims decide to tell stories to pass the time. The poem begins with a wonderful prologue which documents the characters in the group. This collection of people and their stories gives a brilliant insight into medieval England. However, it is much more than this. The characters are timeless and they present all shades of human characters and types. *The Tales* give a picture of medieval England but the same character types can be seen today. Chaucer was commenting on the social and political concerns of his day, many of which are the same as our concerns today. Superimposed on this cavalcade is the fun and satire which Chaucer himself creates. Similar to monologues, for example *My Last Duchess* and *Porphyria's Lover* by Robert Browning and *Talking Heads* by Alan Bennett, the characters reveal themselves as they speak. The tales range from the bawdy to the pious and are great fun to read.

Thanks to the invention of the printing press by William Caxton in about 1476, Chaucer's work was published. This marvellous invention had the effect of formalising English spelling, of creating a more permanent text and making texts more widely available.

Translating 'English' into 'English'!

However, the language of Chaucer's poetry may at first be considered a barrier. In 1700 John Dryden updated *The Tales* and wrote this in his preface to *Fables Ancient and Modern; translated into verse*:

I find some people are offended that I have turned these tales into modern English; because they think them unworthy of my pains and look on Chaucer as a dry old fashioned Wit, not worth receiving ... Chaucer, I confess is a rough diamond, and must first be polished e'er he shines.... Another poet, in another age may take the same liberty with my writings.... It was also necessary sometimes to restore the sense of Chaucer which was lost or mangled in the errors of the press.

Dryden acknowledges that 'Chaucer has taken onto the compass of the tales ... the whole English nation. Not a single character has escaped him ... here is God's plenty'.

Modern 'translations'!

More recently the tales have been translated into modern English by Nevill Coghill. He comments in his introduction

the present version of this master work is intended for those who feel difficulty in reading the original, yet would like to enjoy as much of that 'plenty' as the translator has been able to convey in more modern idiom.

Coghill's version was first published in paperback in 1951. Chaucer's original poetry has thus been transformed into poetry in a modern idiom.

More recently still the British writer/director Jonathan Myerson has created a cartoon version of the tales with latex puppets. Myerson's background is as a script writer for the BBC (*The Bill* and *Eastenders*). There are voice-overs by British actors Sean Bean, Bob Peck, Billie Whitelaw and Imelda Staunton. The tales are produced in English, Welsh and Middle English. Myerson said in an interview:

I wrote the script like it was an episode from *The Bill*. I don't believe in venerating old texts. I was deliberately modernising it and the language the characters speak. This opens up a classic text to a wider audience. . . . We're making Chaucer accessible and saying that it doesn't have to be done in that terribly difficult and pompous tone. You can just have fun and it will come through.

ACTIVITY 124

Do you think 'old' texts should be adapted for a modern reader? What should be the criteria for this and what would be the value of it?

Key skills: Communication – discussion

ACTIVITY 125

Below is Chaucer's original description of one of his story-teller pilgrims, the miller. Read it and answer **true** or **false** to the questions which follow. It may help to read the passage out loud.

The MILLER was a stout carl for the nones;
Ful byg he was of brawn, and eek of bones.
That proved wel, for over al ther he cam.
At wrastling he wolde have always the ram.
He was short-sholdred, brood, a thikke knarre;
Ther was no dore that he nolde heve of harre,
Or breke it at a rennyng with his heed.
His berd as any sowe or fox was reed,
And therto brood, as though it were a spade.
Upon the cop right of his nose he hade
A werte, and theron stood a toft of herys,
Reed as the brustles of a sowes erys;
His nosethirles blake were and wyde.
A swerd and bokeler bar he by his syde.
His mouth as greet was as a greet forneys.
He was a janglere and a goliardeys,
And that was most of synne and harlotries.
Wel koude he stelen corn and tollen thries;
And yet he hadde a thombe of gold, pardee.
A whit cote and a blew hood wered he.
A baggepipe wel koude he blowe and sowne,
And therwithal he broghte us out of towne.

Answer true or false to these questions and quote the evidence for your decision:

1 The miller was thin
2 He was very strong

3 He had a grey beard
4 It was a goatee beard
5 He had a wart on his nose
6 There was a tuft of hair on a wart on his nose

7 His nostrils were black
8 He had a mouth like a furnace
9 He wore a red coat and hood
10 He played the piano

You might like to draw the miller!
Check your answers by looking at Coghill's translation.

> The MILLER was a chap of sixteen stone,
> A great stout fellow big in brawn and bone.
> He did well out of them for he could go
> And win the ram at any wrestling show.
> Broad, knotty and short-shouldered, he would boast
> He could heave any door off hinge and post
> Or take a run and break it with his head.
> His beard, like any sow or fox, was red
> And broad as well, as though it were a spade;
> And, at its very tip, his nose displayed
> A wart on which there stood a tuft of hair
> Red as the bristles in an old sow's ear.
> His nostrils were as black as they were wide.
> He had a sword and buckler at his side,
> His mighty mouth was like a furnace door.
> A wrangler and buffoon, he had a store
> Of tavern stories, filthy in the main.
> His was a master hand at stealing grain.
> He felt it with his thombe and thus he knew
> Its quality and took three times his due-
> A thumb of gold, by God, to gauge an oat!
> He wore a hood blue and a white coat.
> He liked to play his bagpipes up and down
> And that was how he brought us out of town.

Coghill manages to get most of the flavour of the original without having the change too much in meaning to make the poem easier to understand.

However, he appears to have changed the meaning of 'a thombe of gold'. Coghill interprets this as almost a magic thumb which could judge the corn accurately. Chaucer's comment was based on the old saying that 'an honest miller hath a thumb of gold' meaning there were really no honest millers to be found.

ACTIVITY 126

As well as obvious characters like a miller and various members of the church, for example a prioress, monk and friar, Chaucer includes some characters which we would not instantly recognise today. Find out what these characters were: Reeve, Summoner, Franklin, Pardoner and Manciple. We also find there is a Knight and a Squire.

What do you learn of society in Chaucer's time by the inclusion of these characters?

Imagine you are going to write a contemporary *Canterbury Tales*. The original characters were all on their way to Canterbury. Can you suggest a modern equivalent to this pilgrimage and modern character types? What about a fundraising walk, a music festival or a protest march? Write a modern prologue describing your contemporary people. These could include a New-age traveller, a thug, an academic, a student, a tart and a feminist.

Fleas and funerals

Poetry has an immediacy and vigour. The context in which a poem was written influences how we view it and also the ease with which we understand it. We also interpret it in the light of our present situation and our experience as well as current literary thinking and social factors. There is more on this in Chapters 3 and 4.

Poet/clergyman!

In 1572 a great love poet who also became a clergyman was born. His name was John Donne and he died in 1631 after a career that encompassed a naval expedition, a secret marriage, a spell in prison and a time in the legal profession. He is a major poet and was to become known as a 'metaphysical' poet. He also became an Anglican priest and a preacher and would possibly have been made a bishop had his health been better. He

John Donne

was a prolific writer of love poems, religious work, letters and satires. His work was published in 1633 although it had been widely circulated in manuscript form before this. There is a strong tendency to see his poetry as autobiographical but this, as with all poets, is not necessarily the case. Donne himself, however, suggests that 'Jack Donne' wrote the secular poetry and Dr. Donne the religious verse, thus indicating that he saw his writing life in two distinct parts!

Donne – realist or romantic?

Donne's love poetry is a reaction to the conventional idealised picture of women given in earlier elegant love poetry. In *The Anagram*, he describes a particular woman's teeth as 'jeat' (black) and her skin as 'rough' and her cheeks as 'yellow.'

'Though all her parts be not in the usual place,
She hath the anagram of a good face'.

You might like to look up Shakespeare's Sonnet 130 and compare the two poems. In his poem *The Comparison* Donne writes:

And like a bunch of ragged carrets stand
The short swolne fingers of her hand.

He certainly had a way of cutting his women down to size!

What does metaphysical mean?

Donne was a 'metaphysical poet' along with other Elizabethans, Andrew Marvell, George Herbert, Richard Crashaw and Henry Vaughan. The term 'metaphysical' was used in a derogatory way to indicate their use of witty pseudo-scientific argument. There is more about this poetic movement in Chapter 9 (Studying Poetry). One distinguishing feature of this group of poets is the 'metaphysical conceit'. This is the use of striking similes and metaphors showing an intellectual approach to subjects normally considered emotional. It is the head dictating how the heart should be expressed. These poets were criticised for harking back to medieval scholastic philosophy. The most famous conceit is the comparison of lovers to a pair of compasses in *A Valediction Forbidding Mourning*. Two lovers are about to part but Donne argues that their two souls will never really be separated.

If they be two, they are two so
As stiffe twin compasses are two,
Thy soule the fixt foot, makes no show
To move, but doth, if th'other doe.

And though it in the center sit,
Yet when the other far doth rome,

It leanes, and hearkens after it,
And grows erect, as that comes home.

Such wilt thou be to mee, who must
Like th'other foot, obliquly runne.
Thy firmness makes my circle just,
And makes me end, where I begunne.

ACTIVITY 128

Explain the meaning of these lines to bring out the suitability of this 'metaphysical conceit'. Exactly what is Donne suggesting here? It may make things clearer if you find a pair of compasses or mime or draw the action of this instrument.

Donne – the smooth operator!

Persuasion is one of the elements in Donne's poetry. We can find many examples in his poetry where, as a persona or as himself, he is directly addressing the reader, or some one actually in his company, and is trying to influence their actions. Perhaps the most famous example is *The Flea* where he is encouraging his mistress to yield to him. This is commented on in Chapter 9 (Studying Poetry). Another example is *Breake of Day* where the speaker is persuading his mistress to stay in bed with him even though it is day. He uses a fairly simple but acceptable argument in the first stanza:

Why should we rise? Because 'tis light?
Did we lie down, because 'twas night?

In the second stanza he claims that if daylight could speak, the worst thing it could say would be that the lover wishes to stay in the favourable circumstances in which he finds himself. In the final stanza the speaker complains that if 'businesse' or daily routine is the reason for their parting then that is the worst excuse possible. He ends with the ironic comment:

He which has businesse, and makes love, doth doe
Such wrong, as when a maryed man doth wooe.

Reaction in his time

Contemporary reaction to Donne varied. Ben Jonson called his poem *The Anniversarie* 'profane' and 'full of blasphemies' and also wrote 'Donne, for not keeping of accent (rhythm), deserved hanging'.

Isaac Walton (1593–1683) wrote a short biography of Donne:

'The recreations of his youth were poetry, in which he was so happy, as if nature and all her varieties had been made only to exercise his sharp wit, and high fancy; and in those pieces that were facetiously composed and carelessly scattered it may appear by his choice of metaphors, that both nature and all the arts joined to assist him with their utmost skill'.

After describing Donne's deathbed scene Walton comments:

thus variable, thus virtuous was the life; thus exemplary was the death of this memorable man.

John Dryden, in about 1770, accused Donne of:

affect(ing) metaphysics ... and perplex(ing) the minds of the fair sex with nice speculations of philosophy.

In 1779, Samuel Johnson wrote:

the metaphysical poets were men of learning, and to show their learning was their whole endeavour; but unluckily resolving to show it in rhyme, instead of writing poetry, they wrote only verses, and very often verses that stood the trial of the finger better than of the ear; for the modulation was so imperfect, that they were only found to be verses by counting the syllables.

Strong criticism indeed!

Modern thoughts on Donne

It was not until the beginning of the 20th century that the metaphysical poets again began to be popular. T.S. Eliot insisted (in his review of an anthology in 1921) that unity of thought and feeling was the essence of being a poet and that 'a thought to Donne was an experience; it modified his sensibility'. Thus he praised these poets for the very features which had caused criticism in a earlier age.

Perhaps 20th century self-indulgence enjoys the intellectual, witty incongruity of the metaphysicals.

In 1994 the editor of a paperback volume of Donne's *Complete English Poems*, E.A. Patrides, begins:

Donne is in the first instance coarse. This judgement is ventured in earnest, and is meant not in denigration but in praise.

Donne would have enjoyed this comment!

ACTIVITY 129

Here are four extracts from Donne's poetry. Read them carefully and find the answers to these questions.

1 What ideas do these extracts have in common?
2 What do you learn about Donne's attitude to women?

3 What do you learn about Elizabethan burial customs?
4 Make some comments on Donne the man, based on these extracts.

The Relique

When my grave is broken up againe
Some second guest to entertain,
(for graves have learned that woman-head
To be to more than one a bed)

And he that digs it spies
A bracelet of bright hair about the bone,
Will he not let us alone,
And thinke that there a loving couple lies
Who thought that this device might be some way
To make their soules, at the last busie day,
Meet at this grave, and make a little stay?

The Dampe

When I am dead and doctors know not why
And my friends curiositie
Will have me cut up to survay each part,
When they shall find thy picture in my heart,
You think a sodaine dampe of love
Will through all their senses move,
And work on them as me, and so prefere
Your murder, to the name of massacre.

Dampe – a noxious vapour
Preferre – promote

The Apparition

When by thy scorn, o murdresse, I am dead
And that thou thinkst thee free
From all solicitation from me
Then shall my ghost come to thy bed,
And thee, fain'd vestall in worse arms shall see;

The Funeral

Whoever comes to shroud me, do no harm
Nor question much
That subtle wreath of hair which crowns my arm;
The mystery, the signe you must not touch,
For tis my outward soule
Viceroy to that, which unto heaven being gone,
Will leave this to controule
And keep these limbes, her Provinces from dissolution.

ACTIVITY 130

Here is a complete poem by John Donne called *The Canonization*. In this poem Donne at first abuses anyone who interrupts the love of the poet and his mistress. As their love offends no-one and cannot change the course of events, they should be left alone to enjoy it. However, by the third verse the poet has begun to imply the importance of their love as it makes sense of other events. Their love is then suggested as suitable for poetic tributes however short they might be. Finally the love of the poet and his mistress is seen as a symbol or pattern for all other love. Therefore, far from being private, it has become hugely important and 'public property'! Read the poem yourself and then consider these questions.

Discuss the tone of this poem bearing in mind what you already know about Donne. The 'tone' is the attitude of the writer to the subject he is writing about or to the reader. You might use words like 'angry' or 'bitter'.

What words do you consider suggest an Elizabethan background rather than a modern one?

If you were editing this poem, for which words would you provide a glossary?

The Canonization

For Godsake hold your tongue and let me love,
Or chide my palsie or my gout,
My five gray hairs, or ruin'd fortune flout,
With wealth your state, your mind with Arts improve,
Take you a course, get you a place
Observe his honour, or his grace,
Or the king's reall, or his stamped face
Contemplate, what you will, approve
So you will let me love.

Alas, alas, who's injured by my love?
What merchants ships have my sighs drown'd?
Who saies my tears have overflowed his ground?
When did my colds a forward spring remove?
When did the heats which my veines fill
Adde one more to the plaguie Bill?
Soldiers finde warres, and Lawyers find out still
Litigious men, which quarrels move,
Though she and I do love.

Call us what you will, wee are made such by love;
Call her one, mee another flye
We'are Tapers too, and at our owne cost die,
And wee in us finde the'Eagle and the dove,
The Phoenix riddle hath more wit
By us, we two being one, are it.
So, to one neutrall thing both sexes fit,
Wee dye and rise the same, and prove
Mysterious by this love.

Wee can dye by it, if not live by love,
And if unfit for tombes and hearse
Our legend bee, it will be fit for verse;
And if no peece of Chronicle we prove
We'll build in sonnets pretty room;
As well a well wrought urne becomes
The greates ashes, as half acre tombs,
And by these hymnes, all shall approve
Us canoniz'd for love.

And thus invoke us; you whom reverend love
Made one anothers hermitage;
You, to whom love was peace, that now is rage
Who did the whole worlds soul contract, and drove
Into the glasses of your eyes
So made such mirrors, and such spies,
That they did all to you epitomize
Countries, Townes, Courts; Beg from above
A patterne of our love.

ACTIVITY 131

Look back at the information and poetry already discussed in this section. Then find out all you can about Donne's life. What do you think is 'modern' about him and his poetry?

Write this up either as the introduction to a new edition of his poems or as an article in a magazine about books to encourage someone to buy the book or attend a reading.

Key skills: Communication – writing Information Technology – present information

ACTIVITY 132

Collect some lyrics to popular songs. Discuss whether there is any similarity between these and Donne's poetry in theme, content or approach.

Key skills: Communication – discussion

Marriage, money and misunderstandings

Between 1642 and 1660 no plays were produced in England. This was the time of civil war and the authorities felt that theatre could influence people's behaviour. When the theatres re-opened with the restoration of the monarchy, they were quite different from the ones that had existed in Shakespeare's time. New theatres were private and were attended by courtiers and wealthy 'gallants'. Audiences wanted to see comedy which reflected their way of life. Hence the 'comedy of manners' was born with its references to contemporary issues and its reliance on humour. A real innovation was that for the first time women were allowed to act. Consider the difference this might make to the types of plays written and how they were staged.

Samuel Pepys' diary contains many references to his visits to the theatre between 1660 and 1669. Here are three brief references:

31st September 1668. To the Duke of York's play house and saw *Hamlet* which we have not seen this year before, or more; and mightily pleased with it, but above all, with Betterton, the best part, I believe that ever a man acted.

25th September. My wife and I to the Duke of York's House to see *The Duchess of Malfi,* a sorry play, and sat with little pleasure for fear of my wife's seeing me look about; and so I was uneasy all the while.

12th May 1669 After dinner my wife and I to the Duke of York's play house, and there, in the side balcony, over against the music did hear, but not see, a new play the first day acted, *The Roman Virgin*, an old play but ordinary, I thought; but the trouble of my eyes with the light of the candles did almost kill me.

ACTIVITY 138

The extract below describes Satan addressing the fallen angels. Enthroned in Hell in Pandemonium, he addresses the fallen angels to raise their spirits and requests a debate on their future actions. His skill as an orator is displayed here. Try to read this passage from Book Two of *Paradise Lost* aloud as it is written to be 'declaimed'.

High on a Throne of Royal State, which far
Outshon the wealth of Ormus and of Ind,
Or where the gorgeous East with richest hand
Show'rs on her Kings barbaric Pearl and Gold,
Satan exalted sat, by merit rais'd
To that bad eminence; and from despair
Thus high uplifted beyond hope, aspires
Beyond thus high, insatiat to persue
Vain war with Heav'n, and by success untaught
His proud imaginations thus displayed.
Powers and Dominions, Deities of Heav'n
For since no deep within her gulf can hold
Immortal vigor, though opprest and fall'n
I give not heaven for lost. From this descent
Celestial Vertues rising, will appear
More glorious and more dread than from no fall,
And trust themselves to fear no second fate:
Mee though just right and the fixt Laws of Heav'n
Did first create your Leader, next free choice,
With what besides, in Counsel or in Fight,
Hath bin achiev'd of merit, yet this loss
Thus farr at least recovered, hath much more
Establisht in a safe unenvied throne
Yielded with full consent. The happier state
In Heav'n, which follows dignity, might draw
Envy from each inferior; but who here
Will envy whom the highest place exposes
Formost to stand against the Thunderes aime
Your bulwark, and condemns to greatest share
Of endless pain? Where there is then no good
For which to strive, no strife can grow up there
From Faction; for none sure will claim in hell
Precedence, none, whose portion is so small
Of present pain, that that with ambitious mind
Will covet more. With this advantage then
To union, and firm Faith, and firm accord,
More than can be in Heav'n, we now return
To claim our just inheritance of old
Surer to prosper than prosperity
Could have assur'd us: and by what best way,
Whether of open Warr or covert guile
We now debate; who can advise can speak.

What methods of persuasion is Satan using to encourage his fellow angels to take a positive stance? These will not be quite the same as the ones suggested by your role play but they will be similar.

Satan's speech is probably full of propaganda and lies. He gives three reasons for being their leader. Can you find them in the passage? Why does he feel safe from opposition?

ACTIVITY 139

Satan is obviously the villain of the piece and villains are easier to portray than saints! Good characters are boring! Can you think of any popular TV heroes who are admired for their deviousness and dishonesty rather than their goodness? Can you think of any likeable rogues in literature or film?

ACTIVITY 140

Here are some more extracts from Book Two. These are describing personifications of Sin and Death. Can you draw them from this description? You may come up with a very good depiction of Sin and Death or you may find that Milton's words are more successful as they leave much to your imagination. You cannot draw the sounds Milton describes, but you can probably have a go at the rest of the 'formidable shape' of Sin. Notice how much is left to your imagination with such phrases as 'If shape it might be called that shape had none' and 'what seemed his head'.

Describing *Sin*:
> Before the gates there sat
> On either side a formidable shape;
> The one seemd Woman to the waist, and fair,
> But ended foul in many a scaly fold
> Voluminous and vast, a serpent armd
> With moral sting: about her middle round
> A cry of Hell Hounds never ceasing barkd
> With wide cerberean mouths full loud, and rung
> A hideaous Peal, yet, when they list, would creep
> If aught disturbd thir noise, into her womb,
> And kennel there, yet there still bark'd and howld
> Within unseen.

Describing *Death*:
> The other shape,
> If shape it might be calld that shape had none
> Distinguishable in member, joint of limb,
> Or substance might be calld that shaddow seemd
> For each seemed either; black it stood as night,
> Fierce as ten Furies, terrible as Hell
> And shook a dreadful Dart; what seemd his head
> The likeness of a kingly crown had on.

ACTIVITY 141

From the extracts given in this section, find examples of the following aspects of Milton's style – classical references, reversed word order, long involved sentences, patterning of some sort, balance, repetition, similes, vivid description, appeals to the senses.

You are probably thinking that what Milton wrote was not 'English'. In fact he seemed to be writing English as though it were Latin! However by the late 18th century the pendulum had swung and poetry became the language of emotion and of the young again.

Revolution and Romanticism

The movement in poetry called Romanticism was roughly between 1797 and 1860. There is more on Romanticism in Chapter 9 (Studying Poetry). The birth of one of the poets of this period, William Wordsworth, in 1770, is a marker in the subject specifications for English which suggests its importance as a literary landmark.

William Wordsworth

Samuel Taylor Coleridge

The poets usually considered Romantics are Wordsworth and Coleridge followed by a second 'wave' Byron, Shelley and Keats. 1789 marks the beginning of the French Revolution which was seen by young poets as the birth of freedom and reform. In *The Prelude*, a long autobiographical poem by Wordsworth, he wrote 'Bliss was it in that dawn to be alive, but to be young was very heaven'.

The idealism of the young poets

Some general themes emerge in the mosaic of poems and poets under this general title of 'Romanticism'. These young poets wanted to free poetry from the establishment and find new audiences and new subjects. They saw industrialisation as a curse and wrote about pastoral settings and rural characters. (Their ideas were taken up in the 19th century by the novelist George Eliot whose work is about ordinary rural people and their lives). Although they wrote about the common man, the individual and his thoughts and feelings, they also enjoyed myths, dreams and fantasy. They believed strongly in the power of the individual and in poetry as the expression of feelings. They rejected reason in favour of the imagination.

'Lyrical Ballads' – imaginative and horrific or just plain 'down to earth'?

Wordsworth and Coleridge published *Lyrical Ballads* in 1798. In this anthology one of the contradictions of Romanticism is displayed. Wordsworth's contribution includes poems entitled *The Idle Shepherd-boy, Poor Susan, To a Sexton, The Two April Mornings, The Pet Lamb, The Childless Father, The Old Cumberland Beggar, Michael, Nutting, The Foster Mother's Tale, The Female Vagrant* and *The Idiot Boy*.

ACTIVITY 142

Find a copy of the *Lyrical Ballads* and from looking at the titles of the poems, say what issues concern the poets most. It does not take much analysis to notice the rural and simple subject matter of these poems.

In the same book we find Coleridge's *The Rime of the Ancient Mariner*. This narrative poem describes the horrific tale told by the mariner of his sea voyage. His rash killing of an Albatross brings retribution on the crew who die of thirst. The mariner escapes only to be visited by 'Life in Death'. After acknowledging the beauty of some water snakes, he is forgiven but is condemned to wander the earth telling his tale to all who will listen. It is a ghostly and disconcerting tale – the stuff of nightmares.

Ordinary language?

Wordsworth wrote an 'advertisement' and later a preface to *Lyrical Ballads* in which he set out his philosophy and poetic ideas. He wrote (he hoped) 'in a selection of language really used by men'.

They were written chiefly with a view to ascertain how far the language of conversation in the middle and lower classes of society is adapted to the purposes of poetic pleasure.

Wordsworth acknowledges the:

readers of superior judgement may disapprove of the style in which many of these pieces are executed.

Reaction in his time

Contemporary reaction to *Lyrical Ballads* was mixed. Southey, himself a poet, considered the *Preface* 'tiresome' and that with regard to *The Rime of the Ancient Mariner*, 'genius has here been employed in producing a poem of little merit'. In 1798 he wrote 'the experiment, we think, has failed, not because the language of conversation is little adapted to the purposes of poetic pleasure, but because it has been tried upon uninteresting subjects.' In the same year a commentator in *The Analytical Review* wrote that *The Ancient Mariner* has the extravagance of a mad German poet! By 1802, however, at least one commentator stated that a few of the ballads 'will rank with the first rate compositions in the language'. The same writer calls Wordsworth 'a feeler and a painter of feelings'.

The Ancient Mariner is probably the only poem in *Lyrical Ballads* which is famous in its own right. Very many illustrations have been drawn for this poem. The only ones seen by the poet were those of David Scott (1806–1849). Other versions include an oratorio by John Francis Barnett performed in 1863, dancing to a recitation of the poem by John Gielgud (1993), an adaptation by Bogdanov in 1984 for the National Theatre and a film by Mark Lavender called *Shooting the Albatross*.

ACTIVITY 143

Here is a list of illustrators of *The Ancient Mariner*: Doré (1832–1883), Jones (1895–1974), Peake (1911–1968) and Pogány (1882–1955). Some of their illustrations are reproduced in the following pages. See if you can find some others. Three modern painters have also produced illustrations – Berlin (b.1911), Procktor (b.1936) and Palmer (b.1933). Perhaps the most appealing modern version is a comic strip by Hunt Emerson (b.1952) (see page 162). In this the whole text is preserved but humour is added in the comic strip pictures and in the improvised additional dialogue.

"I looked upon the rotting sea,
And drew my eyes away." Gustave Doré

David Jones

"The sun came upon the left" Mervyn Peake

"The water-snakes" Patrick Procktor

"The very deep did rot" Willy Pogány

Hunt Emerson

You can consider which version best captures your imagination. Read the whole poem if you can and if you are artistic you could design your own illustrations. This can form the basis of a presentation.

Key skills: Information Technology – present information

A reviewer in 1799 said 'each ballad is a tale of woe'! Below is one of the short poems in *Lyrical Ballads*. Comment on the poem in the light of what has been said about the Romantics in this chapter. Look at the subject matter and the language.

Old Man Travelling

       The little hedge-row birds,
That peck along the road, regard him not.
He travels on, and in his face, his step,
His gait, is one expression; every limb,
His look and bending figure, all bespeak
A man who does not move in pain, but moves
With thought – He is insensibly subdued
To settled quiet: he is one by whom
All effort seems forgotten, one to whom
Long patience has such mild composure given,
That patience now doth seem thing, of which
He hath no need. He is by nature led
To peace so perfect, that the young behold
With envy, what the old man hardly feels.
– I asked him whither he was bound, and what
The object of his journey; he replied
Sir! I am going many miles to take
A last leave of my son, a mariner,
Who from a sea-fight has been brought to Falmouth,
And there is dying in an hospital.

An autobiographical poem

Wordsworth's most famous poem is *The Prelude*, a long autobiographical poem completed in 1805 but published posthumously in 1850. In this poem Wordsworth writes about the events in his life which shaped his poetic character.

In this extract from *The Prelude*, Wordsworth describes a skating excursion. What poetic techniques can you find here? Chapter 9 (Studying Poetry) will help. Would you consider this extract to be written in 'the language really used by men'?

And in the frosty season, when the sun
Was set, and visible for many a mile
The cottage windows blazed through twilight gloom,
I heeded not their summons: happy time
It was indeed for all of us – for me
It was a time of rapture! Clear and loud
The village clock tolled six, – and wheeled about,
Proud and exalting like an untired horse
That cares not for his home. All shod with steel,
We hissed along the polished ice in games
Confederate, imitative of the chase

And woodland pleasures, – the resounding horn,
The pack loud chiming, and the hunted hare
So through the darkness and the cold we flew,
And not a voice was idle; with the din
Smitten, the precipices rang aloud;
The leafless trees and every icy crag
Tinkled like iron; while far distant hills
Into the tumult sent an alien sound
Of melancholy not unnoticed, while the stars
Eastward were sparkling clear, and in the west
The orange sky of evening died away.
Not seldom from the uproar I retired
Into a silent bay, or sportively
Glanced sideway, leaving the tumultuous throng
To cut across the reflex of a star
That fled, and, flying still before me, gleamed
Upon the glassy plain; and oftentimes,
When we had given our bodies to the wind,
And all the shadowy banks on either side
Came sweeping through the darkness, spinning still
The rapid line of motion, then at once
Have I, reclining back upon my heels,
Stopped short; yet still the solitary cliffs
Wheeled by me – even as if the earth had rolled
With visible motion her diurnal round!
Behind me did they stretch in solemn train,
Feebler and feebler, and I stood and watched
Till all was tranquil as a dreamless sleep.

COMMENTARY   You have probably identified the strong appeals to the senses in this extract. Sight, sound and touch are very clear. The figurative language is very simple with the similes being easy to appreciate. The extended image of the hunt is accessible to all. In content the extract is more complicated as Wordsworth is exploring his ideas of communion with Nature, and Nature as his companion and teacher – ideas which are explored in more detail in the rest of *The Prelude*. The appeal of solitude is shown when he leaves his companions to retreat 'into a silent bay'. The sensation of giddiness when he stops quickly and notices the world still spinning is quite graphic. The power of reflection and the imagination is touched on with his reference to the tranquillity found after the intense activity.

On the whole the language of this extract is accessible, with perhaps only 'diurnal round' being rather pretentious. However, the thoughts and feelings are to some extent obscure and personal to the poet.

The second wave

The second group of Romantic poets included Byron (1788–1824), Shelley (1792–1822), and Keats (1795–1821).

Byron died in Greece of a fever aged 36. Shelley was drowned in a storm near Italy aged 30. Keats died of tuberculosis at the age of 26. It seems that Romanticism and longevity did not coincide! (Although Wordsworth lived until he was 80, he lost his idealism and to some extent his inspiration.

Coleridge lived until he was 62 although his best work was written before he was 28 and much of that was unfinished.)

John Keats is most famous for his odes. He also wrote some delightful long narrative poems including *Hyperion*, *The Eve of St Agnes*, *The Pot of Basil* and *Lamia*.

ACTIVITY 146

Lamia is the fascinating story of a serpent woman who wishes to become a human woman once more in order to gain her lover. She bribes the young god Hermes to change her shape. The whole thing ends in disaster when her lover realises she is really a serpent in disguise! Here is an extract from the poem which describes the serpent woman. Study it and decide what its qualities are and how far it fits in with what has been considered the Romantic movement.

> She was a gordian shape of dazzling hue,
> Vermilion spotted, golden, green and blue;
> Striped like a zebra, freckled like a pard,
> Eyed like a peacock and all crimson barr'd;
> And full of silver moons, that as she breathed,
> Dissolv'd, or bright shone, or interwreathed
> Their lustres with the gloomier tapestries-
> So rainbow-sided, touched with miseries,
> She seem'd, at once, some penanced lady elf,
> Some deamon's mistress, or the demon's self.
> Upon her crest she wore a wannish fire
> Sprinkled with stars, like Ariadne's tiar;
> Her head was serpent, but ah, bitter sweet!
> She had a woman's mouth with all its pearls complete:
> And for her eyes: what could such eyes do there
> But weep, and weep that they were born so fair?
> As Proserpine still weeps for her Sicilian air.

Key skills: Communication – discussion

COMMENTARY

You have probably realised that this extract does not confine itself to the real language of men. Neither does its subject matter seem rural and simple. There are classical references in 'gordian knot', 'Ariadne'and 'Proserpine'. This is the type of reference that the Romantic poets are reputed to be reacting against! It does, however, have something in common with *The Ancient Mariner* in its supernatural aspect and its vivid description. You may have noticed the conflict of beauty and threat in the extract.

The passage describing the change of Lamia into a woman is well worth examination. It can be found in part one of the poem, lines 146 to 170.

ACTIVITY 147

Romanticism is full of contradictions. Make up a chart in which you identify the contradictions you have noticed. Use the extracts in this chapter and any other material you have studied. Here are two areas to begin with:

- Look at the subject matter of the poems and say what differences there are.

- Examine the language and see if it really is 'the language of ordinary men'.

Give examples to show these contradictions.

Key skills: Communication – discussion

ACTIVITY 148

This chapter has dipped into literature from the 14th to the 19th century. See how much you have learnt by answering the short quiz below. Find the answers either in the chapter or in your personal research.

1

Of wealthy lustre was the banquet room,
Fill'd with pervading brilliance and perfume:
Before each lucid panel fuming stood
A censer fed with myrrh and spiced wood,
Each by a sacred tripod held aloft,
Whose slender feet wide-served upon the soft
Wool-woofed carpets: fifty wreaths of smoke
From fifty censers their light voyage took
To the high roof, still mimick'd as they rose
Along the mirror'd walls by twin clouds odorous.

2

Her lips are red, her looks are free,
Her locks are yellow as gold:
Her skin is white as leprosy,
And she is far liker death than he;
Her flesh makes the still air cold.

3

'Tis true, 'tis day, what though it be:
O wilt thou therefore rise from me?
Why should we rise because 'tis light?
Did we lie down because 'twas night?
Love which in spight of darkness brought us hither,
Should in despight of light keepe us together.

B Which poets were writing during the French revolution? Find out all you can about this Revolution. You might like to check which novelists were writing too and see if their work reflects the same influence!

C What is the significance of these dates: 1476, 1660, 1770, 1789

D In this chapter which writer is 'Elizabethan'?

A Which poets do you think wrote the verses 1–6 and what are your reasons?

4

. . . long is the way
and hard, that out of Hell leads up to light;
Our prison strong, this huge convex of Fire,
Outrageous to devour, immures us round
Ninefold, and gates of burning Adamant
Barrd over us prohibit all egress.

5

Bifil that in that season on a day,
In Southwerk at the Tabard as I lay
Redy to wenden on my pilgrymage
To Caunterbury with ful devout corage,
At night was come into that hostelrye
Wel nyne and twenty in a compaignye
Of sondry folk, by aventure yfalle
In fellowshipe and pilgrimes were they all,
That toward Caunterbury wolden ryde.

6

I saw an aged Beggar in my walk
And he was seated on the highway side
On a low structure of rude masonry
Built at the foot of a huge hill, that they
Who lead their horses down the steep rough road
May thence remount at ease.

Find out all you can about the social and political situation at this time. You might like to find out about other famous Elizabethan writers.

E Which poet wrote political pamphlets as well as poetry during the Commonwealth? He was also imprisoned for his views. Find out what you can about the Commonwealth.

Answers to quiz

A 1 John Keats. An extract from the wedding feast in *Lamia*
    2 Coleridge. The description of Life in Death
    3 John Donne. From *Breake of Day*
    4 Satan describing his proposed journey out of Hell
    5 Chaucer. From near the beginning of *The Canterbury Tales*
    6 Wordsworth. An extract from *The Old Cumberland Beggar*

B Wordsworth and Coleridge

C 1476 – the invention of the printing press
    1660 – the restoration of the monarchy after the 'Commonwealth'
    1770 – the birth of William Wordsworth
    1789 – the beginning of the French Revolution

D John Donne

E John Milton

9 Studying Poetry

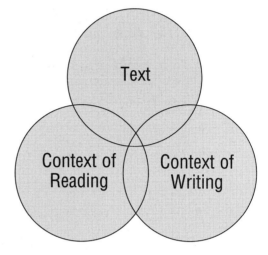

Poetry is always closer to being an experience than to being an explanation – William C. Cavanaugh.

Poetry is probably more popular today than ever before. We have Poetry on the Underground in London; the Nation's Favourite Poems; and the Nation's Favourite Comic Poems – voted for in a poll-winner style television show. But it remains for many people one of the more challenging aspects of any literature syllabus. Poetry is different. Poetry, more than any other literary form, breaks the rules. But what kinds of rules?

- Novels, biographies and travel writing usually tell stories. Poetry doesn't always.
- Novels and plays usually depict life-like situations. Poetry doesn't always.
- The language of plays and novels generally obeys grammatical rules. Poetry can break them.
- Poetry looks different on the page from other kinds of writing.

And yet poetry is all around us. Much of the language of everyday life – slang and advertising for example – is rich in metaphor and therefore suggests a poetic use of language, as in the following expressions:

Don't bottle it up.
You shouldn't slag her off.
When it gets difficult you have to fudge it.
Can you beef up your argument?
He doesn't know whether he's coming or going.

This chapter provides an outline of poetry written in English; it suggests ways in which you can read poetry and details some of the features of poetry to look out for. It also shows how contexts and others' readings of poems can be incorporated into your own responses.

Where does this fit in?

Poetry plays an important part in A level English Literature. All AS and A2 specifications require some kind of response to poetry. Poetry is often more closely associated with its writer than other forms of literature and therefore the biographical context of writing is a powerful tool. In addition to this, it is worth remembering that Shakespeare uses poetry and that novelists and other playwrights use poetic techniques.

AO2 asks you to write using appropriate terminology.

Writing about poetry probably uses its own specialist terminology to a greater extent than writing about other kinds of literature. In the glossary of one A level textbook (Shiach 1984) about half of the terms listed referred to poetry rather than other literary genres.

In some ways these terms are hooks to hang your ideas upon – knowing the appropriate terminology arguably enables you to look for features that otherwise you would not see. On the other hand, terminology can give the impression that analysing poetry is all about spotting features and giving them labels. Your individual reading of the poem is more important than these terms, although, if possible, they should help to improve your personal response. The trick is to find a balance between these two extremes.

Health Warning!

Don't let the terminology take over.

What do you mean, poetry?

ACTIVITY 149

1 On your own think about what poetry is and then write a short statement to define it.
2 Discuss the following comments on poetry. Rank order them from favourite to least favourite and argue out any differences of opinion.
3 Decide whether each statement emphasises the context of writing, the text itself or the context of reading.

Key skills: communication – discussion

A 'The difference between genuine poetry and the poetry of Dryden, Pope and their school is briefly this: their poetry is conceived and composed in their wits, genuine poetry is conceived and composed in the soul'. Matthew Arnold (1822–1888)

B '... poetry makes nothing happen'. W.H. Auden (1907–1973)

C 'Poetry is not a turning loose of emotion, but an escape from emotion; it is not the expression of personality, but an escape from personality'. T.S. Eliot (1888–1965)

D 'If poetry comes not as naturally as leaves to

a tree it had better not come at all'. John Keats (1795–1821)

E 'Music begins to atrophy when it departs too far from the dance; … poetry begins to atrophy when it gets too far from music.' Ezra Pound (1885–1927)

F 'Poetry is a record of the best and happiest moments of the happiest and best minds.' Percy Bysshe Shelley (1792–1822)

G 'Poetry is the breath and finer spirit of all knowledge; it is the impassioned expression which is in the countenance of all science.' William Wordsworth (1770–1850)

H 'Poetry is what gets lost in translation.' (attributed to Robert Frost 1874–1963)

I 'The poem is not a record of experience; it is

the experience.' A.S.P. Woodhouse in J. Hardy and M.Westbrook, *Twentieth Century Criticism: The Major Statements* (The Free Press) 1974, p. 336

J 'Not the poem which we have *read*, but that to which we *return*, with the greatest pleasure, possesses the genuine power, and claims the name of *essential poetry*.' Samuel Taylor Coleridge (1772–1834)

K 'A poem should not mean but be'. (Wallace Stevens 1879–1955)

L 'The language of imagination expressed in verse.' (Collins New English Dictionary)

M 'Expression in verse of noble thoughts or feelings.' (The Oxford School Dictionary, 1960)

COMMENTARY The above statements about poetry can be assigned to the three circles as follows, although there is definitely some room for debate here:

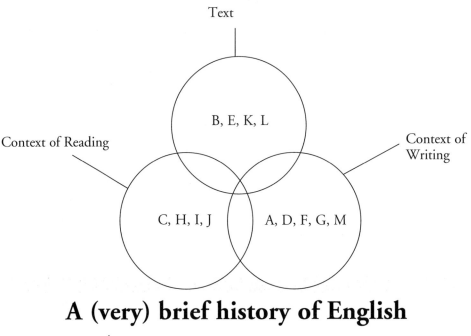

A (very) brief history of English poetry

Poetry is older than novels and short stories. The Anglo-Saxons were fond of poetry, producing dramatic poems and riddles. Although ancient civilisations told stories they were transmitted orally – that is, they were usually recited rather than written down and so they had to be full of poetic uses of language to make them memorable: for example, alliteration. The earliest known poem (and literary work) in English is *Beowulf* which was written anonymously in the 8th century.

Here is a list of some of the dead and living poets who have contributed to British poetry. The list is not definitive.

Geoffrey Chaucer (1340–1400) wrote *The Canterbury Tales* which were about a band of pilgrims who tell each other stories to while away the time on their journey. These tales were essentially tales told in poetic form.

William Shakespeare (1564–1616) It is worth reminding yourself that Shakespeare was not only a dramatist but also a poet. His plays are, of course, poetry in themselves but Shakespeare also wrote sonnets, some of which are so well-known that they have become part of the language. See Chapter 7 for a complete coverage of Shakespeare as a playwright.

The Metaphysical Poets (e.g. John Donne) wrote during the early 17th century. Their work was characterised by unusual metaphors and original angles on their subjects.

John Milton (1608–1674) Milton was responsible for one of the greatest poems in the language, *Paradise Lost*, but he also wrote many others. You can find an activity on one of his poems on page 49.

The Romantic Poets (William Blake, William Wordsworth, Samuel Taylor Coleridge, John Keats, Percy Bysshe Shelley, Lord Byron). These poets wrote from the late 18th century until midway through the 19th. Somewhat revolutionary in their way, they wrote about nature and other subjects, their influence being traceable up to the present day.

The Victorian Poets (Tennyson, Browning, Hopkins) These poets had very little in common but all wrote during the reign of Queen Victoria (1837–1901).

Poetry of the First World War (Wilfred Owen, Isaac Rosenberg, Siegfried Sassoon).

Modernist poetry (T.S. Eliot, Ezra Pound). This marked a revolution in style in the 1920s. It was often difficult, fragmented and littered with obscure references and quotations from earlier poetry.

Post-war poetry (Philip Larkin, Seamus Heaney, Ted Hughes) These three do not represent a movement. The latter two can be considered primarily as nature poets.

ACTIVITY 150

No history or list of great poets should be treated as simply true. Discuss the following aspects of the above list:

a What is missing from it?

b In what ways is the list biased? i.e. what kind of people are the poets?

For **b** you may need to find out a little more using an encyclopedia.

COMMENTARY   There are at least two serious omissions from list. Firstly there are no women and secondly there is no reflection of the diversity of ethnic influences on English writing today. The second point raises the question: what do we mean by English literature? Is it literature written in English (whether it is American, African or Caribbean) or is it literature from the British Isles? Even then, where do we draw the line?

ACTIVITY 151

Compare the above history of English poetry with the contents page of a historical book about English poetry e.g. *An Outline of English Literature* – Edited by Pat Rogers. Look carefully at:

a how each age is labelled (e.g. by the style of

the poetry, by the name of the monarch, etc.)

b the similarities and differences between each account

c any bias that seems to emerge.

Key skills: Communication – reading

ACTIVITY 152

The poet Andrew Motion was appointed Poet Laureate (the poet who is officially appointed to write about state occasions for the Queen) at the end of the last millennium. This appointment was hotly disputed as there were several other strong contenders for the title: Tony Harrison, Carol Ann Duffy, Seamus Heaney, Simon Armitage, etc. Here is a list of possible criteria for being poet Laureate:

- political views that are acceptable to the establishment
- no skeletons in your closet (no embarrassing secrets!)
- quality poet
- able to conform to the requirements of the job

- highly respected
- popular
- easy to understand

a Research: using the Internet or encyclopedias, find out why each of the other poets might not have been selected for the job. *The Reader's Companion to Twentieth Century Literature* (Ed. Peter Parker, Helicon, 1995) is a useful starting point.

b Personal Laureate. Which of the above poets (or you may like to investigate another) would you most like to have written poems about you and your life? What would your criteria be?

How to read poetry?

ACTIVITY 153

With a partner discuss how you read poetry compared with other kinds of writing. It might help to have a piece of prose and a piece of poetry for this and compare the way you read them.

a Make a list of dos and don'ts
b Compare your findings with the list of suggestions below.

Key skills: Communication – discussion

You may wish to consider:

- what you expect from a poem in the first place
- how many times you read it
- what you do when you come across difficulties
- what the ends of lines mean to you
- when you know you've finished
- whether or not you would read it aloud; etc.

Below are seven basic things to remember about reading poetry that will help avoid disappointment:

1 Don't try to work out 'what it means' right from the start. Go with the flow. Tolerate misunderstanding and remember that even the best critics are uncertain.
2 Reading poetry is a process – that is, it continues through time and never really comes to an end. All ends in your situation may be artificial – you have to get your ideas together for an essay, you have to sit an exam etc.
3 Poetic language is often dense and it may therefore take a while for you to untangle it.
4 You are unlikely to be able to explain everything. Concentrate on what you like and what you think you can explain.
5 Focusing on your difficulties can help you to come to terms with the poem. So, read *yourself* whilst you are reading the poem.
6 Look through the words (in the sense of what they stand for or depict) but also look at the words themselves – their sounds, their origins, how they are usually used.
7 Read with the ear and with the eye. It is important how a poem sounds and how it looks.

According to this view we reflect on our own experience as we read a poem, whilst also trying to uncover the poet's experience or point of view, bearing in mind that the persona (character) created in a poem may not be identical with that of the poet.

To put all of this another way, there are five things to do when you are reading a poem:

- focus on the words on the page and what they say to you.
- focus on patterns of language. Have any of the words got anything in common? Do they remind you of language from another context? e.g. newspapers.
- focus on yourself and the context in which you are reading. This might include your knowledge, memories, beliefs, or those of someone else reading the poem. Also think about the society in which you live and how it might respond to the poem you are reading.
- focus on the underlying meaning or experience, if necessary drawing on the context of writing, i.e. is there anything you know about this poet, their beliefs or the time they were writing in, that might influence your reading? (see Chapter 3).
- above all, be independent in your beliefs about the poem as long as you can justify yourself with reference to the poem.

ACTIVITY 154

The following example illustrates how we began to come to terms with a poem. Read the poem yourself several times.

a Make notes in the margin using the above advice.

b Compare your responses with ours.
c Read our comments on our own response and then try to make similar comments on your own responses.

The Tyre by Simon Armitage

1   Just how it came to rest where it rested,
    miles out, miles from the last farmhouse even,
    was a fair question. Dropped by hurricane
    or aeroplane perhaps for some reason,
    put down as a cairn or marker, then lost.
    Tractor-size, six or seven feet across,
    it was sloughed,* unconscious, warm to the touch,   * Cast-off, like a
    its gashed rhinoceros, sea-lion skin   snake's skin.
    nursing a gallon of rain in its gut.
10 Lashed to the planet with grasses and roots,
    it had to be cut. Stood up it was drunk
    or slugged, wanted nothing more than to slump,
    to spiral back to its circle of sleep,
    dream another year in its nest of peat.
    We bullied it over the moor, drove it,
    pushed from the back or turned it from the side,
    unspooling a thread in the shape and form
    of its tread, in its length and in its line,
    rolled its weight through broken walls, felt the shock
20 down to meadows, fields, onto level ground.
    There and then we were one connected thing,
    five of us, all hands steering a tall ship
    or one hand fingering a coin or ring.
    Once on the road it picked up pace, free-wheeled,
    then moved up through the gears, and wouldn't give
    to shoulder-charges, kicks; resisted force
    until to tangle with it would have been
    to test bone against engine or machine,
    to be dragged in, broken, thrown out again
30 minus a limb. So we let the thing go,
    leaning into the bends and corners,
    balanced and centred, riding the camber,
    carried away with its own momentum.
    We pictured an incident up ahead:
    life carved open, gardens in half, parted,
    a man on a motorbike taken down,
    a phone-box upended, children erased,
    police and an ambulance in attendance,
    scuff-marks and the smell of burning rubber,
40 the tyre itself embedded in a house
    or lying in the gutter, playing dead.
    But down in the village the tyre was gone,
    and not just gone but unseen and unheard of,
    not cornered in the playground like a reptile,
    or found and kept like a giant fossil.
    Not there or anywhere. No trace. Thin air.

    Being more in tune with the feel of things
    than science and facts, we knew that the tyre
    had travelled too fast for its size and mass,
50 and broken through some barrier of speed,
    outrun the act of being driven, steered,
    and at that moment gone beyond itself
    towards some other sphere, and disappeared.

1 For a start I like this poem. I like its humour and I suppose I recognise the kind of experience I might have had as a boy although, as yet, I cannot claim to fully understand it. I know that it tells the simple story of the finding of a tyre and its mysterious disappearance. But I expect the poem to be saying something more than this ... so I will look for it.

> The response is personal. Reader is thinking about himself, his personal context and the poem.

> The reader is not afraid of uncertainty.

> The reader expects more than a story.

2 As I re-read the first two lines I wonder if the repetition of the exaggerated 'miles' is supposed to be childlike language, and then the words 'was a fair question' make me wonder where and when this is being told from – its point of view, in other words. No answers to this as yet.

> Focusing on the words although he doesn't yet know why this language is used.

> He raises questions but does not expect answers yet.

3 There are several 'large scale' references in the early lines – 'hurricane', 'planet' and I wonder if these are intended to provide a sense of mystery or perhaps the excesses of childish imagination.

> Attempts to connect language pattern with childhood. This also links with personal experiences.

4 The early descriptions of the tyre are sympathetic. The *metaphors* compare the tyre with live animals, especially ones that have suffered at the hands of man ('rhinoceros', 'sea lion'). The fact that the tyre is 'lashed' to the planet also implies capture.

> Brings in some technical terminology.

> Uses language as key to some underlying ideas.

5 When the tyre is moved it becomes almost comic for a few lines and then the poem becomes kind of geometric in its precise description of movement. And then there is emphasis on the effect the tyre has on the five of them who are moving it ('we were one connected thing'). I am struck by the words 'tall ship', 'coin' or 'ring' which all seem to hint at the past or perhaps something mythical – these are all elements that you might put into a ballad. There is also something else going on in the word play on 'hands' as in 'all hands on deck'.

> This is his feeling about the poem – he finds it funny.

> Disconnected observations about language.

> Attempting to find common element.

6 At the moment I feel like my students when they say that the language is just

'normal' because I'm not struck by anything until the last stanza. Here I am amused by the logic, wondering if the poet is making fun of childish imagination.

> Tries to verbalise his difficulties and get at poet's intentions.

7 Partly in frustration, I am reminded of the little criticism of Armitage that I have read. Sean O'Brien says that Armitage's poetry is sometimes like language running around with its head cut off. He has certainly made me feel like such a chicken.

> Relates poem to his current context – his own reading.

8 Looking back at my own comments I am tempted to look at the Sean O'Brien article to see if he makes any statements about Armitage that I can test against the poem. But I feel that it is too early for this. I need to look back at my comments and find a way forward from there.

> Reflection on his own responses and deciding how to proceed.

9 At the moment the theme of child-like imagination seems the most fruitful. Through imagination this ordinary thing is transformed into something mystical. At this point I remember that the section of the anthology that this poem appears in contains other poems that find something mystical in mundane things. This is where I start to make contact with the context of writing.

> He is attempting to find underlying themes.

> Relates to own context of reading.

10 Another context of writing is beginning to emerge for me. The Romantic poets of the early 19th century tended to idealise childhood and they also elevated nature as something that can raise people up from their everyday lives. It strikes me that this poem has something of both of those points of view in it. But the joke is that an old tyre is just about as far from the subject of a Romantic poem as you could possibly get! Is Armitage a new nature poet in this respect?!

> He is trying to connect the poem with a context of writing – the influence of Romantic poetry.

> Identifies a theme that builds on ideas about childhood. Raises a new question as a result.

ACTIVITY 155

Use the above response as the basis for your own response to a poem you are studying or to another poem in this book. Remember: respond to the poem and to your own developing feelings. Use the advice given in the above checklists.

Forms and structures of poetry

In recent years literary theory has given readers a great deal of freedom but you mustn't get the impression that a poem is an empty football pitch waiting for you to kick the ball wherever you want. You must be prepared to abide by the rules and that means learning about some of the forms and conventions of poetry that have grown up over the last few hundred years. Here we can provide only a brief sketch.

Sonnet: a 14 line poem densely woven. Some variation in the precise form exists. Typically it contains a 'turn' after the first eight lines when the poem turns towards its concluding thought. There are many possible themes but many sonnets are love poems, as in Shakespeare's best known ones.

Ballad: this tends to be a longer poem in short stanzas that rhyme and it tells a story, e.g. *The Ballad of Sir Patrick Spens.*

Epic: a narrative poem that celebrates the life of a classical hero or mythological figure, e.g. Milton's *Paradise Lost.* A mock epic uses the same grand style but the content is trivial, e.g. Pope's *The Rape of the Lock.*

Lyric/Lyrical poetry: a loose term that refers to relatively short poems expressing a poet's thoughts and feelings, and that cannot be fitted into any other category. Lyrical poems often try to capture the spirit of a single moment. Much of the work of Ted Hughes and Philip Larkin can be classed as lyrical.

Free verse: poetry that conforms to no apparent structure. Such poetry breaks away from regularity and invents its own form to suit the meaning it is communicating, e.g. *Hare in the Snow* below.

Haiku: a Japanese form that has been popular in England for several centuries. It contains three lines, one of five syllables, a second of seven and a third of five. It traditionally deals with static images of nature.

ACTIVITY 156

Choose one of the above forms of poetry that you think is best suited for each of the purposes below and justify your answers. You do not have to write the poems!

1 You want to tell the story of a football team's journey to the cup final.
2 You want to write a love poem for your partner.
3 You want to capture the moment when you saw a fox.
4 Irritated recently by the speed at which time passes, you try to capture your feelings in a poem.
5 You want to re-tell the story of Adam and Eve from Eve's point of view.
6 You want to write a poem about your cat.

Poetry is characterised by:

- lines of varying lengths
- rhythmic effects creating by stressed and unstressed syllables
- other sound effects such as alliteration (see page 181)
- use of space, i.e. the layout of the words on the page
- use of metaphorical language (see page 103)

These features are an important part of what the poet is saying and should be mentioned selectively when you are writing about poetry. There are no precise rules but here are some rules of thumb about the layout of poetry:

- short lines fragment a poem and might suggest a slower reading
- look for regularities and irregularities in the rhythm. Irregularities draw attention to themselves and to the words they use
- words stand out if they are stressed. This might arise from
  a the rhythm
  b their position on the page
  c rhyme
- linked ideas are often in the same stanza but a poet might deliberately flout this to make a point

The following poem shows how some of these ideas can be applied:

Hare in the Snow – lines and stanzas

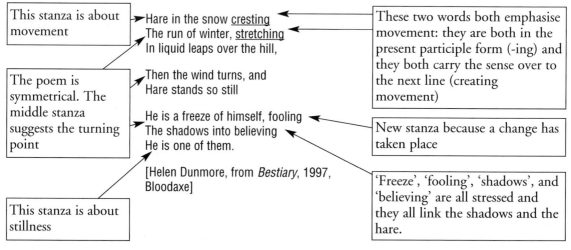

This stanza is about movement

Hare in the snow <u>cresting</u>
The run of winter, <u>stretching</u>
In liquid leaps over the hill,

Then the wind turns, and
Hare stands so still

He is a freeze of himself, fooling
The shadows into believing
He is one of them.

[Helen Dunmore, from *Bestiary*, 1997, Bloodaxe]

The poem is symmetrical. The middle stanza suggests the turning point

This stanza is about stillness

These two words both emphasise movement: they are both in the present participle form (-ing) and they both carry the sense over to the next line (creating movement)

New stanza because a change has taken place

'Freeze', 'fooling', 'shadows', and 'believing' are all stressed and they all link the shadows and the hare.

ACTIVITY 157

Opposite are four versions of the Siegfried Sassoon poem, *Suicide in the Trenches* – the original has been altered for this exercise. Each version uses a slightly different form for the poem.

a Make notes on the way the lines are set out and how the rhyme is organised.

b Then work out how these different ways of organising the poem affect you as a reader. Do they help to emphasise things that should be emphasised? Does the structure reflect the logic of the poem? Does the organisation influence the way that you physically read the poem? Discuss your feelings with a partner.

c Decide which is the original poem and give your reasons.

Note that the word 'crumps' refers to the sound of shells exploding.

Key skills: Communication –
reading/discussion/presentation

A *Suicide in the Trenches* by Siegfried Sassoon

I knew a simple soldier boy
who grinned at life in empty joy,
slept soundly through the lonesome dark,
and whistled early with the lark.
In winter trenches, cowed and glum,
with crumps and lice and lack of rum,
he put a bullet through his brain.
No one spoke of him again.
You smug-faced crowds with kindling Eye
who cheer when soldier lads march by,
sneak home and pray you'll never know
the hell where youth and laughter go.

B *Suicide in the Trenches* by Siegfried Sassoon

I knew a simple soldier boy
who grinned at life in empty joy,
slept soundly through the lonesome dark,
and whistled early with the lark.

In winter trenches, cowed and glum,
with crumps and lice and lack of rum,
he put a bullet through his brain.
No one spoke of him again.

You smug-faced crowds with kindling eye
who cheer when soldier lads march by,
sneak home and pray
you'll never know the hell
where youth and laughter go.

C *Suicide in the Trenches* by Siegfried Sassoon

I knew a simple soldier boy
who grinned at life
in empty joy,
slept soundly through
the lonesome dark,
and whistled early
with the lark.
In winter trenches,
cowed and glum,
with crumps and lice
and lack of rum,
he put a bullet
through his brain.
No one spoke
of him again.
You smug-faced crowds
with kindling eye
who cheer when
soldier lads march by,
sneak home and pray
you'll never know
the hell where
youth and laughter go.

D *Suicide in the Trenches* by Siegfried Sassoon

I knew a simple soldier boy
Who grinned at life in empty joy,

Slept soundly through the lonesome dark,
and whistled early with the lark.

In winter trenches, cowed and glum,
With crumps and lice and lack of rum,

He put a bullet through his brain.
No one spoke of him again.

You smug-faced crowds with kindling eye
Who cheer when soldier lads march by

Sneak home and pray you'll never know
The hell where youth and laughter go.

COMMENTARY   Commentaries are provided for the first two texts:

A The rhyme is regular throughout and there is no division of stanzas. The poem seems to march easily towards its conclusion. This perhaps increases the impact of the last two lines as they seem to carry on in the same thoughtless manner – at the same time the poem gives us something to think about.

B The division of the stanzas divides the poem logically into three sections. Separating them helps to emphasise their differences. The rhyme pattern is regular until it reaches the all-important last stanza where the poem makes its point. Here, in order to emphasise this point, the poem breaks the pattern, thus also breaking the rhythm.

ACTIVITY 158

Using a poem that you are studying, try setting it out in various ways. Compare these alternatives with the original and make notes on the way that they affect the reader.

Punctuating poetry

Although poetry often breaks the rules, most poems use conventional punctuation. Punctuation guides the reader by showing where pauses and breaks are to be inserted and by indicating the relationships between parts of the poem. It is easy to see the punctuation of a poem as a secondary thing – but the activity below shows how punctuation can in unusual circumstances, completely change the meaning of a single set of words.

ACTIVITY 159

In the 15th century, punctuation was not a fixed system like it is today. 'Points' (full-stops) were used but so too were *virgula suspensiva* (a forward slash /) to indicate brief pauses. In the following poem about priests, two very different interpretations are possible, depending on which set of punctuation marks is read – the commas or the forward slashes. Write out the two interpretations and with a partner explain their different meanings. Note that 'v' can be either a modern 'u' or a 'v'. You can probably work out other spelling variations yourself. 'Creator' = creature. 'Parde' = in the name of God.

Trvsty. seldom/to their Frendys vniust./
Gladd for to helpp. no Crysten creator/
Willing to greve. setting all their ioy & lust
Only in the pleasour of god. havyng no cvre/
Who is most ryche. With them they wylbe sewer/
Wher nede is. gevyng neyther reward ne Fee/
Vnresonably. Thus lyve prestys. parde./

[Source: Crystal, D. – *Cambridge Encyclopedia of the English Language* – page 282, 1995]

ACTIVITY 160

Discuss how the punctuation of *The Tyre* and *Suicide in the Trenches* contributes to the meanings of these poems. Consider the amount of punctuation at various points in the poem – how does this physically make you read the poem? Look especially at points where the punctuation is at odds with the lineation (the way the lines are set out) – why, for example, does Armitage choose to use two extra full-stops in line 46? Do the same with any poem you have been studying.

Sound effects

Read poetry aloud! Don't forget that poetry is performance. Poetry was heard for thousands of years before anyone thought of writing it down. So use your voice, listen to others and experiment with different ways of reading a poem.

Critics have developed a range of terminology for describing sound effects and you will be expected to use it. But don't allow the terms to get in the way; they may help you to find what you are looking for but they are also only tools, and should not, in themselves, be the focus of your attention. So, for example, avoid writing like this (note that monosyllabic words are words of one syllable):

'The final line of Seamus Heaney's poem 'Mid Term Break' is:
'A four foot box, a foot for every year'.
Here Heaney is suggesting the finality of the death of a child and this is reflected in his choice of vocabulary. Words like 'four', 'foot', 'box' and 'year' are examples of monosyllabic words.'

The last sentence is the offending one: 'monosyllabic' should be incorporated into a sentence describing the effect of the monosyllabic words. This would show the examiner that you know how to *use* that word, rather than pointing out that you know what it *means*.

As in much of this book, the golden rule is to always consider the context. This usually means connecting the sound effect with the meaning that comes across at a particular point in the poem.

The following are examples of some types of sound effects in poetry.

Rhythm: patterns of stressed and unstressed syllables.
Rhyme: repetition of vowel and consonant combinations at the ends of lines.
Assonance: repetition of the same vowel sound.
Stressed syllables: syllables in a word that are naturally stressed.
Onomatopoeia: words that imitate sounds.
Alliteration: repetition of the same consonant sound, especially at the beginnings of words. When the consonants are not at the beginnings of words the term **consonance** is sometimes used.

You should be aware of the effects of certain sounds created by particular letters. For example, in the first line of Robert Frost's poem *Out Out* (see page 14 for the whole context):

The buzz-saw snarled and rattled in the yard
And made dust and dropped stove-length sticks of wood

a Identify the letter 'a' in the first line of the poem and write down the sound that is associated with it in each case. Do this by indicating a word that rhymes with the sound. For example, in the second line there is:

M**a**de ------------------ sh**a**de

b What sounds or kinds of sound dominate the second line? Make connections with the meaning.

a In the first line, Frost uses near assonance to subtly bring out the winding sound of an electric saw as its tone shifts. The 'a's produce the following sounds:

'a' word in the poem	'a' sound produced
Saw	paw
Snarled	car
And	cat (arguably it is closer to the 'ion' in 'attention')
Rattled	cat
Yard	car

If you say these various 'a' sounds aloud, missing out all other letters, the resultant effect is something similar to that of an electric saw heard at a distance!

b In the second line you might have argued that much harder sounds begin to dominate, perhaps in imitation of the sound made by the short pieces of wood as they hit the ground. These sounds are: the 'p' and 'd' of 'dropped'; the 'st' of 'stove' and 'sticks'; the 'k' of 'sticks' and the 'd' of 'wood'.
Notice that these are rather isolated effects so you would need to connect them with other aspects of the poem, such as the way that the poem builds a pattern of sounds in the reader's auditory imagination as it sets the scene. Note too that there may be other sound effects in the poem that strike you more strongly, so describe those. You most certainly must not attempt to describe every sound effect produced in the poem.

Here are two poems that illustrate a range of sound effects:

Hare in the Snow – Sound Effects

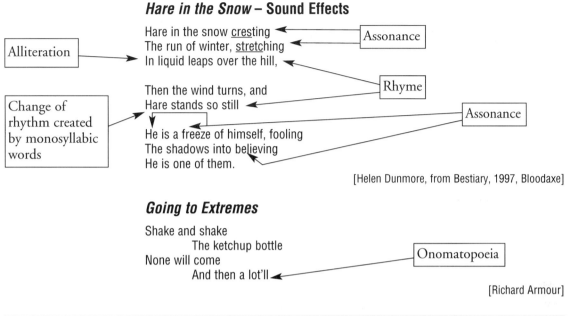

[Helen Dunmore, from Bestiary, 1997, Bloodaxe]

Going to Extremes

Shake and shake
      The ketchup bottle
None will come
      And then a lot'll ← Onomatopoeia

[Richard Armour]

ACTIVITY 162

It cannot be stressed enough that these concepts and the terms that go with them are only tools, not ends in themselves. Using the above analysis as a starting point and the one on page 178, write a full analysis of *Hare in the Snow*, using the appropriate terminology. That is, put emphasis on the effects created in you, the reader, and then refer to the terms to explain how these are achieved. There is a commentary at the end of the chapter.

Poetic movements as contexts of writing

As implied by much of this book, no literary work can be considered in isolation. Poetry can usefully be read as part of a literary movement. In other words, poets influenced each other or were influenced by the spirit of the time so that their work is seen, sometimes not until many years later, as a part of a movement. Some movements were mentioned on page 171 but here is a more detailed look at two of them.

ACTIVITY 163

Look at the two lists below. They describe two groups of poets and the ways in which they wrote. With a partner decide:

a which kind of poetry you would have preferred to read for pleasure;
b which kind you would like to study for A level;
c which kind you would send to your mother in a card.

A

1 Ingenious, extended metaphors (referred to as conceits).
2 Intellectual concepts beyond the conventional.

3 An understanding of the abstract through the concrete.

4 Demand on the mind rather than on the senses.

5 The representation of a persuasive, logical argument.

6 Wit and humour.

7 Dramatic quality.

8 Frequent use of paradox – that is, use of ideas that seem to contradict each other but actually make sense.

9 Colloquial tone (like everyday speech) and rhythm, varied in order to emphasise a thought.

10 Concise and concentrated language.

(Adapted from Burns and McNamara, MacMillan 1983).

B

1 It expressed the value of individual experience.

2 There was a sense of the infinite.

3 The main feature of style is intensity.

4 The power of the imagination was important.

5 Inspiration was sometimes taken from the Eastern and the exotic.

6 They stressed links between people and nature.

7 Some key ideas were: dreams, creativity.

8 Common themes were: unrequited love, remembered childhood, the exiled hero.

9 'The movement was a revolt against: classical form, conservative morality, authoritarian government, personal insincerity and human moderation.'(*Oxford Companion to Literature*).

10 In the poem the poet often discovers something about the world or himself.

11 The role of the poet is to awaken the minds of others to some fresh sensation concerning an object.

COMMENTARY

'**A**' describes the characteristics of 17th century poetry known as Metaphysical, as written by John Donne, Andrew Marvell, George Herbert and others. '**B**' describes Romantic poetry which spanned the period from 1790 until about 1830. This was written by poets such as Wordsworth, Coleridge, Keats, Shelley and Byron.

In the activity, which kind you preferred is very much a matter of personal opinion. Your answers to **a**, **b** and **c** may have varied according to your purpose.

ACTIVITY 164

Below are two poems. One is an example of a Romantic poem, the other a Metaphysical poem. In a small group, discuss which of the above criteria apply to which poem. For example, does **B1** apply to Poem 1, Poem 2 or to both?

Key skills: Communication – discussion

The first poem is about a poet who sees a woman working and singing in the fields in Scotland. He focuses on the subject of her singing. In the second the poet is attempting to persuade his lover to make love with him. The main weapon in his argument is a flea that has just sucked blood from her.

See the commentary at the end of this chapter.

Poem 1

The Solitary Reaper

Behold her, single in the field,
Yon solitary Highland lass!
Reaping and singing by herself;
Stop here, or gently pass!
Alone she cuts and binds the grain,
And sings a melancholy strain;
O listen! for the Vale profound
Is overflowing with the sound.

No Nightingale did ever chaunt
More welcome notes to weary bands
Of travellers in some shady haunt,
Among Arabian sands:
A voice so thrilling ne'er was heard
In spring-time from the Cuckoo-bird,
Breaking the silence of the seas
Among the farthest Hebrides.

Will no one tell me what she sings? –
Perhaps the plaintive numbers flow
For old, unhappy, far-off things,
And battles long ago:
Or is it some more humble lay,
Familiar matter of today?
Some natural sorrow, loss, or pain,
That has been, and may be again?

What'er the theme the maiden sang
As if her song could have no ending;
I saw her singing at her work,
And o'er the sickle bending; –
I listened motionless and still;
And, as I mounted up the hill,
The music in my heart I bore,
Long after it was heard no more.

Poem 2

The Flea

Mark but this flea, and mark in this,
How little that which thou deniest me is;
It sucked me first, and now sucks thee,
And in this flea our two bloods mingled be;
Thou know'st that this cannot be said
A sin, nor shame, nor loss of maidenhead;
Yet this enjoys before it woo,
And, pampered, swells with one blood of two;
And this, alas, is more than we would do.

Oh stay, three lives in one flea spare,
Where we almost, yea, more than married are.
This flea is you and I, and this
Our marriage bed and marriage temple is;
Though parents grudge, and you, we're met,
And cloistered in these living walls of jet.
Though use make you apt to kill me,
Let not to that, self-murder added be,
And sacrilege, three sins in killing three.

Cruel and sudden, hast thou since
Purpled thy nail in blood of innocence?
Wherein could this flea guilty be,
Except in that drop which it sucked from thee?
Yet thou triumph'st and say'st that thou
Find'st not thyself, nor me, the weaker now.
'Tis true, then learn how false fears be:
Just so much honour, when thou yield'st to me,
Will waste, as this flea's death took life from thee.

Health Warning!

Finding the features typical of a poetic movement will help you to understand the poetry but it cannot replace your own independent judgements about the poem.

ACTIVITY 165

a Could it be argued that the Romantic poem satisfies criteria for the Metaphysical poem and vice-versa? Test this claim by re-reading each poem.

b Find three more examples of each kind of poem and demonstrate that they belong to the appropriate movement.

Key skills: IT – different sources

Imagist poetry

The Imagists are an interesting modern example of a poetic movement. Although the movement itself produced little of real significance, it had a lasting effect on the poetry of the 20th century. It began in the early decades and its most famous practitioner was Ezra Pound who strongly influenced T.S. Eliot.

The Imagists believed:

- in writing using concrete and natural images, avoiding abstractions
- that every word must contribute to the whole poem
- that philosophy should be left to essay writers
- that description should be left to painters
- that rhythms should not sound like a metronome

ACTIVITY 166

Read and respond to the two versions of the following Imagist poem by F.S. Flint and answer the questions below:

Version 1

A Swan Song

Among the lily leaves the swan,
The pale, cold lily leaves, the swan,
With mirrored neck, a silver streak
Tipped with a tarnished copper beak,
Towards the dark arch floats slowly on;
The water is deep and black beneath the arches . . .

Version 2

A Swan Song

Over the green cold leaves
and the rippled silver
and the tarnished copper
of its neck and beak,
towards the deep black water
beneath the arches,
the swan floats slowly.

a List the differences between the two versions in terms of vocabulary, rhythm, lineation, structure, repetition and any other differences you can find.

b Try to describe what difference these changes make to your response to the poem.

c The critic C.H. Sisson writes the following about the second version: 'The rhythm has gone; the emotion has gone. One is almost tempted to say that Flint, the poet, was killed by Imagism. At any rate the comparison may cause one to reflect on the extreme danger of literary theories which are supposed to bind the poet who, after all, if he is a poet, knows better.' [C.H. Sisson – *English Poetry 1900–1950*, p 60]

To what extent do you agree with Sisson here?

Using other readers' responses

It is important that you are able to use other readers' responses to a piece of literature. Critics' views can often be rather daunting and so persuasive that it is difficult to disagree with them. Because of this, it is a good idea to use the thoughts of other students as a way of developing your own response to a piece of literature. Probably the best time to do this is when other readers and yourself are in the early stages of responding to a poem. This way you will be more prepared to change and adapt your views.

ACTIVITY 167

Read D.H. Lawrence's poem *Piano* several times, responding to it in any way that suits you but using the advice given in this chapter. The student responses that follow are spontaneous rather than crafted pieces of writing. Give your views on the comments. To what extent do you agree with each? Write your own short response to the poem using the method shown on page 173 or another you are comfortable with.

Key skills: Communication – reading/writing

Piano

Softly, in the dusk, a woman is singing to me;
Taking me back down the vista of years, till I see
A child sitting under the piano, in the boom of the tingling strings
And pressing the small, poised feet of a mother who smiles as she sings.

In spite of myself the insidious mastery of song
Betrays me back, till the heart of me weeps to belong
To the old Sunday evenings at home, with winter outside
And hymns in the cosy parlour, the tinkling piano our guide.

So now it is vain for the singer to burst into clamour
With the great black piano appassionato. The glamour
Of childish days is upon me, my manhood is cast
Down in the flood of remembrance, I weep like a child for the past.

D.H. Lawrence

Tips for using other readers' responses:

1 Try to develop some ideas of your own before you look at the views of other readers.
2 Pick out statements that you agree or disagree with. Then go back to the poem and find evidence to support your views.
3 Try to question any assumptions that the other reader has made in order to weaken their argument e.g. Response number 2 seems to make a large number of assumptions about what poetry should be.

Response 1
After about 3 readings decide I don't like this. It makes me angry... I feel myself responding to it and don't like responding. I think I feel hypnotised by the long boomy lines. But the noise when I stop myself being hypnotised seems disproportionate to what's being said. A lot of emotion is being stirred up about nothing much. The writer seems to love feeling sobby about his pure spotless childhood and to enjoy thinking of himself as a world-worn wretch. There's too much about 'insidiousness' and 'appassionato' for me. The whole comparison between childhood's Sunday evenings and passionate manhood etc. is cheap by which I

mean (1) It is easy; (2) It is unfair both to childhood and manhood.

Response 2

The general effect upon me of [this poem] is mild. I consider it sentimental verse rather than poetry but it doesn't strike me as being of the really nauseating type. The emotion described might well be sincere as far as it went but to be enthusiastic over the poem I should have to be convinced that the poet's miseries were worth weeping about or casting down his manhood, and I certainly am not convinced. It seems to me to be full of 'appeals to the gallery', e.g. 'small poised feet' – anyhow they're certainly not worth weeping about, nor is a hymn in a cosy parlour, and to a great number of people a tinkling piano.

Response 3

It is difficult to pass judgement on this poem. The communication is excellent, and the experience one familiar to most people. I suppose this emotional reversion to an ordinary incident of one's childhood, and the indulgence in grief for it simply because it is past, is really sentimental. The striking thing is, that the poet ... knows quite well that it is so, and does not try to make capital out of the sentiment. The simplicity and accuracy with which he records his feelings – and the justness of the expression,

not pitching the thing up at all – somehow alters the focus; what might have been merely sentimental becomes valuable – the strength of the underlying feeling becoming apparent through the sincerity and truthfulness of the expression.

Response 4

One is made keenly aware of the strange relationship of past and present experience – one feels the emotion the poet experienced through his identity with and separation from his past self. He has succeeded in conveying the acute emotion he experienced and he has succeeded in dealing with a situation fraught with the danger of sentimentality, without sentimentalism. The idea of motherhood – the past – Sunday evenings etc. all lend themselves to insincere emotion. In the second verse it seems to me, the poet recognises and dispels that danger. He recognises there the difference between his man's outlook and his childish outlook and we share his experience of being 'betrayed back' by 'the insidious mastery'. I'm not sure if this explains how sentimentality is missed. I am convinced it is missed by the fact that the poem moves me more as I read it more often. An insincere emotion betrays itself by slovenly expression if one watches it closely I think.

COMMENTARY These responses were written by Cambridge undergraduates in 1929 as part of some research. You probably found these responses very judgmental which should have given you plenty to work against. Did you find the poem a lot of fuss over nothing? Did you agree that the comparison is an easy one to make and if so, why should poets have to make 'difficult' comparisons? Did you feel that Response number 2 could not identify with the poet's situation? To what extent is the poem merely sentimental and can 'sincerity' alter it?

This chapter has offered a brief introduction to the study of poetry. It provided basic information on historical contexts, forms of poetry and sound effects. It has suggested a way of working with poetry that emphasises informed personal response, grounded in the reader's experience, the words on the page and the context in which the poem was written.

COMMENTARY ON ACTIVITY 162

Hare in the Snow is a snapshot of a hare in a winter environment. It shows the hare moving and then, as the wind turns it becomes still – these three factors determine the poem's whole organisation.

In the first stanza the hare is speed, suggested by the use of the two active present participles 'cresting' and 'stretching' which also, coming at the ends of lines plunge the reader into the next line, as if there is no time to stop. 'Cresting' itself reminds us of 'on the crest of a wave' which is reflected in 'liquid leaps'; the latter combination stands out because it is alliterative (and it is appropriate that this should be on a soft sound such as 'l') and metaphorical. The whole poem is symmetrical so it is correct that the middle stanza is the turning point that changes the behaviour of the hare. The impact of the changes in the hare is heightened by the alliteration of 'stands so still' and the fact that the reader senses the change of rhythm created by the monosyllabic words in the second stanza. The third stanza sees the hare as static. The stressed words 'freeze', 'fooling', 'shadows' and 'believing' are the important ideas here. They show how the hare is able to merge in with his background to such an extent that he almost becomes a shadow. Although the poet has used the same pattern as the opening stanza, this time the present participles are not about action but are mental, internal processes that, like the hare, are invisible to the eye. The assonance of 'freeze' and 'believing' links cause and effect, and 'freeze' itself has several meanings: firstly its suggests stillness, secondly its coldness implies that the hare is part of winter and thirdly there is a likely pun here on 'frieze' – which is a pattern or picture around the top of a wall.

This analysis is not complete and it does avoid answering some more difficult questions like the poet's tendency to see the hare in human terms, especially in the last stanza. Usually such questions should be considered in a wider context such as alongside other poems by the same writer or other poems about animals by different writers.

COMMENTARY ON ACTIVITY 164

The first poem was written in the 19th century by William Wordsworth, the poet who most embodies the Romantic movement. The second was written by John Donne, one of the Metaphysical poets, in the 17th century. These poets are further contextualised on pages 142 and 155. *The Solitary Reaper* bears elements of criteria 1, 4, 5, 6, 11. *The Flea* uses the flea's blood sucking as a metaphor for the union of the two people (criteria 1–3). The poet's use of argument to persuade uses criteria 4–6. The language is certainly concentrated and takes some untangling (criterion 10) but it has elements of conversation (criterion 9) and because sections of it do not seem to make sense at first, it could be argued that it contains elements of criterion 8. The most debatable criterion is probably 7.

Further reading

How To Study Modern Poetry by Tony Curtis (1990) Macmillan.
Provides a method for studying poems and demonstrates it.

Double Vision by Michael and Peter Benton (1990) Hodder and Stoughton.
Links the study of poetry with looking at paintings. Practical and creative.

Twentieth Century Poetry: From Text to Context edited by Peter Verdonk (1993) Routledge.
A challenging book for A level. Takes a linguistic approach.

A Linguistic Guide to English Poetry by Geoffrey N. Leech (1969) Longman.
An excellent technical guide.

10 Studying Novels

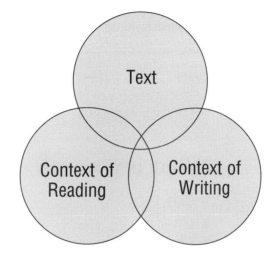

In this chapter, the novel will be explored. Some approaches to studying novels are discussed with reference to:

1 beginnings and endings
2 creation of the world of the novel
3 creation of the characters in the novel
4 role of the narrator
5 structure

This is followed by a brief history of the novel.

Where does this fit in?

All Assessment Objectives are covered in this section but in particular 4, 5(i) and 5(ii). You will be studying at least one complete novel whichever specification you are following.

Today we use the word 'novel' without a second's thought. The word itself means 'new' and it was in the 18th century that this new literary form appeared. A novel is a fictional text that we read and enjoy and gives us some insight into human behaviour. Bookshops are full of novels with attractive covers which encourage us to buy them. Lists of best sellers are produced. There's bedtime reading, holiday reading, Christmas reading, beach reading. . . . The best novels are adapted for television or the cinema.

Prizes are awarded for the best novels each year. The most famous prize is the 'Booker Prize' for which books are short-listed and then a winner chosen by a panel of 'experts'. Each year the winner is controversial!

Health Warning!

In this chapter there are many cross references to other chapters.

You may also be tempted to read the whole of some of the books mentioned. Try not to resist the temptation!

A good reference book to develop your understanding is David Lodge's *The Art of Fiction* (1992) This is a collection of articles originally published in quality newspapers. It explains technical terms and explores many features of how the novel works.

What is a novel?

A novel:

- is written to be enjoyed
- attracts the interest and sympathy of the reader
- is fictional
- is written in prose
- has a beginning, a middle and an end
- has characters with personalities
- has a plot
- is set in a well defined, believable place or world
- observes human nature
- has chapters
- is longer than a short story

ACTIVITY 168

Check this list against a novel you have read. Are any general features of the novel form missing from this list? Are there any unusual features in the novel you have chosen?

Key skills: Communication – discussion

Some approaches to studying novels

You probably read modern novels for relaxation. Sometimes you will come across 'a real gem' which you recommend to a friend, or other times you read one and wonder why you even picked it up!

What distinguishes the good novel from the mediocre? An analysis of the skills of various novelists should help to develop your critical appreciation so that you can give informed opinions about modern prose.

In this section various aspects of studying the modern novel will be discussed. The ways into these texts would be equally appropriate for older and more modern texts.

1 Beginnings and endings

Beginnings

Enduring Love by Ian McEwan has one of the most riveting openings written in recent years. Read the extract from the book below which is the first three pages. Write down anything intriguing or interesting in the way this is written. What do you find out about the characters and the incident? What do you think will happen next? Make close reference to the text to support your ideas. Compare your ideas with the commentary which follows the text.

The beginning is simple to mark. We were in sunlight under a turkey oak, partly protected from a strong, gusty wind. I was kneeling on the grass with a corkscrew in my hand, and Clarissa was passing me the bottle – a 1987 Daumas Gassac. This was the moment, this was the pinprick on the time map: I was stretching out my hand, and as the cool neck and the black foil touched my palm, we heard a man's shout. We turned to look across the field and saw the danger. Next thing, I was running towards it. The transformation was absolute: I don't recall dropping the corkscrew, or getting to my feet, or making a decision, or hearing the caution Clarissa called after me. What idiocy, to be racing into this story and its labyrinths, sprinting away from our happiness among the fresh spring grasses by the oak. There was the shout again, and a child's cry, enfeebled by the wind that roared in the tall trees along the hedgerows. I ran faster. And there, suddenly, from different points around the field, four other men were converging on the scene, running like me.

I see us from three hundred feet up, through the eyes of the buzzard we had watched earlier, soaring, circling and dipping in the tumult of currents: five men running silently towards the centre of a hundred-acre field. I approached from the south-east, with the wind at my back. About two hundred yards to my left two men ran side by side. They were farm labourers who had been repairing the fence along the field's southern edge where it skirts the road. The same distance beyond them was the motorist, John Logan, whose car was banked on the grass verge with its door, or doors, wide open. Knowing what I know now, it's odd to evoke the figure of Jed Parry directly ahead of me, emerging from a line of beeches on the far side of the field a quarter of a mile away, running into the wind. To the buzzard Parry and I were tiny forms, our white shirts brilliant against the green, rushing towards each other like lovers, innocent of the grief this entanglement would bring. The encounter that would unhinge us was minutes away, its enormity disguised from us not only by the barrier of time but by the colossus in the centre of the field that drew us in with the power of a terrible ratio that set fabulous magnitude against the puny human distress at its base.

What was Clarissa doing? She said she walked quickly towards the centre of the field. I don't know how she resisted the urge to run. By the time it happened – the event I am about to describe, the fall – she had almost caught us up and was well placed as an observer, unencumbered by participation, by the ropes and the shouting, and by our fatal lack of co-operation. What I describe is shaped by what Clarissa saw too, by what we told each other in the time of obsessive re-examination that followed: the aftermath, an appropriate term for what happened in a field waiting for its early summer mowing. The aftermath, the second crop, the growth promoted by that first cut in May.

I'm holding back, delaying the information. I'm lingering in the prior moment because it was a time when other outcomes were still possible; the convergence of six figures in a flat green space has a comforting geometry from the buzzard's perspective, the knowable, limited plane of the snooker table. The initial conditions, the force and the direction of the force, define all the consequent pathways, all the angles of collision and return, and the glow of the overhead light bathes the field, the baize and all its moving bodies, in reassuring clarity. I think that while we were still converging, before we made contact, we were in a state of mathematical grace. I linger on our dispositions, the relative distances and the compass point – because as far as these occurrences were concerned, this was the last time I understood anything clearly at all.

What were we running towards? I don't think any of us would ever know fully. But superficially the answer was, a balloon. Not the nominal space that encloses a cartoon character's speech or thought, or, by analogy, the kind that's driven by mere hot air. It was an enormous balloon filled with helium, that elemental gas forged from hydrogen in the nuclear furnace of the stars, first step along the way in the generation of multiplicity and variety of matter in the universe, including our selves and all our thoughts.

We were running towards a catastrophe, which itself was a kind of furnace in whose heat identities and fates would buckle into new shapes. At the base of the balloon was a basket in which there was a boy, and by the basket, clinging to a rope, was a man in need of help.

COMMENTARY   This incident is told from the point of view of the narrator who is telling of a personal experience. He was with his girlfriend having a picnic when a hot air balloon with two passengers landed in a field nearby. The passengers were obviously in need of help and four other people came to the rescue along with the narrator.

This itself is quite an exciting story line but McEwan relates the incident so that it is not only vivid but also of immense significance to the narrator. The world of the novel is created by a clear description of the setting and sounds, particularly the relaxed picnic under the oak which is disturbed and punctuated by the cries for help.

The use of the buzzard is interesting as it puts the action in a different perspective and gives an overview of the situation. The event is seen as part of a pattern which is overseen by an almost 'godlike' presence. The buzzard can see these people, who have not yet met, converging on the scene and we can only begin to imagine the way these characters will interact. There seems an inevitability and a threat in the activity. The narrator is intrusive and self-conscious. He uses expressions like 'knowing what I know now' and 'innocent of the grief this entanglement would bring' and 'I'm holding back, delaying the information'. The narrator tries to distance himself from the event and becomes reflective.

The monumental nature of the event is stressed by 'what idiocy to be racing into this story and its labyrinths, sprinting away from our happiness among the fresh spring grasses by the oak'. The whole passage is scattered with words signifying the importance of the event – 'enormity', the balloon is a 'colossus'. There is 'power 'and 'magnitude'. Against this, man is seen as 'puny' and expendable. Man is seen as a victim and the outcome, whatever that may be, is inevitable.

These are just some of the feelings evoked by the passage.

What then, makes it an effective opening for a novel?

In outline, we learn about:

■ the narrator and how important this moment becomes to him
■ the place – with its original calm relaxed atmosphere, its sights and sounds
■ the event that takes on a metaphorical meaning with the characters rushing into their own destruction.

We want to know if the passengers can be saved but also what other terrible events are to be unfolded. The language arouses our interest because the event is made to sound monumentally important. We are given enough information to be enticed into the world of the novel and our curiosity aroused so that we wish to read on. Suspense is created and hints of further action are given. The story of this novel is fascinating. The first pages are to some extent a red herring i.e. not the real focus of the plot. It is the people who meet in this tragic situation by accident who are the main focus of the story – in particular Joe Rose and the obsessive Jed Parry.

You might like to return to this passage after you have studied the rest of this chapter. You will then have more information about the importance of place, character, narrator and structure.

Another interesting beginning is from a novel by Charles Frazier called *Cold Mountain*. This story centres around the parallel stories of a soldier returning to his loved one after the American Civil War and the story of the hardship which the woman endures. Their stories are interwoven. As they get closer together, each oblivious of the other's situation, the reader becomes even more intrigued: as a reader we have an overview of the situation.

ACTIVITY 169

Read this extract from *Cold Mountain* and write down your first reactions. What do we learn about the events, the place, the person? What is interesting in the structure of the extract?

At the first gesture of morning, flies began stirring. Inman's eyes and the long wound at his neck drew them, and the sound of their wings and the touch of their feet were soon more potent than a yardful of roosters in rousing a man to wake. So he came to yet one more day in the hospital ward. He flapped the flies away with his hands and looked across the foot of his bed to an open triple-hung window. Ordinarily he could see to the red road and the oak tree and the low brick wall. And beyond them to a sweep of fields and flat piney woods that stretched to the western horizon. The view was a long one for the flatlands, the hospital having been built on the only swell within eyeshot. But it was too early yet for a vista. The window might as well have been painted grey.

Had it not been too dim, Inman would have read to pass the time until breakfast, for the book he was reading had the effect of settling his mind. But he had burned up the last of his own candles reading to bring sleep the night before, and lamp oil was too scarce to be striking the hospital's lights for mere diversion. So he rose and dressed and sat in a ladderback chair, putting the gloomy room of beds and their broken occupants behind him. He flapped again at the flies and looked out the window at the first smear of foggy dawn and waited for the world to begin shaping up outside.

The window was tall as a door, and he had imagined many times that it would open onto some other place and let him walk through and be there. During his first weeks in the hospital, he had been hardly able to move his head, and all that kept his mind occupied had been watching out the window and picturing the old green places he recollected from home. Childhood places. The damp creek bank where Indian pipes grew. The corner of a meadow favored by brown-and-black caterpillars in the fall. A hickory limb that overhung the lane, and from which he often watched his father driving cows down to the barn at dusk. They would pass underneath him, and then he would close his eyes and listen as the cupping sound of their hooves in the dirt grew fainter and fainter until it vanished into the calls of katydids and peepers. The window apparently wanted only to take his thoughts back. Which was fine with him, for he had seen the metal face of the age and had been so stunned by it that when he thought into the future, all he could vision was a world from which everything he counted important had been banished or had willingly fled.

By now he had stared at the window all through a late summer so hot and wet that the air both day and night felt like breathing through a dishrag, so damp it caused fresh sheets to sour under him and tiny black mushrooms to grow overnight from the limp pages of the book on his bedside table. Inman suspected that after such long examination, the grey window had finally said about all it had to say. That morning, though, it surprised him, for it brought to mind a lost memory of sitting in school, a similar tall window beside him framing a scene of pastures and low green ridges terracing up to the vast hump of Cold Mountain. It was September. The hayfield beyond the beaten dirt of the school playground stood pant-waist high, and the heads of grasses were fuming yellow from need of cutting. The teacher was a round little man, hairless and pink of face. He owned but one rusty black suit of clothes and a pair of old overlarge dress boots that curled up at the toes and were so worn down that the heels were wedgelike. He stood at the front of the room rocking on the points. He talked at length through the morning about history, teaching the older students of grand wars fought in ancient England.

After a time of actively not listening, the young Inman had taken his hat from under the desk and held it by its brim. He flipped his wrist, and the hat skimmed out the window and caught an updraft and soared. It landed far out across the playground at the edge of the hayfield and rested there black as the shadow of a crow squatted on the ground. The teacher saw what Inman had done and told him to go get it and to come back and take his whipping. The man had a big paddleboard with holes augered in it, and he liked to use it. Inman never did know what seized him at that moment, but he stepped out the door and set the hat on his head at a dapper rake and walked away, never to return.

The beginning of a novel must attract our attention and fire our imagination. It must give a clear indication of the world of the novel and raise questions in our minds which need to be answered.

Endings

Endings are often similarly intriguing. A surprise ending is a common tool of the classic short story but often a novel has the same feature.

ACTIVITY 170

Find out about the alternative ending of *Great Expectations* by Charles Dickens and why Dickens wrote a different ending. See also Chapter 3 (Contexts of Writing).

Endings that feel like beginnings!

At the end of *Things Fall Apart* by Chinua Achebe the whole book is put in a new perspective and the reader is shocked by the behaviour of a new character. The novel tells of the Nigerian village of Umuofia and its inhabitants. We live through its ups and downs and recognise the people as a civilised and respected race. The white colonists and missionaries arrive and cause havoc. This challenges our expectations somewhat! One of the main warriors of the tribe commits suicide – a great sin. The final paragraph, however, is a brutal reminder that these people with whom we have lived throughout the novel are seen as savages by the white colonists.

The Commissioner went away taking three or four of the soldiers with him. In the many years in which he had toiled to bring civilisation to different parts of Africa he had learnt a number of things. One of them was that a District Commissioner must never attend to such details as cutting down a hanged man from a tree. Such attention would give the natives a poor opinion of him. In the book which he planned to write he would stress that point. As he walked back to the court he thought about that book. Every day brought him some new material. The story of this man who had killed a messenger and hanged himself would make interesting reading. One could almost write a whole chapter on him. Perhaps not a whole chapter but a reasonable paragraph, at any rate. There was so much else to include, and one must be firm in cutting out details. He had already chosen the title of the book, after much thought: 'The Pacification of the Primitive Tribes of the lower Niger'.

The reader is incensed by his attitude and the whole book becomes a tribute to the tribe of Umuofia.

ACTIVITY 171

Take a novel you know well and look at the final paragraph. How significant is it? Does it tie up the loose ends or does it create some more? Is it satisfying or do you feel cheated? Does it shed any light on the meaning of the novel? Does it change the focus of the book? Can you rewrite it in such a way that it does change the focus of the book as a whole?

Key skills: Communication – discussion

2 The importance of place – creation of the world of the novel

ACTIVITY 172

Novels must have clear settings to keep us involved in them. Here are three descriptions of places you would **not** wish to visit in reality. Look at them carefully and see how the writer has made them so vivid. Consider the appeals to the senses and what atmosphere the writer has created. A commentary on extract A has been provided to guide you.

Text A from *Archangel* by Robert Harris

Kelso opened the heavy door and the stale air hit him like a wall. He had to clamp a hand to his mouth and nose to keep from gagging. The smell that pervaded the whole house seemed to have its source in here. It was a big room, bare, lit from the opposite wall by three tall, net-curtained windows, high oblongs of translucent grey. He moved towards them. The floor seemed to be strewn with pools of tiny black husks. His idea was that if he pulled back the curtain, he could throw light on the room, and see what he was treading on. But as his hand touched the rough nylon net, the material seemed to split and ripple downwards and a shower of black granules went pattering across his hand and brushed the back of his neck. He twitched the curtain again and the shower became a cascade, a waterfall of dead, winged insects. Millions of them must have hatched and died in here over the summer, trapped in the airless room. They had a papery, acid smell. They were in his hair. He could feel them rustling under his feet. He stepped backwards, furiously brushing at himself and shaking his head.

Text B from *Great Expectations* by Charles Dickens

I crossed the staircase landing, and entered the room she indicated. From that room too the daylight was completely excluded, and it had an airless smell that was oppressive. A fire had been lately kindled in the damp old-fashioned grate, and the reluctant smoke which hung in the room seemed colder than the cleared air – like our own marsh mist. Certain wintry branches of candles on the high chimney piece faintly lighted the chamber: or, it would be more expressive to say, faintly troubled its darkness. It was spacious, and I dare say had once been handsome, but every discernible thing in it was covered with dust and mould, and dropping to pieces. The most prominent object was a long table with a table cloth spread on it, as if a feast had been in preparation when the house and the clocks all stopped together. An epergne or centrepiece of some kind was in the middle of this cloth; it was so heavily overhung with cobwebs that its form was quite undistinguishable; and as I looked along the yellow expanse out of which I remember it seeming to grow, like a black fungus, I saw speckled-legged spiders with blotchy bodies running home to it, and running out from it, as if some circumstance of the greatest public importance had just transpired in the spider community.

Text C from *The English Patient* by Michael Ondaatje

Between the kitchen and the destroyed chapel a door led into an oval shaped library. The space inside seemed safe except for a large hole at portrait level in the far wall, caused by mortar-shell attack on the villa two months earlier. The rest of the room had adapted itself to this wound, accepting the habits of the weather, evening stars, the sound of birds. There was a sofa, a piano covered in a grey sheet, the head of a stuffed bear and high wall of books. The shelves nearest the torn wall bowed with the rain which had doubled the weight of the books. Lightning came into the room too, again and again, falling across the covered piano and carpet.

COMMENTARY ON TEXT A

The atmosphere that has been created is unpleasant and stifling. There are several references to smell in this passage – 'the stale air hit him like a wall', 'the smell that pervaded the whole house', 'They had a papery, acid smell'.

Touch is also noticeable – the heavy door, the rough nylon net, the black granules 'brushed the back of his neck', 'he could feel them rustling under his feet' (sound and touch!).

We hear sounds in the granules 'pattering' on his hand and 'rustling' under his feet.

There is also quite a lot of movement. The character opens the door, puts his hand to his mouth, moves towards the windows, pulls back the curtain and brushes off the dead insects.

We are given details of the contents of the room but the colours are only grey and black.

The writer also tells us what the character is thinking. He moves the curtain to give himself more light and deduces what has caused this huge number of dead insects. Words indicating Kelso's thoughts are 'the floor **seemed** to be strewn', 'his idea was'. The statement that the insects 'must have' been there over the summer echoes the words he said to himself.

ACTIVITY 173

Here are three descriptions of court scenes. Study each one and decide the main focus of each – the way the author creates a different atmosphere. Bring out their different purposes and attitudes by comparing them. Take each extract in turn and respond to the following:

- Is the place pleasant or unpleasant?
- What appeals to the senses are there?
- What is the significance of this and what atmosphere does it create?

- What is the tone of each piece? (This may not be significant in every piece. Tone means what is the attitude of the writer to the subject matter. Some useful words might be: 'sarcastic', 'humorous' 'witty', 'serious,' 'detached', 'involved', 'critical').
- What is the main focus – is it the people or the place?

Compare the three extracts bearing in mind these questions.

Text A from *Snow Falling on Cedars* by David Guterson

This courtroom, Judge Llewellyn Fielding's, down at the end of a damp drafty hallway on the third floor of the Island County Courthouse, was run-down and small as courtrooms go. It was a place of gray-hued and bleak simplicity – a cramped gallery, a bench for a judge, a witness stand, a plywood platform for the jurors, and scuffed tables for the defendant and his prosecutor. The jurors sat with studiously impassive faces as they strained to make sense of matters. The men – two truck farmers, a retired crabber, a bookkeeper, a carpenter, a boat builder, a grocer, and a halibut schooner deckhand – were all dressed in coats and neckties. The women all wore Sunday dresses – a retired waitress, a sawmill secretary, two nervous fisher wives. A hairdresser accompanied them as alternate.

The Bailiff, Ed Soames, at the request of the judge, had given a good head of steam to the sluggish radiators, which now and again sighed in the four corners of the room. In the heat they produced a humid, overbearing swelter – the smell of sour mildew seemed to rise from everything.

Text B from *The Runaway Jury* by John Grisham

The main courtroom of the Biloxi courthouse was on the second floor, up the tiled staircase to an atrium where sunlight flooded in. A fresh coat of white paint had just been applied to the walls, and the floors gleamed with new wax.

By eight Monday a crowd was already gathering in the atrium outside the large wooden doors leading to the courtroom. One small group was clustered in a corner, and was comprised of young men in dark suits, all of whom looked remarkably similar. They were well groomed, with oily short hair, and most either wore horn-rimmed glasses or had suspenders showing from under their tailored jackets. They were Wall Street financial analysts, specialists in tobacco stocks, sent South to follow the early developments of *Wood v. Pynex*.

Another group, larger and growing by the minute, hung loosely together in the centre of the atrium. Each member awkwardly held a piece of paper, a jury summons. Few knew one another, but the papers labeled them and conversation came easily. A nervous chatter rose quietly outside the courtroom. The dark suits from the first group became still and watched the potential jurors.

The third group wore frowns and uniforms and guarded the doors. No fewer than seven deputies were assigned to keep things secure on the opening day. Two fiddled with the metal detector in front of the door. Two more busied themselves with paperwork behind a makeshift desk. They were expecting a full house. The other three sipped coffee from paper cups and watched the crowd grow.

The guards opened the courtroom doors at exactly eight thirty, checked the summons of each juror, admitted them one by one through the metal detector, and told the rest of the spectators they would have to wait awhile. Same for the analysts and same for the reporters.

Text C from *Bleak House* by Charles Dickens

On such an afternoon, if ever, The Lord High Chancellor ought to be sitting here – as here he is – with a foggy glory round his head, softly fenced in with crimson cloth and curtains, addressed by a large advocate with great whiskers, a little voice, and an interminable brief, and awkwardly directing his contemplation to the lantern in the roof, where he could see nothing but fog. On such an afternoon, some score of the members of the High Court of Chancery Bar ought to be – as here they are – mistily engaged in one of the ten thousand stages of an endless cause, tripping one another upon slippery precedents, groping knee deep in technicalities, running their goat-hair and horsehair warded heads against walls of words, and making a pretence of equity with serious places, as players might. On such an afternoon, the various solicitors of the cause some two or three of whom have inherited it from their fathers, who made a fortune by it, ought to be, as are they not? – ranged in a line, in a long matted well (but you might look in vain for Truth at the bottom of it), between the registrar's red table and the silk gowns, with bills, cross bills, answers, rejoinders, injunctions, affidavits, issues, references to masters, masters' reports, mountains of costly nonsense, piled before. Well may the court be dim, with wasting candles here and there; well may the fog hang heavy in it, as if it would never get out; well may the stained glass windows lose their colour, and admit no light of day into the place; well may the uninitiated from the streets, who peep in through the glass panes in the door, be deterred from entrance by its owlish aspect, and by the drawl languidly echoing to the roof from the padded dais where The Lord High Chancellor looks into the lantern that has no light in it, and where all the attendant wigs are all stuck in a fog-bank! This is the Court of Chancery which has its decaying houses and blighted lands in every shire; which has its worn out lunatic in every madhouse, and its dead in every churchyard; which has its ruined suitor, with his slipshod heels and thread bare dress, borrowing and begging through the round of everyman's acquaintance; which gives to monied might, the means abundantly of wearying out the right; which exhausts finances, patience, courage, hope; so overthrows the brain and breaks the heart; that there is not an honourable man among its practitioners who would not give – who does not often give – the warning, 'Suffer any wrong that can be done you, rather than come here!'

You can see from these extracts that creation of place is often intertwined with creation of character.

3 The importance of people – creation of characters in the novel

Creation of character is as important as creation of place and plot in a novel. Not all characters are fully rounded or developed but the central ones need to be. Characters are rounded if we know what they look like, how they speak and what makes them behave the way they do. Characters who change during the course of a novel are perhaps more likely to engage our attention than those who do not. Also recurrent mannerisms and idiosyncrasies in speech lend familiarity and realism to a character.

ACTIVITY 174

Here is the beginning of *Snow Falling On Cedars* by David Guterson where one of the characters is introduced. Exactly what do you learn about the character here?

The accused man, Kabuo Miyamoto, sat proudly upright with rigid grace, his palms placed softly on the defendant's table – the posture of a man who has detached himself insofar as this is possible at his own trial. Some in the gallery would say later that his stillness suggested a disdain for the proceedings; others felt certain it veiled a fear of the verdict that was to come. Whichever it was, Kabuo showed nothing – not even a flicker of the eyes. He was dressed in a white shirt worn buttoned to the throat and gray, neatly pressed trousers. His figure, especially the neck and shoulders, communicated the impression of irrefutable physical strength and of precise, even imperial bearing. Kabuo's features were smooth and angular; his hair had been cropped close to his skull in a manner that made its musculature prominent. In the face of the charge that had been levelled against him he sat with his dark eyes trained straight ahead and did not appear moved at all.

A few paragraphs later we are given more information to help us build up the character:

The accused man, with one segment of his consciousness, watched the falling snow outside the windows. He had been exiled in the county jail for seventy seven days – the last part of September, all of October and all of November, the first week of December in jail. There was no window anywhere in his basement cell, no portal through which the autumn light could come to him. He had missed autumn, he realised now – it had passed already, evaporated. The snowfall, which he witnessed out of the corners of his eyes – furious, wind-whipped flakes against the windows – struck him as infinitely beautiful.

What additional information here helps us to understand and believe in this character?

Using a novel that you know well investigate how well a particular character is drawn. Choose a character and them assemble the following evidence.

a What does the person look like?
b What are the mannerisms in speech and action?
c What does the character do that is significant?

d What are the motivations for the actions of the character? These might be kept a secret until quite late in the book.
e What do other people think and say about this character?
f What does this character think?

You might like to hot seat this character. See Chapter 7 (Studying Shakespeare) if you are not sure what this means.

4 The role of the narrator – who is telling the story and what do they think?

Think of an occasion where you have been told of an event by two different people. You may remember that the emphasis and tone may have been quite different. Perhaps even a different outcome was narrated. The stories you were listening to were told from a different point of view and this is a key factor in the novel.

All novels are obviously written by a novelist. However, the actual telling of the story of the novel is more complex than this. A story must be told by someone and this 'someone' has a 'point of view' or a particular stance from which they are telling the story. It is important to distinguish between the author and the narrator. Establishing the 'point of view' of a novel is interesting and intriguing.

Here are the main possibilities.

a The author tells the story as if he or she knows everything. This is called the omniscient narrator. It is a third person narrative in which the narrator describes the characters as 'he/she' and describes what they do. We are introduced to all the thoughts and feelings of the major characters and the narrator has all the information and chooses when to tell the reader. Sometimes suspense is created here by the reader knowing more than the characters and anticipating what will happen when the character does finally have all the information. Within this category the narrator can be:
  1 objective (telling the story from a balanced and unbiased view point)
  2 subjective (making judgements and commenting on the action)
  3 intrusive (pointing out that this is a story or hinting about what will happen next). This could also be called a self-conscious narrator. *Tom Jones* is an example of this. If the narrator has an axe to grind, the novel is 'didactic'
  4 unobtrusive. The reader is unaware of the story teller. This is the un-selfconscious narrator.

b The author narrates the story as above, but concentrates on telling the story mostly through the eyes of one of the main characters. The reader then has a restricted view of events. This would give a subjective/biased point of view. It also leads to suspense. Jane Austen's *Emma* is a good example of this.

c The story can be told by one of the characters in the novel – a '*persona*'. This means that we have all the thoughts and feelings and also the misconceptions of the character. The story is told in the first person – that is, 'I saw' and 'I went' etc. This narrator can of course be reliable or unreliable. Is the character really telling the truth to the reader/him/herself? Does the character only see what he/she wants to see or is there a misinterpretation of what happens? This leads to a great deal of interest for the reader who can agree/disagree or be misled or feel superior! The style can be fairly straightforward narrative or it can echo the confused emotions and thoughts of the narrator. This latter type of writing, where the thought processes are expressed, is called 'steam of consciousness'.

ACTIVITY 176

Tell the story of Cinderella from the point of view of one of the characters. Perhaps different members of the group could retell the story from different viewpoints. You could tell it from the point of view of an intrusive narrator passing judgement on the characters.

ACTIVITY 177

Look through the extracts from novels used in this chapter and define the point of view of each. The chart below may help. Only circle one category from each pair for each novel. You may not be able to categorise all of the options from the short extracts here.

The narrator is:

first person	third person
omniscient	limited viewpoint
reliable	unreliable
subjective	objective
a persona	the author
obtrusive	unobtrusive
didactic	entertaining
selfconscious	un-selfconscious

ACTIVITY 178

Retell the beginning of *Enduring Love* (the extract is on pages 193–194 of this chapter) from the point of view of Clarissa or one of the other men at the scene.

5 How is the story structured?

We have already mentioned that some novels may be epistolary i.e. written in the form of letters. In these we get a clear picture of the character with no interference from an external narrator and we are left to our own devices to decide whether the story is biased or not. We can make our own judgement on the actions of the *'persona'*.

Early novels were published in serial form and this has an effect on the structure.

A simple story can be made much more interesting by changing the order in which events are narrated. It may be that the reader is told everything and anticipates the revelation to the characters. It may be that secrets are kept from the reader and so suspense is created. Sometimes the narrator shifts so that we see the same incident from various viewpoints. *As I Lay Dying* by William Faulkner is an example of this. *Last Orders* by Graham Swift has the same technique on a similar topic. Other lively books with this structure are *Talking It Over* by Julian Barnes and *Paradise* by Toni Morrison. Sometimes situations of different characters in the same story are told concurrently as in *Cold Mountain*. The possibilities are many!

Perhaps one of the most complex structures is that of *Wuthering Heights* by Emily Brontë where the persona telling the story visits a lonely farm house and is told a long story by the housekeeper which explains the present situation in very vivid detail. He returns years later to hear the rest of the story and again he hears the explanation of the circumstances which he can see around him. Some readers find this intriguing – others find it tedious and unnecessarily complex.

It is fairly rare to find a novel that begins at the real beginning and tells the story chronologically. Often the novel begins well into the story with a series of flashbacks giving the explanation.

ACTIVITY 179

Examine the structure of a novel you know well and comment on it. Briefly retell the story chronologically or change the order and see what effect this has on the reader. Make a time line showing the main events in chronological order. Superimpose on this, a brief linear outline of the book's chronology. Identify what the significance is of the change in order of the revelation of events. There are some useful comments on this in the section called 'Gaps' in Chapter 5 (Methodologies).

You could do this with a retelling of a well-known fairy story to see its effect. Try Cinderella!

A brief glance at narrative theory!

Narrative theory is a particularly powerful tool for analysing novels. One branch of this theory looks at how narrative is organised according to three factors:

1 **Order**: how are the events in the story ordered compared with chronological order? What is the part played by flashbacks/flashforwards? Why is the reader given the events in this particular order?

2 **Duration**: how long does it actually take to tell parts of the story? Dialogue often takes just as long to tell as it would if it was really happening. But events can be summarised in just a few words, or a simple act can be slowed down and described in immense detail. So the important questions are: why are some events given a longer treatment than others?

3 **Frequency**: how many times is something actually narrated? Normally, if something happens once, you narrate it once: 'She woke up that morning to find ...' But it is quite possible to narrate something several times in different ways as, for example, when a story tells of events from different points of view; the same event could be narrated several times by different characters.

We will now briefly look at how the modern novel came about.

The 18th century novel – adventures (amorous and otherwise)

The early novels in English were really adventure stories. The very first novel as such was probably *The Pilgrim's Progress* which was written before the 18th century. In this work John Bunyan (1628–88) has described a literal and spiritual journey of Christian to the Celestial City. On the way he meets characters such as Faithful, Hopeful and the giant Despair and visits such places as Mount Caution and Doubting Castle. An edition published in 1928 by 'The Religious Tract Society' sings its praises:

This book, which is equally a favourite in the nursery and in the study, has received the commendation of men of the highest order of intellect. It has been translated into numerous languages, some of which were unknown to Europe in the days in which Bunyan lived. Missionaries have carried with them this book to almost every part of the earth; and now Pilgrim tells his tale to the Chinese in the East, to the Negroes in the West, to Greenlanders in the North, and islanders of the Pacific in the South. The Religious Tract Society has aided, up to the present year (1928), in printing editions of this work in one hundred and twenty languages.

There are still new paperback and hardback versions available today. The main purpose of this 'tract' was to inform and instruct. Real adventure stories which were intended to entertain were written much later.

Sailors, rogues and whores

Daniel Defoe (1660–1731) can be credited with two texts which are important to the development of the novel. He wrote *Moll Flanders* and

Robinson Crusoe. These are told in the first person. This means they are written as if the main character is talking to the reader and uses 'I' a great deal. The character is **not** the actual author but a character created by the author to narrate the story. This is called a *persona.* Men can write as women as in *Moll Flanders* or the other way round. Both books are lively accounts of the lives and adventures of the narrators. There are no chapter divisions and there is limited psychology but nevertheless they make interesting reading. *Robinson Crusoe* is a worthy predecessor of *Coral Island* and *Lord of the Flies* which also chart the life of people isolated from society. A more recent book on this subject, which is a good read, is *The Beach* by Alex Garland. *Moll Flanders* is a 'romp' worthy of a modern farce. In both books, personas are created who tell their personal stories.

Below are two extracts from these early texts at crucial moments in the story.

ACTIVITY 180

Robinson Crusoe tells of the adventures of a man shipwrecked on a deserted island – or so he thinks. One day to his horror he sees a footprint which is not his!

I happen'd one day about noon going towards my boat, I was exceedingly surpriz'd with the print of a man's naked foot on the shore, which was very plain to see in the sand. I stood like one thunderstruck, or as if I had seen an apparition; I listen'd. I look'd around me, I could hear nothing, nor see anything; I went up to a rising ground to look farther; I went up to the shore and down to the shore, but it was all one, I could see no other impression but that one. I went to it again to see if there were any more, and to observe if it might not be my fancy; but there was no room for that, for there was exactly the print of a foot, toes, heel and every part of a foot; how it came hither I knew not, nor could in the least imagine. But after innumerable fluttering thoughts, like a man perfectly confus'd and out of myself, I came home to my fortification, not feeling, as we say, the ground I went on, but terrify'd to the last degree, looking behind me at every two or three steps, mistaking every bush and tree, and fancying every stump at a distance to be a man; nor is it possible to describe how many various shapes affrighted imagination represented things to me in, how many wild ideas were found every moment in my fancy, and what strange unaccountable whimsies came into my thoughts by the way.

a Make a list of expressions which show that this is not a modern text. Suggest modern alternatives. In your study of Literature at A2 level you are required to study a text written before 1770 and you should try to develop your understanding of how language has changed since that time and also develop your close reading skills.

b In your own words explain what Crusoe's reaction is and what he does. Do you think that this is the likely reaction to the situation? Are you told how he feels as well as what he does?

ACTIVITY 181

This is an extract from *Moll Flanders*. She is a woman who has made her way in life by marrying well and often! Here she has discovered something which changes her life. She has emigrated to Virginia with her latest husband to join his mother (a transported convict who has made good). When she hears the story of her mother-in-law's past and how she had a baby in Newgate prison, Moll realises that this woman is really her mother who had to leave her behind as a baby when she was transported. Moll's husband is therefore her brother and at this time she is pregnant with her husband's child.

I was now the most unhappy of all women in the world. Oh! had the story never been told to me, all had been well; it had been no crime to have lain with my husband, if I had known nothing of it.

I had now such a load on my mind that it kept me perpetually waking; to reveal it I could not find would be to any purpose, and yet to conceal it would be next to impossible; nay, I did not doubt but that I should talk in my sleep, and tell my husband of it whether I would or no. If I discovered it, the least thing I could expect would be to lose my husband, for he was too nice and too honest a man to have continued my husband after he had known I had been his sister; so that I was perplexed to the last degree.

I leave it to any man to judge what difficulties presented to my view. I was away from my native country, at a distance prodigious, and the return to me impossible. I lived very well, but in a circumstance unsufferable in itself. If I had discovered my self to my mother, it might be difficult to convince her of the particulars, and I had no way to prove them. On the other hand, if she had questioned or doubted me, I had been undone, for the bare suggestion would have immediately separated me from my husband, without gaining my mother or him; so that between the surprise on one hand, and the uncertainty on the other, I had been sure to be undone.

a Pick out words or phrases which identify this as an 'old text'.

b Outline in note form Moll's main thoughts.

Do you think that her thoughts are believable and natural?

COMMENTARY

You should have found these extracts easy to understand even if you found quite a few words which are not used today.

In the extract from *Robinson Crusoe* you may have picked out:

- 'fancy' meaning 'imagination'
- 'It was all one' meaning 'it was what I thought 'or 'it was still the same'
- 'Hither' meaning 'there'
- 'Affrighted imagination' would be 'scary thoughts'.

From *Moll Flanders* you may have chosen to include:

- 'waking' meaning 'awake'
- 'to any purpose' meaning 'be of any use'
- 'discovered it' meaning 'told anyone about it'
- 'at a distance prodigious' meaning 'a very long way'
- 'I had been undone' meaning 'I was in a mess' or 'I would be found out'

Although these early novels are considered to be entertaining adventures with little realism, you will probably agree that the thoughts and feelings portrayed here are believable and 'human' even if they seem more controlled than a modern version might be. Robinson Crusoe shows quite understandable fear when his illusion of isolation is shattered. He thinks he might have imagined the footprint and returns to check it. He is naturally terrified and fears the worst. He begins to imagine that he is being watched. His actions of looking constantly behind him and not really remembering how he got to a place of relative safety ring true. He lets his imagination run riot!

Moll's reactions are similarly real and engaging. She wishes she did not know the truth and then everything would remain as it was. She cannot, however, remain as she is, now that she knows the truth. She looks at the possibilities of telling her husband or not. She realises she is a great distance from 'home'. She fears she may not be believed. Even if her mother does not believe her, she would cause doubts in her husband's mind and lose him any way! She feels like she is in a 'no win' situation.

Sordid and comic stories

Early forerunners of Alice Walker's *The Color Purple* were written at this time. *Pamela* and *Clarissa* are novels written in the form of letters (epistolary novels) by Samuel Richardson (1689–1761). Margaret Doody in her introduction to the Penguin Classic edition (1980) writes:

When *Pamela* appeared in two volumes in November 1740 it was soon what we should call a 'best seller', the first example of that phenomenon in the history of English fiction. Everybody read it; there was 'Pamela' rage, and Pamela motifs appeared on teacups and fans. Many praised the novel enthusiastically both for its liveliness and its morality, but some condemned the work as undignified and low, seeing in the servant girl's story a pernicious levelling tendency. *Pamela* has never ceased being a controversial work. It is certainly a revolutionary book. It changed the life of the novel as a literary genre, pointing out new directions in subject style and form.

Can you suggest any recent books, plays or films that have received this type of 'hype'? Are they really ground-breaking or simply creations that are given high coverage for commercial gain?

Pamela tells the story of a servant who resists the advances of the son of her dead mistress – yet another exploration of the sex and power theme. Events are retold in detail and the emotions aroused are realistically portrayed. The exchange of letters is intriguing and again there is evidence of psychological understanding. Many of the letters are a cry from the heart:

I can write no more. My heart is almost broken! Indeed it is! O when shall I get away? Send me, good God, in safety once more to my father's peaceful cot – and there the worst that can happen will be joy in perfection to what is now borne by Your distressed daughter.

This would pull at the heart strings of any parent!

Another 'epistolary novel' is *The Expedition of Humphry Clinker* by Tobias Smollett (1721–1771).

ACTIVITY 182

What are the advantages and disadvantages of telling a story in the form of letters?

Choose a novel you know well. Reduce the story to a few sentences. Choose one of the characters and plan a series of letters which would in effect tell the story from the point of view of that character. Write one of the letters. List the effects on the knowledge of the reader of telling the story in this way. How does this make the story more interesting?

Key skills: Communication – writing

Tom Jones by Henry Fielding (1707–1754) tells of the adventures of an abandoned child who is eventually restored to his rightful inheritance, but not before a large number of sexual escapades. Through his adventures we can get a glimpse of English society in the mid-18th century. Like many 18th and 19th century novels there seems to be a conspiracy between the narrator/writer and the reader when the narrator/writer comments on the action being unfolded. Fielding interprets the action for the reader, explaining and moralising on the situation.

Below is what the narrator says at the beginning of Chapter Six of Book Four:

There are two sorts of people who, I am afraid, have already conceived some contempt for my hero on account of his behaviour to Sophia. The former of these will blame his prudence in neglecting an opportunity to possess himself of Mr. Western's fortune; and the latter will no less despise him for his backwardness to so fine a girl, who seemed ready to fly into his arms if he would open them to receive her.

Also at the end of Chapter Three of Book Seven:

... poor Sophia was all simplicity. By which word we do not intend to insinuate to the reader that she was silly which is generally understood as a synonymous term with simple. For she was indeed a most sensible girl, and her understanding was of the first rate, but she wanted all that useful art which females convert to so many good purposes in life and which, as it arises from the heart than from the head, is often the property of the silliest of women.

The Victorians found this novel too vulgar but it did resurface in the 1880s and was a popular feature film and television production in the 20th century. Its comedy and light-hearted vulgarity were appreciated at last!

The most innovative writer at this time was Lawrence Sterne (1713–1768). His highly original, bawdy and challenging novel *The Life and Opinions of Tristram Shandy* is an interesting read. It is intriguing and challenging. The hero, the narrator, is not born until half way through the book and there are constant reminders of the relationship between the reader and the writer. Blank pages and sections in French inserted in the text add to the challenge! Reminders to the reader about the nature of a novel abound. James Joyce (1842–1941) an Irish novelist, short story writer and poet was the next writer to employ such innovative techniques. His most famous works would be interesting for you to read. These are *Portrait of the Artist as a Young Man* and *Ulysses*.

The English novel really came into its own in the 19th century.

The 19th century novel

Find out what was happening in Britain and Europe between 1770 and 1850. Look at political and social events here and on the continent. The most important events would be the Industrial Revolution, the French Revolution and the Napoleonic Wars.

Look also at the writers of literature other than novelists at this time and find out their main interest and concerns. Chapter 8 will give you a starting point.

Key skills: Communication – reading

Female writers

Women novelists (Jane Austen, the Brontë sisters and George Eliot) dominated the early part of the 19th century. Up to this time very little writing by women had been published. Can you suggest why women might be successful novelists?

Jane Austen (1775–1817) 'A highly cultivated garden'

The most enduring novels of the 19th century were those which can be considered to be commentaries on and criticisms of the society of that time. Jane Austen's novels are wonderfully comic accounts which mostly centre around the trials and tribulations of gaining both self-knowledge and a husband – usually concurrently. Jane Austen's work has always been popular and is now frequently adapted for television and film. This has also helped to revive interest in it as literature.

Her novels, although written in the third person, are seen through the eyes of the heroine. Readers share her mistakes and ignorance. We feel her confusion as the truth is revealed. There are few more delightful moments in literature than the moment in *Pride and Prejudice* when Mr Darcy reveals his love for Elizabeth Bennet (Chapter 11 of Volume Two if you want to look it up!).

There are recurrent themes of misunderstanding and misinterpretation – the hero who appears a villain and vice-versa. The tales are of fortune hunting and scandal – lost and regained love. Jane Austen is most noted for her irony and wit, her criticism of the morality and beliefs of her age. Her thumbnail sketches of her characters contain some gems! Mrs Bennet is described early in *Pride and Prejudice* as:

a woman of mean understanding, little information, and uncertain temper. When she was discontented she fancied herself nervous. The business of her life was to get her daughters married; its solace was visiting and news.

And that's her cut down to size! Irony is Jane Austen's chief weapon. When describing the spoilt sisters of the rich and handsome Bingley she writes:

Their powers of conversation were considerable. They could describe an entertainment with accuracy, relate an anecdote with humour, and laugh at their acquaintance with spirit.

There are few more amusing proposals of marriage than that of Mr Collins to Elizabeth in Chapter 19 of *Pride and Prejudice*.

ACTIVITY 184

Try to watch a video of one of Jane Austen's stories and see what character types are still alive and well in society today.

If you know one of her novels in detail, see if you can identify any changes or additions that have been made in a film version and suggest why.

What would feminists make of Jane Austen? Certainly her heroines develop into strong autonomous women on the whole and they usually get what they want! (Information about feminism can be found in Chapter 5 on page 85).

Key skills: Communication – discussion

Reaction in her time and since

When it was published, Jane Austen's work was received very positively. A brief account of contemporary response is given in the *Macmillan Masterguide to Pride and Prejudice* by Raymond Wilson. *Pride and Prejudice* was seen as a demonstration of what can happen if parents do not keep proper restraint on young girls (a reference to the elopement of one of the Bennet sisters with a good-for-nothing handsome suitor!) and as such was considered worthy of reading and digesting. Annabelle Milbanke, who later married Lord Byron, comments in a private letter in 1813 that it is:

'a superior work. It depends not on any of the common resources of novel writers, no drownings, no conflagrations, nor runaway horses, nor lap dogs and parrots, no chambermaids and milliners, nor rencontres and disguises. I really think it is one of the most probable I have read.'

The admiration of Sir Walter Scott and Jane Austen was mutual. In 1826 Scott compared his 'big bow-wow strain' of writing to the 'exquisite touch' of Jane Austen. 20th century criticism of Jane Austen has been complimentary, seeing the work as of value both as a social document of its time and as a triumph of the art of the novel.

However, Charlotte Brontë, one of the famous Brontë sisters who were also novelists at this time, wrote a scathing comment on *Pride and Prejudice* in a letter in 1848.

I got the book. And what did I find . . . a carefully fenced, highly cultivated garden, with neat borders and delicate flowers; but no glance of a bright, vivid physiognomy, no open country, no fresh air, no blue hill, no bonny beck. I should hardly like to live with her ladies and gentlemen, in their elegant but confined houses.

The Brontë sisters: 'a bleak and rocky landscape'

If Jane Austen writes like 'a highly cultivated garden' then Charlotte's sister, Emily, writes like a 'bleak, rocky landscape'!

Anne (1820–1849), Emily (1818–1848), and Charlotte Brontë (1816–1855), clergyman's daughters, were making their names as novelists at this time. They were to some extent self-educated and lived fairly isolated lives. Their books are about women who live in difficult situations where they gain independence and self-knowledge. They had great difficulty in getting their work published even though they wrote under male pseudonyms. Charlotte's *Jane Eyre* and Emily's *Wuthering Heights* remain classics today.

Jane Eyre is the story of an orphan child who makes her own way in the world and finally marries when her would-be husband has shown himself worthy of her. She marries when she has gained her independence and the love of her life will, for the most part, be dependent on her. Feminists appreciate this tale. See Chapter 11 (Studying Plays) and Chapters 3 and 4 (Contexts).

Wuthering Heights is read today by students of literature at all levels. It is a love story with a complicated time scale and two narrators. It begins in the middle of the tale. For some students there are too many Cathys, Earnshaws, Heathcliffs and Lyntons! However, it remains one of the triumphs of its genre.

Reactions to the Brontës

A good resumé of contemporary reaction to the novels of these sisters is given in *Charlotte and Emily. Literary Lives* by Tom Winnifrith and Edward Chitham (Macmillan *Literary Lives*):

Reading contemporary reviews of the Brontë novels is a depressing business. The English critical factories did not exist and reviewers were amateurs who tended to concentrate on content rather than style, quoting in addition large sections of the novels in order to give their readers a flavour of what they might expect.... Both contemporary praise and contemporary blame should not be taken too seriously when considering the real merits of *Wuthering Heights* and *Jane Eyre*. It is a useful reminder of the vanity of contemporary judgements to read in the same journals that damned the Brontës, either with faint praise or with loud condemnations, reviews of totally forgotten novels that are full of eulogies about high moral and artistic standards. The failure of the Brontës to live up to these standards can be explained by their isolation which had forced them into reading books of a previous generation or from a foreign culture. The fact that *Jane Eyre* and to some extent *Wuthering Heights* definitely have remained popular with all cultures and generations is a tribute to that universal appeal which is the hall mark of great art.

ACTIVITY 185

What factors do you think a critic takes into account when he/she reviews a book? Examine some contemporary reviews of a book you know well (perhaps in newspapers or on the Internet). What different factors should a reviewer consider when writing a review of a new edition of an old text? Look at the covers of new editions of old texts as these give a clue to their relevance today. *Jane Eyre* and *Wuthering Heights* would be good texts to look for.

Key skills: Information Technology – different sources/Communication – reading

If you know an 18th or 19th century book well, write a review of it for a magazine aimed at A level students that will show its appeal to a modern audience. Cover such things as its style, method of narration, content, themes and issues that were relevant in its time and how these themes and issues are interpreted today. See the earlier sections of this chapter and other sections in this book for help with this.

Key skills: Communication – writing

Find out more details about the lives of the Brontës and how their books reflect their experiences – if they do! Juliet Barker has written two useful books – *The Brontës: A Life in Letters* and *The Brontës*.

Key skills: Information Technology – different sources

Yet another woman novelist – George Eliot

George Eliot (1819–1880) is the pseudonym of Mary Anne Evans and unlike the Brontës her pseudonym stayed with her. She was not the daughter of a clergyman (as the Brontës and Jane Austen were). Her upbringing was very serious and academic and she was also quite a freethinker. She travelled abroad with a married man and returned to England to live as his wife. They could not marry because he was unable to divorce his real wife – rather an outrageous thing to do in the middle of the 19th century. She made a great deal of money from her writing which again distinguishes her from many of her contemporaries. She was highly respected in her lifetime.

Her novels show a respect and love for ordinary people. Her criticisms are genial and she, as a narrator, excuses her characters when they behave badly. She delves into the motivations of her characters and explains and understands their actions. She fell out of favour after her death as she was seen to be too locked into Victorian values. However, a renewed interest in her work was generated by Virginia Woolf, a famous 20th century novelist who called Eliot's *Middlemarch* a 'magnificent book which for all its imperfections is one of the few novels for grown-up people'.

The genius of Charles Dickens

So much has been written about Charles Dickens (1812–1870) that there is little point in trying to cover this prolific writer in an introductory book such as this. A biography of him by Peter Ackroyd begins with a stirring picture of his death:

Charles Dickens was dead. He lay on a narrow green sofa – but there was room enough for him, so spare had he become – in the dining room of Gad's Hill Place. He had died in the house which he had first seen as a small boy and which his father had pointed out to him as a suitable object of his ambitions; so great was his father's hold upon his life that, forty years later he had bought it. Now he had gone. It was customary to close the blinds and curtains, thus enshrouding the corpse in darkness before its last journey to the tomb; but in the dining room of Gad's Hill the curtains were pulled apart and on this June day the bright sunshine streamed in, glittering on the large mirrors around the room. The family beside him knew how he enjoyed the light; they understood too that none of the conventional sombreness of the late Victorian period – the year was 1870 – had ever touched him.

Dickens was full of fun. Although he was very interested in social issues and was a social reformist, pointing out the social evils of his time, he has created some of the most enduring and comic characters in literature.

ACTIVITY 188

Find out which novels these famous characters appear in (the answers are at the end of the chapter).

a Fagin
b Mr Micawber
c Miss Havisham
d Scrooge
e Sydney Carton
f Little Nell
g Jaggers
h Uriah Heep
i Lady Dedlock
j Gradgrind

Much of Dickens' work is autobiographical, at least it contains places and situations with which he was familiar. His work gives a detailed picture of the life of his times in all social classes. There are frequent situations involving education, the law, employment, criminals, prison and so on.

ACTIVITY 189

Research the life of Dickens and find out which of his books are autobiographical. Find specific examples of incidents about education, the law, criminals and prison. You do not need to read the books in the original to do this. Find some synopses or look them up on the Internet.

Present the information in the form of a literary encyclopaedia entry.

Key skills: Information Technology – different sources

ACTIVITY 190

Many novels at this time were published in three volumes and then later they were serialised in magazines.

Many of Dickens' books were published in weekly or monthly parts. Readers thought his characters were real and the death of Little Nell in *The Old Curiosity Shop* and Paul Dombey in *Dombey and Son* sent the nation into mourning. Make a list of the effects of publishing novels in weekly or monthly parts. You should consider

the following: the effect on character and plot, financial considerations, the effect on the reader, the advantages and disadvantages of publishing a novel in this way.

Think about soap operas today and how they are structured. Share your ideas. See Chapter 3 (Contexts for Writing) for more about this.

Key skills: Communication – discussion

Dickens' novels today are analysed by academics for their plot, characters, comedy, theme, style and structure. He is considered to be a brilliant caricaturist. He has none of the delicacy of Jane Austen, of whom he did not approve, and none of the passion of the Brontës. He is much less serious than George Eliot. Perhaps one criticism of him today would be his inability to portray woman as anything other than angels or monsters!

Thomas Hardy: his body's in Westminster Abbey but his heart's in Dorset!

Thomas Hardy (1840–1928) is as popular a writer today as he was during his life. Like Dickens, much of his work was serialised but unlike Dickens there is a sadness and feeling of inevitability of human suffering about his work. He was criticised in his life-time by prudish readers for the passionate sexual relationships he describes. He even had to change a small incident in his most famous novel *Tess of the d'Urbervilles* to make it more acceptable and less suggestive. In present editions, the supposed 'hero' of the novel, Angel Clare carries milkmaids over a flooded path in his arms. However, in the earliest editions Angel had to enlist the help of a wheelbarrow for this purpose to avoid touching the female bodies! Such sensitivity would not be an issue today.

Hardy's work is characterised by:

■ the creation of a place called Wessex with fictitious place names mingled with real ones. Wessex is the Dorset Hardy loved
■ the representation of the inevitability of fate
■ the futile struggle of mankind against this fate
■ the use of surroundings and weather as integral 'characters' in the story
■ the portrayal of clear characters and setting

Anyone interested can visit Dorchester in Dorset and follow walking tours of the places mentioned in Hardy's novels and imagine the characters as they may have lived there. Hardy's body is buried next to Dickens in 'Poet's Corner' in Westminster Abbey but his heart is buried in Stinsford Church in Dorset where he would have wished to remain.

ACTIVITY 191

Search the Internet for synopses of *Tess of the d'Urbervilles, Jude the Obscure, Far from the Madding Crowd, The Mayor of Casterbridge* and *Return of the Native*. Note the similarities in the stories and identify the main preoccupations of Hardy the novelist. You might like to read some of his poetry too. There is more on *The Mayor of Casterbridge* in Chapter 5.

Using this information and anything else you can find out, write an article for a guidebook to Stinsford Church which will give a visitor some insight into Hardy the novelist.

Key skills: Information Technology – present information

Below is a description of the murder of Alec by Tess in *Tess of the D'Urbervilles*. Read it and then answer the questions which follow. Tess had been persuaded and betrayed by Alec into believing that the real love of her life, Angel, her husband, was lost to her forever. However, she had just met Angel again and realised how she had been betrayed by Alec. You may need to refer back to earlier sections of this chapter.

Mrs. Brooks, the lady who was the householder at The Herons, and owner of all the handsome furniture, was not a person of an unusually curious turn of mind. She was too deeply materialized, poor woman, by her long and enforced bondage to that arithmetical demon Profit and Loss, to retain much curiosity for its own sake, and apart from possible lodgers' pockets. Nevertheless, the visit of Angel Clare to her well-paying tenants, Mr and Mrs d'Urberville, as she deemed them, was sufficiently exceptional in point of time and manner to reinvigorate the feminine proclivity which had been stifled down as useless save in its bearings on the letting trade.

Tess had spoken to her husband from the doorway, without entering the dining-room, and Mrs Brooks, who stood within the partly-closed door of her own sitting-room at the back of the passage, could hear fragments of the conversation – if conversation it could be called – between those two wretched souls. She heard Tess re-ascend the stairs to the first floor, and the departure of Clare, and the closing of the front door behind him. Then the door of the room above was shut, and Mrs Brooks knew that Tess had re-entered her apartment. As the young lady was not fully dressed Mrs Brooks knew that she would not emerge again for some time.

She accordingly ascended the stairs softly, and stood at the door of the front room – a drawing-room, connected with the room immediately behind it (which was a bedroom) by folding-doors in the common manner. This first floor, containing Mrs Brooks's best apartments, had been taken by the week by the d'Urbervilles. The back room was now in silence; but from the drawing-room there came sounds.

All that she could at first distinguish of them was one syllable, continually repeated in a low note of moaning, as if it came from a soul bound to some Ixionian wheel 0 – 0 – 0!

Then a silence, then a heavy sigh, and again – 0 – 0 – 0!'

The landlady looked through the keyhole. Only a small space of the room inside was visible, but within that space came a corner of the breakfast table, which was already spread for the meal, and also a chair beside. Over the seat of the chair Tess's face was bowed, her posture being a kneeling one in front of it; her hands were clasped over her head, the skirts of her dressing-gown and the embroidery of her night-gown flowed upon the floor behind her, and her stockingless feet, from which the slippers had fallen, protruded upon the carpet. It was from her lips that came the murmur of unspeakable despair.

Then a man's voice from the adjoining bedroom –

'What's the matter?'

She did not answer, but went on, in a tone which was a soliloquy rather than an exclamation, and a dirge rather than a soliloquy. Mrs Brooks could only catch a portion:

'And then my dear, dear husband came home to me ... and I did not know it! ... And you had used your cruel persuasion upon me ... you did not stop using it – no – you did not stop! My little sisters and brothers and my mother's needs – they were the things you moved me by ... and you said my husband would never come back –

never; and you taunted me, and said what a simpleton I was to expect him! . . . And at last I believed you and gave way! . . . And then he came back! Now he is gone. Gone a second time, and I have lost him now for ever . . . and he will not love me the littlest bit ever any more – only hate me! . . . O yes, I have lost him now – again because of – you!' In writhing, with her head on the chair, she turned her face towards the door, and Mrs Brooks could see the pain upon it; and that her lips were bleeding from the clench of her teeth upon them, and that the long lashes of her closed eyes stuck in wet tags to her cheeks. She continued: 'And he is dying – he looks as if he is dying! . . . And my sin will kill him and not kill me! . . . O, you have torn my life all to pieces . . . made me be what I prayed you in pity not to make me be again! My own true husband will never, never – O God – I can't bear this! – I cannot'.

There were more and sharper words from the man: then a sudden rustle; she had sprung to her feet. Mrs Brooks, thinking that the speaker was coming to rush out of the door, hastily retreated down the stairs.

She need not have done so, however, for the door of the sitting-room was not opened. But Mrs Brooks felt it unsafe to watch on the landing again, and entered her own parlour below.

She could hear nothing through the floor, although she listened intently, and thereupon went to the kitchen to finish her interrupted breakfast. Coming up presently to the front room on the ground floor she took up some sewing, waiting for her lodgers to ring that she might take away the breakfast, which she meant to do herself, to discover what was the matter if possible. Overhead, as she sat, she could now hear the floorboards slightly creak, as if some one were walking about, and presently the movement was explained by the rustle of garments against the banisters, the opening and the closing of the front door, and the form of Tess passing to the gate on her way into the street. She was fully dressed now in the walking costume of a well-to-do young lady in which she had arrived, with the sole addition that over her hat and black feathers a veil was drawn.

Mrs Brooks had not been able to catch any word of farewell, temporary or otherwise, between her tenants at the door above. They might have quarrelled, or Mr d'Urberville might still be asleep, for he was not an early riser.

She went into the back room which was more especially her own apartment, and continued her sewing there. The lady lodger did not return, nor did the gentleman ring his bell. Mrs Brooks pondered on the delay, and on what probable relation the visitor who had called so early bore to the couple upstairs. In reflecting she leant back in her chair.

As she did so her eyes glanced casually over the ceiling till they were arrested by a spot in the middle of its white surface which she had never noticed there before. It was about the size of a wafer when she first observed it, but it speedily grew as large as the palm of her hand, and then she could perceive that it was red. The oblong white ceiling, with this scarlet blot in the midst, had the appearance of a gigantic ace of hearts.

Mrs Brooks had strange qualms of misgiving. She got upon the table, and touched the spot in the ceiling with her fingers. It was damp, and she fancied that it was a blood stain. Descending from the table, she left the parlour and went upstairs, intending to enter the room overhead, which was the bedchamber at the back of the drawing-room. But, nerveless woman as she had now become, she could not bring herself to attempt the handle. She listened. The dead silence within was broken only by a regular beat.

Drip, drip, drip.

a Through whose eyes is this seen? Give evidence for your view. What effect does this have on the way it is told. (Look at the information about 'point of view' earlier in the chapter to help with this.)

b What do you learn about Mrs. Brooks, Tess and Mr. d'Urberville in this extract?

c How does Hardy create suspense in this section?

d Look at the dialogue here. What are its characteristics and what is its effect? Does it have the qualities of real speech (incoherence, repetition, pauses . . .)?

After this incident Tess flees from the scene of the crime with her true love Angel Clare but is eventually surrounded by the police at Stonehenge on Salisbury Plain and arrested. She is hanged for murder at Wintonchester Prison (Winchester) at the end of the book.

ACTIVITY 193

Find the description of the murder of Nancy by Bill Sykes in *Oliver Twist* by Charles Dickens (Chapter XLVII and the beginning of the following chapter) and answer the same questions substituting different names. Compare the two descriptions.

What sort of novel do you enjoy?

ACTIVITY 194

As a group list as many modern novels as you can and try to fit them into categories. Create some sensible sub genres.
In *The English Novel*, (Longman) Ian Milligan has classified novels thematically as follows:

1 the hero in the making
2 the young woman facing her destiny
3 love and marriage
4 the family
5 society
6 politics
7 utopias (and distopias)
8 inner worlds
9 adventures

Do the novels you have chosen for the previous exercise fit into these categories?

You might also like to consider novels from the viewpoint of 'realism', 'naturalism' 'expressionism' and 'feminism'.

Check Chapter 5 and Chapter 11 for more information about this.

Key skills: Communication – discussion

ACTIVITY 195

Take a novel you have read recently, preferably one you read for pleasure and enjoyed. Write a critical commentary or review. Bring out the significance of its opening and ending and note any good descriptions of place and character. Examine the point of view, structure, its genre and language features etc.

If you are studying the same novel as a group, divide into small groups and each take an aspect of the novel. Assemble the information and ideas and present them to the whole group.

Answers to the quiz – Activity 188

a *Oliver Twist*
b *David Copperfield*
c *Great Expectations*
d *A Christmas Carol*
e *A Tale of Two Cities*
f *The Old Curiosity Shop*
g *Great Expectations*
h *David Copperfield*
i *Bleak House*
j *Hard Times*

Further reading

York Handbook. *The English Novel* by Ian Milligan (1984) Longman.

The Art of Fiction by David Lodge (1992) Penguin.

11 Studying Plays

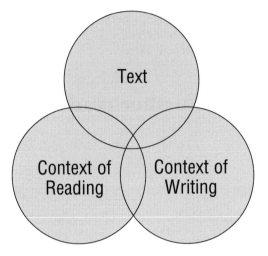

Text

Context of Reading

Context of Writing

Where does this fit in?

All Assessment Objectives are covered in this section but in particular 2(i), 4, 5(i) and (ii). You will study a play of some kind no matter which specification you follow. It is likely that you will study at least one play written before 1900.

In this chapter we shall be looking at the following aspects of drama:

1 the broad categories of tragedy and comedy
2 some broad 'movements' e.g. realism, expressionism
3 the creation of character
4 the stage set – creation of place
5 the 'stage manager'

Health Warning!

Plays are written to be performed and not simply studied as literature. Beware when you go to see a play you know well. It may have been subjected to quite a radical interpretation. You may also find you need to use your imagination more in studying plays than you do when studying other texts!

The play's the thing

Plays have always been important to society. They have often been seen as subversive or threatening to the established order. *An Inspector Calls* written by J.B. Priestly in 1945 was first performed in Moscow in 1946. There was an acclaimed production in the 1990s by Stephen Daldry. Priestley was an experimental dramatist and, although his play was set in 1912, he was consciously trying to promote a Labour victory in the election after the Second World War in 1945. The 1912 setting of the play was transferred in the 1990s production to a World War Two bomb site, thus showing its relevance to the time it was written. Priestley had strong social and political interests. The message of the play, the disintegration of society and the need for social reform, is seen clearly in the disintegration of the actual set.

Another example of the social importance of plays is Arthur Miller's *The Crucible*, written in 1953. On the surface this play is about witch hunts in Salem, Massachusetts in the 17th century but its alternative message was a commentary on the hysteria and betrayal of Senator Joseph McCarthy's anticommunist investigations in the early 1950s in the United States.

Remember also that plays had been banned in England from 1642 to 1660 because they were considered too dangerous. Plays were censored in England until 1968 when censorship in general was abolished and private prosecutions were left to do this job.

All the world's a stage

In this chapter you will be thinking about the staging of plays. You need to be aware of the different ways in which plays can be staged. New theatres can usually be adapted for particular performances and have flexible acting areas.

1 **Proscenium Arch Stage**. This is where there is a wall separating the audience and the actors and there is a hole in the wall so the audience can see! This is usually covered by a curtain between acts and at the beginning and end of the performance. In this type of staging, scene changes and some entrances and exits can be hidden from the audience. It is one of the most impersonal types of staging. It is also called a picture frame stage and there is the idea that the audience is the fourth wall of the room or whatever is depicted on stage.

2 **Thrust or Apron stage**. This is where some of the stage is in the auditorium (where the audience sits) so that the actors are surrounded on three sides by the audience. This is obviously more intimate. The stage does tend to be more bare with the scenery being restricted to the back of the stage.

3 **Theatre in the round** or **Arena Stage** This is exactly what it says with the actors surrounded on all sides by the audience. This leads to more involvement still by the audience and needs careful staging as props and scenery can hide the view of some of the audience. Any change of scene or entrances and exits are completely visible by the audience.

The diagram below shows these possibilities and others more clearly.

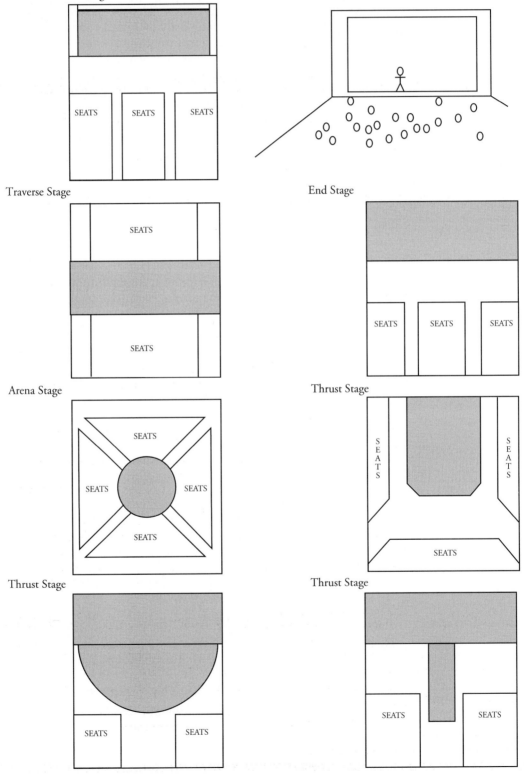

Proscenium Arch Stage

Traverse Stage

End Stage

Arena Stage

Thrust Stage

Thrust Stage

Thrust Stage

Revolving stages, trap doors and many different exits and entrances can also be incorporated into the set. Many West End musicals are well known for their elaborate sets. In the musical *Starlight Express* the actors race through the auditorium on roller skates on specially constructed paths and in *Cats* some of the audience revolves on the revolving stage. It is fairly common for actors to appear from the auditorium at some point.

ACTIVITY 196

Discuss any plays in which you have taken part – even plays in first school – and decide what you or the audience gained from them. What did you learn about yourself and other people by working with them on a play? Do you think your experience of acting changed you or your relationships in any way? Are there any plays you have seen that have influenced your life or made you more aware of an issue?

Key skills: Communication – discussion

COMMENTARY

Perhaps Ben Elton's play *Popcorn* (1996) might make you more aware of the role of the media. Perhaps Shakespeare's *King Lear* might make you consider parent/child relationships in a different light. Willy Russell's *Educating Rita* (1980) might make you consider the purpose and value of education.

Do you think there should be more censorship of plays which are politically sensitive or vulgar in someway? For example O'Casey's play *Juno and the Paycock* (1924) is about the 'troubles' in Ireland. *The Resistible Rise of Arturi Ui* by Bertold Brecht (1958) parodies the rise of Hitler. Brian Friel's *Making History* (1988) shows how there can be more than one 'truth' in History. Ibsen's *A Doll's House* (1879) looks feminist in approach. In 1965 Edward Bond's play *Saved* was refused a licence for public performance because of a scene which showed a baby being stoned in its pram.

You may have started to think of the various different ways in which plays may be introduced to you. For example you may read it as a text or you may see the play as it was intended or a modernised production on stage. You may have seen a production made for television or a film version of a play. Plays were written to be performed on stage, not to be read in a comfortable chair or in a classroom. The way you visualise it at home may be very different to what you would experience in a live production.

ACTIVITY 197

Make a list of the different factors which are involved in producing a play for the stage and on film. Think about the restrictions of performing on a stage and the freedom of recording 'on location'. Think about storm scenes or crowd scenes. What sort of changes or innovations can be made by film? What restrictions does a playwright face when writing for the stage? Do the same restrictions apply to a radio play? You may have seen a video or stage production of a play you know well. This will help you to see specific differences.

Key skills: Communication – discussion/presentation

Having said all this, remember that it is the play as literature that is the main focus of study for this course. Productions and innovations should be seen in the light of how they help us to understand the play itself and its writer.

Quotable quote!

A novelist selects words so far as possible to create a precise image in the mind of the reader. A dramatist writes blank cheques for the collaboration of others.

Thornton Wilder

It is true that dramatists have less control over how their work is produced than novelists and that there is more scope for change and innovation in plays than there is in novels. However, there are still theatrical movements and theatrical conventions which are worthy of study.

This chapter will highlight some theatrical movements and theories and look also at creation of character, structure and atmosphere.

1 Tragedy and comedy

The first broad distinction to draw is between the two poles – tragedy and comedy.

Look at this extract from *Educating Rita* by Willy Russell (1980). The play is about a hairdresser who, through the Open University, is trying to find an understanding of life through literature and hopefully enjoy herself at the same time. Her tutor is a cynical alcoholic academic called Frank. The extract is from Act One Scene Six. Rita has just discovered *Macbeth* when she went for the first time to the theatre.

RITA   Look, I went out an' bought the book. Isn't it great? What I couldn't get over is how excitin' it was.
FRANK   *puts his feet up on the desk*
RITA   Wasn't his wife a cow, eh? An' that fantastic bit where he meets Macduff an' he thinks he's all invincible, I was on the edge of me seat at that bit. I wanted to shout out an' tell Macbeth, warn him.
FRANK   You didn't, did you?
RITA   Nah, Y' can't do that in a theatre, can y'? It was dead good. It was like a thriller.
FRANK   Yes, you'll have to go and see more.
RITA   I'm going to. Macbeth's a tragedy, isn't it?
FRANK   *nods*
RITA   Right.
RITA   *smiles at* FRANK *and he smiles back at her*
         Well I just—I just had to tell someone who'd understand.
FRANK   I'm honoured that you chose me.
RITA   (*moving towards the door*) Well, I better get back. I've left a customer with a perm lotion. If I don't get a move on there'll be another tragedy.
FRANK   No. There won't be a tragedy.

RITA   There will, y' know. I know this woman; she's dead fussy. If her perm doesn't come out right there'll be blood an' guts everywhere.

FRANK   Which might be quite tragic—
He throws the apple from his desk which she catches
—but it wouldn't be a tragedy.

RITA   What?

FRANK   Well—erm—look; the tragedy of the drama has nothing to do with the sort of tragic event you're talking about. Macbeth is flawed by his ambition—yes?

RITA   (*going and sitting in the chair by the desk*) Yeh. Go on. (*She starts to eat the apple*)

FRANK   Erm—it's that flaw which forces him to take the inevitable steps towards his own doom. You see?

RITA   *offers him a can of soft drink. He takes it and looks at it*

FRANK   (*putting the can down on the desk*) No thanks. Whereas, Rita, a woman's hair being reduced to an inch of stubble, or—or the sort of thing you read in the paper that's reported as being tragic, 'Man Killed By Falling Tree', is not a tragedy.

RITA   It is for the poor sod under the tree.

FRANK   Yes, it's tragic, absolutely tragic. But it's not a tragedy in the way that *Macbeth* is a tragedy. Tragedy in dramatic terms is inevitable, pre-ordained. Look, now, even without ever having heard the story of *Macbeth* you wanted to shout out, to warn him and prevent him going on, didn't you? But you wouldn't have been able to stop him would you?

RITA   No.

FRANK   Why?

RITA   They would have thrown me out of the theatre.

FRANK   But what I mean is that your warning would have been ignored. He's warned in the play. But he can't go back. He still treads the path to doom. But the poor old fellow under the tree hasn't arrived there by following any inevitable steps, has he?

RITA   No.

FRANK   There's no particular flaw in his character that has dictated his end. If he'd been warned of the consequences of standing beneath that particular tree he wouldn't have done it, would he? Understand.

RITA   So—so Macbeth brings it on himself?

FRANK   Yes. You see he goes blindly on and on and with every step he's spinning one more piece of thread that will eventually make up the network of his own tragedy. Do you see?

RITA   I think so. I'm not used to thinkin' like this.

FRANK   It's quite easy, Rita.

RITA   It is for you. I just thought it was a dead exciting story. But the way you tell it you make me see all sorts of things in it. (*After a pause*) It's fun, tragedy isn't it?

ACTIVITY 198

What features of 'tragedy' in its technical sense have you learnt along with Rita here? Take a close look at what Frank says.

Traditional tragedy

The first person to write about tragedy in this technical sense was Aristotle who wrote his *Poetics* in the fourth century BC which set down the basic ideas of 'tragedy' and which influenced the Elizabethans and many playwrights since. Aristotle's ideas are the benchmark against which tragedy is measured. Here are some features. The words in brackets are the original Greek words used by Aristotle.

1 The story is of one main character who is the protagonist.
2 The protagonist is responsible for his fate in that he has a tragic flaw (*hamartia*) which leads to his downfall.
3 The play shows reversal of fortune *(peripeteia)*.
4 There are moments of discovery *(anagnorisis)*.
5 The audience feels pity and terror – pity that the misfortune is greater than the protagonist deserves and terror that we may suffer the same fate ourselves.
6 After watching tragedy the audience feels elated rather than depressed as if the emotions have purged them *(catharsis)*.

Many of Shakespeare's tragedies fulfil all or some of these requirements. In modern tragedy the protagonist is more likely to be an ordinary person than a king! Do you think it is right that a 'protagonist' can be ordinary or do you think drama should be about people whose fate really matters?

ACTIVITY 199

Write the story outline for a tragedy yourself. Begin with a popular group of musicians who are world-famous and hugely successful. One of the group decides to 'go it alone'. What happens next and why? Write a commentary to show which conventions of tragedy you are following. Consider the same plot with the main characters just ordinary students who want to be famous. Is the play so significant?

ACTIVITY 200

Write out the outline story of a Shakespeare play or any play you know well and suggest how far it fulfils the ideas of Aristotle's definition of tragedy.

Is comedy meant to be funny?

ACTIVITY 201

In small groups think of the funniest thing that has happened to you. Then think about the funniest television show you watch. Make a list of the things that make up comedy. Some suggestions are given later in this section: see

Comedy – why do we laugh? Share your ideas with the group and look for similarities.

Key skills: Communication – discussion

Shakespearean comedy

If comedy is seen solely in its Shakespearean sense then it means simply the opposite of tragedy. There is potential for mishap but everything is all right in the end. In comedy, no-one dies. In Shakespearean tragedy it seems that everybody does! At the end of *King Lear* the king himself and his three daughters are dead, the lover of two of them and his father are dead and the king's faithful servant indicates he has not long to live himself and that's just the last scene! Marriage is the usual ending of many comedies. Look at the section about the ending of *Measure for Measure* in Chapter 7. In the Shakespearean sense, comedy has only a little to do with laughter. It has more to do with a happy ending, with much confusion and deception on the way. In modern productions much is made of stage business to promote laughter. In Shakespeare's time laughter may have been produced through the witty words and topical references understood by the audience as well as slapstick.

Here is an extract from Act One Scene Two of *Measure for Measure*. Two characters are discussing their relative wickedness.

A. Well, there went but a pair of shears between us.
B. I grant: as there may between the lists and the velvet. Thou art the list.
A. And thou the velvet. Thou art good velvet. Thou'rt a three piled piece, I warrant thee. I had as lief (*prefer*) be a list of an English kersey (*coarse woven woollen cloth*) as be piled, as thou art piled, for a French Velvet.

This probably makes little sense to a modern audience but an Elizabethan audience would recognise the play on words. The first line means the equivalent of 'we were cut from the same cloth'. 'List' refers to the selvedge on a piece of cloth: the firm edge at the sides to prevent it from fraying. It is usually hidden in a seam or cut off when a garment is made. 'Three piled' refers to the most expensive velvet but also the word 'piles' has the same meaning as it has today, that is haemorrhoids and also refers to baldness. Both of these conditions are signs of syphilis. 'French velvet' alludes to the best quality velvet and also reminds the audience of 'the French disease' (syphilis) and 'velvet women' prostitutes. In other words character A accepts the suggestion that he is the least worthy of the two but then goes on to say that character B has the signs of syphilis acquired no doubt from his relationship with prostitutes.

Much easier for a modern audience to follow is the scene later in the play (Act Two Scene One) where a minor character 'misplaces' his words and actually says the opposite of what he means. He brings 'benefactors' to court instead of 'malefactors' and 'detests' rather than 'respects'. He calls the judges 'varlets' and the wrongdoers 'honourable men'. The humour of this is immediately apparent even to a modern audience.

Modern and traditional comedy revolves around misunderstandings and deception which are resolved before any harm can be done.

ACTIVITY 202

There are also the subdivisions of 'high' and 'low' comedy. Make a list of what the features of each of these might be and then look them up in a dictionary of literary terms.

Farce is where ludicrous and highly improbable situations are shown on stage and seems to involve many doors through which characters disappear and many 'trousers down' situations.

Romantic comedies are exactly what you would expect! You can probably think of films or television programmes which have been described as 'romantic comedies'. *Four Weddings and a Funeral, Notting Hill* and *You've Got Mail* were immensely popular films which would be described like this.

Many television comedies are satirical perhaps because they need to be topical. The popular series *Absolutely Fabulous* satirises the family as does *The Royle Family*. We can all see character types we recognise in *Last of Summer Wine, Dad's Army, 'Allo 'Allo* and *The Young Ones*.

Black comedy is where the events are potentially sad or disturbing but they are treated in a comic manner. It's almost as if you feel you ought not to laugh. Joe Orton's *What the Butler Saw* (1969) is an example of this. It concerns sex in a mental institution.

ACTIVITY 203

Using the information above and any other resources you have, make a chart showing the differences between tragedy and comedy.

Key skills: Communication – reading

Tragicomedy

As the name implies this is a mixture of both forms. There may be a tragic flaw and potential for 'tragedy' but at the last moment all is resolved happily and safely. The action generally concerns people from all sections of society – low as well as high. Some examples are *The Winter's Tale* (1610) by Shakespeare. *Waiting for Godot* by Beckett (1954) and Chekhov's *The Cherry Orchard* (1904).

Comedy – why do we laugh?

When you discussed comedy you may have found it difficult to define the term. The fact that different people find different things amusing suggests that it is what you bring to comedy that makes it funny. We often laugh when we recognise the truth of a comic situation – we've 'been there, done that' etc. When something is familiar and true to life we laugh. Also in comedy there is often some sense of incongruity – something that does not quite fit, for example, a teacher or the college principal, who needs to retain their dignity, slipping on a banana skin outside your class is funnier than some one not in a position of authority. On the other hand any one slipping on a banana skin is funny – as long as it's not ourselves! Humour created by watching the discomfort of someone else is called slapstick. The cover of this book shows three comics of this type – the Marx brothers. These were 20th century comedians most famous for their film comedies in the 1930s. Language can also be funny. It can be witty, ironic or have double meanings. The humour of Julian Clary is a typical example of this, as are the classic 'Carry On' films. Much humour is created by the repetition of actions or words within the text or scene – almost as if we are amused that we can predict something or say 'typical' in an exasperated voice!

ACTIVITY 204

Look back at the extract from *Educating Rita* on pages 224–225. Write an equivalent scene for the play in which Frank explains 'comedy' to Rita. Try to visualise the play and use stage directions as well as trying to create character!

Key skills: Communication – writing

2 -ists and -isms!

In your reading about drama and theatre you may come across some ists and isms. Here is a note on some of these which may help to explain them. Any history of drama will give you more detail. You can find out more about these '-isms' by looking at *Cambridge Paperback Guide to Theatre* by Sarah Stanton and Martin Banham, C.U.P. (1996).

Realism

This term was first used in France in the 1850s to describe texts which were concerned with showing the world as it is rather than as it ought to be. The subjects for drama were the social and domestic problems of everyday life. Actors spoke and moved naturally and there was a swing against artificiality. Towards the middle of the 19th century real objects were used on a stage that resembled a room with the fourth wall removed – the so-called picture frame stage. Although the term realism is now used for plays written in the final quarter of the 19th century, the spirit of realism is the dominant style of modern drama with its realism of set, natural characters and 'ordinary' style of dialogue. The term 'kitchen sink drama' is now usually used to refer to this type of drama.

Examples are *Look Back in Anger* (1956*)* by John Osborne and *All My Sons* (1947) by Arthur Miller.

Naturalism

Although this is often assumed to be the same as realism, there is a distinction. In naturalism, human character and social interaction are seen as the result of genetic and historical factors. This suggests that individual human beings have little control over their lives and their destiny. The struggle of the individual to adapt to the environment and the Darwinian idea of the survival of the fittest become the central concerns of naturalistic fiction and drama.

Mourning Becomes Electra (1931) by Eugene O'Neill and Arnold Wesker's *Roots* (1959) are examples.

Expressionism

Originally this was a term applied to art. It is defined in the *Supplement to the Oxford English Dictionary* as 'a style of painting in which the artist seeks to express emotional experience rather than impressions of the physical world'. This is also shown in the highly visual nature of expressionism in drama. The director would choose dramatic lighting and distorted architecture (for example staircases, revolving sections, treadmills, trapdoors etc.) to extend the use of the stage. A new generation of actors rejected 'true life acting' on the one hand and 'declamation' on the other in order to express passion for its own sake; a strident voice and cadaverous face (a face like that of a corpse) became hallmarks of the expressionist actor.

Ibsen's *Peer Gynt* (1867) and Goethe's *Faust* (1832, published posthumously) are examples.

Absurdism

The theatre of the absurd as a genre was recognised in the 1950s. Literally it means 'out of harmony' and it displays the human situation as one of strangers in an inhuman universe. Journalists used the label in a misleading way to mean 'outrageously comic' and this is how it is usually used today. However, the name is now applied to some dramatic techniques where the story and the characters appear to make little sense and there are ridiculous conclusions.

Examples are *Waiting For Godot* (1952) by Samuel Beckett and Edward Albee's four one act plays beginning with *The Zoo Story* (1959).

Feminism

Feminist theatre developed in the 1970s with female companies and women writers coming to the fore. Feminist writers explored some of the main beliefs and arguments of the very varied feminist movement. Feminist playwriting explored the family, gender roles and sexuality from different political and national class and ethnic perspectives. Possibly, popular feminism is less fashionable than it was. There is more on feminism in Chapter 5.

Caryl Churchill's *Top Girls* (1982) is an example, as is *The Grace of Mary Traverse* by Timberlake Wertenbaker (1985).

ACTIVITY 205

Thinking about plays you know well, categorise them, if you can, by using these definitions. Think if any of the plays would actually be more effective if they were produced in a realistic or expressionist way.

Key skills: Communication – discussion

3 Creating character in drama

Characters in drama can be analysed in a way similar to a novel. You need to look at what a character does, says and thinks and what other people say about them. Their names are also an indication of their characters – for example Captain Brazen and Mr Worthy in *The Recruiting Officer*. What they look like also immediately indicates their character for an audience. The obvious way of establishing character is analysing what they actually say on the stage. You can also look at how they relate to others, what they say which reveals their thoughts and the way they are described by the writer in the form of stage directions.

ACTIVITY 206

Look back at the extract earlier in this chapter from *Educating Rita* and write down what you learn about Frank and Rita. Prove your points with quotations from the text. From your knowledge of Rita as a hairdresser and Frank as a cynical alcoholic academic, what would they look like? What about their clothes, their hair and their movements?

COMMENTARY

Rita is an excited, eager student who is willing to learn from Frank who, she thinks, is an intellectual with all the answers. She settles down to listen when he begins to talk specifically about *Macbeth*. She has a sense of humour and a quaint turn of phrase. In fact her language is not what you would expect to use in the study of a university lecturer or in an A level Literature group. 'Wasn't his wife a cow, eh?' she says of Lady Macbeth and the example of a headline of a man being killed by a tree is greeted with the suggestion that this **is** a tragedy for 'the poor sod under the tree'. Her Liverpool accent is suggested by the lack of a final consonant in words like 'and' and 'going' and the use of 'Nah'. She also uses colloquial expressions like 'It was dead good' and 'she's dead fussy' and 'it was dead exciting'. During the conversation we get the impression of her freshness and vitality. She feels at ease with Frank.

Frank also is at ease with Rita. He puts his feet on the desk when she is talking to him. He is generous when he gives her his apple and refuses her can of soft drink, presumably preferring something stronger. He obviously wants to teach her and is patient with her questions. His speech is quite different from Rita's. He agrees with her statements but his language is much more sophisticated. 'Macbeth is flawed by his ambition' he says and this forces Macbeth to 'take the inevitable steps towards his own doom'. Frank uses figurative language about Macbeth's fate: 'With every step he's spinning one more piece of thread which will eventually make up the network of his own tragedy'. He is not trying to confuse Rita and checks often that she has understood. The way the text is written suggests that his pronunciation is not the local Liverpool one like Rita.

ACTIVITY 207

Here is an extract from the beginning of *Making History* (1988) by Brian Friel. The play, set in Ireland, is about Hugh O'Neill who led an alliance of the Irish and Spanish in an attempt to oust the English from Ireland in 1591. In this scene he has just returned from England and his secretary, Harry Hoveden, tells him what has happened in his absence.

What do you learn about O'Neill and Harry in this extract and about their relationship? Add some adverbs (words which describe **how** something is said for example *angrily* or *impatiently*) before some of the speeches to help another reader realise what your interpretation is or to guide an actor in his interpretation of the character. You could scan the extract into a computer and work directly on the screen.

HARRY	That takes care of Friday. Saturday you're free all day – so far. Then on Sunday – that'll be the fourteenth – O'Hagan's place at Tullyhogue. A big christening party. The invitation came the day you left. I've said you'll be there, all right? (*Pause*) It's young Brian's first child – you were at his wedding last year. It'll be a good day. (*Pause*) Hugh?
O'NEILL	Yes?
HARRY	O'Hagan's – where you were fostered.
O'NEILL	Tell me the name of these again.
HARRY	Broom.
O'NEILL	Broom. That's it.
HARRY	The Latin name is genista. Virgil mentions it some where.
O'NEILL	Does he really?
HARRY	Actually that genista comes from Spain. (*O'Neill looks at the flowers in amazement*)
O'NEILL	Good Lord – does it? Spanish broom – magnificent name, isn't it?
HARRY	Give them plenty of water.
O'NEILL	Magnificent colour, isn't it?

HARRY   A letter from the Lord Deputy –

O'NEILL   They really transform the room. Splendid idea of yours, Harry. Thank you.
            (*O'Neill silently mouths the word 'genista' again and then continues distributing the flowers*)

HARRY   A letter from the lord deputy 'vigorously urging you to have your eldest son attend the newly established College of the Holy Trinity in Dublin founded by the Most Serene Queen Elizabeth'. That 'vigorously urging' sounds ominous, doesn't it?

O'NEILL   Sorry?

HARRY   Sir William Fitzwilliam wants you to send young Hugh to the new Trinity College. I'm told he's trying to get all the big Gaelic families to send their children there. He would like an early response.

O'NEILL   This jacket – what do you think Harry? It's not a bit . . . excessive, is it?

HARRY   Excessive?

O'NEILL   You know . . . a little too strident?

HARRY   Strident?

O'NEILL   All right, damn it, too bloody young?

HARRY   (looking at his papers) It's very becoming, Hugh.

O'NEILL   Do you think so? Maybe I should have got it in maroon.
            (*He goes off to get more flowers*)

HARRY   A reminder that the annual Festival of Harpers takes place next month in Roscommon. They've changed the venue to Roosky. You're Patron of the festival and they would be very honoured if you would open the event with a short – (He now sees that he is alone. He looks through his papers)

ACTIVITY 208

Add stage directions indicating where and how the actors should move so that this section becomes humorous. Indicate facial expressions and body language. In pairs you could work out the moves for this short scene and act it out. You can then analyse each pair and see how comedy has been created and how the relationship between the two people has been demonstrated differently by actions as well as words.

Key skills: Information Technology – information

Soliloquy

Sometimes a character in a play reveals his character without interruption from others. This is called a soliloquy. The character explores his or her feelings by directly addressing the audience. By this method the audience learns the motives of the character. Shakespeare's characters often explore their thoughts in the form of a soliloquy. Hamlet's soliloquy 'To be or not to be' is probably the most famous soliloquy of all time! In John Osborne's ground breaking play *Look Back in Anger* (1956), at times, Jimmy's tirades are soliloquies even though other characters are on stage too.

Another type of individual speech is the dramatic monologue. This is where a single person is speaking the whole time. The most famous dramatic monologues are those by Alan Bennet called *Talking Heads*

(1988). These are short plays in their own right. Poems like *My Last Duchess* and *Porphyria's Lover* by Robert Browning (1812–1889) are also dramatic monlogues.

ACTIVITY 209

In *Look Back in Anger* by John Osborne, written in the 1950s, Jimmy Porter is the original 'angry young man'.

A working class young man with a university education, he has married a middle class woman, Alison, whose background he cannot come to terms with. This play was directly relevant to a society where social barriers were about to dissolve. To some extent Jimmy is expressing Osborne's ideas. Jimmy is attacking all aspects of post-war England that socialism had failed to reform. Because of this the play now seems dated. This speech is early in the play and he is talking to Cliff, their well-meaning lodger, about his new relatives. What do you learn about Jimmy's personality and attitudes here?

JIMMY: Have you ever seen her brother? Brother Nigel? The straightbacked, chinless wonder from Sandhurst? I only met him once myself. He asked me to step outside when I told his mother she was evil minded.

CLIFF: And did you?

JIMMY   Certainly not. He's a big chap. Well, you've never heard so many well-bred commonplaces come from beneath a bowler hat. The Platitude from Outer Space – that's brother Nigel. He'll end up in the cabinet one day, make no mistake. But somewhere at the back of that mind is the vague knowledge that he and his pals have been plundering and fooling everybody for generations. (*Going upstage and turning*). Now Nigel is just about as vague as you can get without being actually invisible. And invisible politicians aren't much use to anyone – not even to *his* supporters! And nothing is more vague about Nigel than his knowledge. His knowledge of life and ordinary human beings is so hazy, he really deserves some sort of decoration for it – a medal inscribed 'for Vaguery in the Field.' But it wouldn't do for him to be troubled by any stabs of conscience, however vague.(*Moving down again*). Besides he's a patriot and an Englishman, and he doesn't like the idea that he may have been selling out his countrymen all these years, so what does he do? The only thing he *can* do – seek sanctuary in his own stupidity. The only way to keep things as much like they always have been as possible, is to make the alternative too much for your poor, tiny brain to grasp. It takes some doing nowadays. It really does. But they knew all about character building at Nigel's school, and he'll make it all right. Don't you worry he'll make it. And what's more, he'll do it better than anybody else!

Creating character through commentary in the text

ACTIVITY 210

Overleaf is an extract from *A Streetcar Named Desire* (1947) by Tennessee Williams. This extract is from Act One Scene Two. Stanley is married to Stella and she has married 'beneath her'. Stella's sister, Blanche, has come to stay in their flat for a while and in fact she has come on hard times and lost the family home. Stanley is not very impressed when he hears this and he resents the situation.

Scan the text into a computer. On your own add some stage directions to show how some of the words should be spoken. Also add a commentary about what the character is actually like in personality as well as words. Try to develop your commentary so that it is almost like introducing a character in a novel. Check with other people to see if you have made the same judgement of character. Obviously in a short extract like this there will be variation. If you knew the play as a whole and read the author's notes you would probably come up with the same interpretation as other students.

Key skills: Information Technology – information

STANLEY	What's all this monkey doings?
STELLA	Oh' Stan. I'm taking Blanche to Galatoires' for supper and then a show because it's your poker night.
STANLEY	How about my supper, huh? I'm not going to no Galatoires' for supper!
STELLA	I put a cold plate on ice.
STANLEY	Well, isn't that just dandy!
STELLA	I'm going to try to keep Blanche out until the party breaks up because I don't know how she would take it. So we'll go to one of those little places in the quarter afterwards and you'd better give me some money.
STANLEY	Where is she?
STELLA	She's soaking in a hot tub to quiet her nerves. She's terribly upset.
STANLEY	Over what?
STELLA	She's been through such an ordeal.
STANLEY	Yeah?
STELLA	Stan, we've lost Belle Reve.
STANLEY	The place in the country?
STELLA	Yes.
STANLEY	How?
STELLA	Oh, it had to be – sacrificed or something. When she comes in be sure to say something nice about her appearance. And, oh! Don't mention the baby. I haven't said any thing yet, I'm waiting until she gets in a quieter condition.
STANLEY	So?
STELLA	And try to understand and be nice to her, Stan.
	Blanche (singing from the bathroom)
STELLA	She wasn't expecting to see us in such a small place, You see I'd tried to gloss over things a little in my letters.
STANLEY	So?
STELLA	And admire her dress and tell her she's looking wonderful. That's important to Blanche. Her little weakness.
STANLEY	Yeah. I get the idea, Now let's skip back a little to where you said the country place was disposed of.
STELLA	Oh yes.
STANLEY	How about that? Let's have a few more details on that subject.
STELLA	It's best not to talk too much about it until she's calmed down.
STANLEY	So that's the deal, huh? Sister Blanche cannot be annoyed with business details right now!
STELLA	You saw how she was last night.
STANLEY	Uh-hum, I saw how she was. Now let's have a gander at that bill of sale.

The importance of a writer's commentary in the text

You have just been asked to add a commentary to a stage play.

Details like this are the writer's way of informing the reader or actor of his intentions with regard to the characters. In some plays these almost resemble the detail you might find in a novel when a character is first introduced. This is how Jimmy Porter is described in the stage directions before Act One of *Look Back in Anger*.

When we do eventually see them, we find that Jimmy is a tall thin young man about twenty five, wearing a very worn tweed jacket and flannels. Clouds of smoke fill the room from the pipe he is smoking. He is a disconcerting mixture of sincerity and cheerful malice, of tenderness and freebooting cruelty; restless, importunate, full of pride, a combination which alienates the sensitive and insensitive alike. Blistering honesty, or apparent honesty, like his, makes few friends. To many he may seem sensitive to the point of vulgarity. To others, he is simply a loud mouth. To be as vehement as he is is to be almost non-committal.

This section serves to show the ambiguity of his character! He is tender and cruel, sensitive yet proud and troublesome. He is honest to the point of arrogance.

ACTIVITY 211

We get the same amount of detail when Blanche is first introduced in *A Streetcar Named Desire.*

Blanche comes around the corner, carrying a valise. She looks at a slip of paper, then at the building. Her expression is one of shocked disbelief. Her appearance is incongruous to this setting. She is daintily dressed in a white suit with a fluffy bodice, necklace and earrings of pearl, white gloves and hat, looking as if she were arriving at a summer tea or cocktail party in the garden district. She is above five years older than Stella. Her delicate beauty must avoid strong light. There is something about her uncertain manner, as well as her white clothes that suggest a moth.

What qualities of Blanche are suggested by this description?

In this play Williams gradually leads the audience into the mind of Blanche until at the end of the play background music and 'cries and noises of the jungle' seem to represent Blanche's unhinged mind. A simple 'hello' 'is echoed and re-echoed by other mysterious voices behind the walls.' On the surface, this play is realistic (see the definition of realism earlier in this chapter) but the set, where both inside and outside of the house are seen at the same time, as well as the use of strange sound effects such as these, is rather surreal (strange and unfamiliar). We seem to be drawn in to the mind of Blanche at the end of the play.

ACTIVITY 212

Write a similar commentary for a short scene of
a play you know well.

4 Creating place – descriptions of the set

Frequently the playwright gives details of the set for the play. This is a
great help for the reader although a director/producer might find this
rather distracting!

ACTIVITY 213

What atmosphere do you think Tennessee
Williams is creating in the extract below from
the beginning of *A Streetcar Named Desire*?

Explain in detail how this atmosphere is created
by the language. If you can, you could draw or
design the set.

Scene One

The exterior of a two storey corner building on a street in New Orleans which is
named Elysian Fields and runs between the L and N tracks *(a railway line for the
Louisiana and Nashville Railroad)* and the river. The section is poor but, unlike
corresponding sections in other American cities, it has a rakish charm. The houses
are mostly white frame, weathered grey, with rickety outside stairs and galleries and
quaintly ornamented gables to the entrances of both. It is the first dark of an evening
early in May. The sky that shows around the dim white building is a peculiarly tender
blue, almost turquoise, which invests the scene with a lyricism and gracefully
attenuates the atmosphere of decay. You can almost feel the warm breath of the
brown river beyond the river warehouses with their faint redolences of bananas and
coffee. A corresponding air is evoked by the music of Negro entertainers at a bar-
room around the corner. In this part of New Orleans you are practically always just
around the corner, or a few doors down the street, from a tinny piano being played
with the infatuated fluency of brown fingers. This 'Blue Piano' expresses the spirit of
the life which goes on here.

Changing the scenery in a play

Often the stage set changes during a play indicating the progress of the
action and usually has some significance. In *Look Back in Anger,* Act One
and Act Three begin with the same setting only the woman character has
changed. A different woman is ironing whilst wearing an old shirt of
Jimmy's in each act. Cliff and Jimmy are reading the Sunday papers as they
were at the beginning. It seems that for all Jimmy's ranting nothing has
changed that is significant.

Change is indicated in *Making History* by a contrast in the set. At the beginning 'the room is spacious and scantily furnished; a large refectory type table; some chairs and stools; a side-board. No attempt at decoration.' The room is described as 'comfortless'.

Scene Two is introduced like this.

Almost a year has passed. The same room as in Scene One, but Mabel has added to the furnishings and the room is now more comfortable and colourful. Mabel is sitting alone doing delicate and complicated lacework. She works in silence for some time. Then there is a sudden and terrifying sound of a girl shrieking. This is followed immediately by boisterous laughter, shouting, horseplay and a rapid exchange in Irish between a young girl and a young man.

Obviously a woman's touch has changed the place. What other indications are there of what has happened or may happen? When you are reading plays it is always worth looking at the off stage noises as well as those on stage. Often they serve to punctuate or forward the action in some way. Here the noises off-stage are seen as threatening by Mabel and she is frightened. In fact, on this occasion, they are simply annoying and not really threatening. However, the atmosphere is ominous.

ACTIVITY 214

Using a play you know well, show how you would indicate the passage of time and the changes that have happened by using scenery or off stage noises at different times in the play. Share your ideas.

Key skills: Communication – discussion

ACTIVITY 215

Design a stage set for *Educating Rita* which would indicate Frank's state of mind and attitudes. Remember to look back at the section at the beginning of this chapter to help you think about different types of staging.

Key skills: Communication – presentation

5 Stage managers

Stage directions help the reader and actors to understand what a playwright is 'getting at'. Sometimes a play is giving us a slice of life. It is as if we are a fly on the wall and are watching reality. Sometimes plays are deliberately 'self-conscious'. (This idea can also be seen in novels.) Sometimes this is in the form of a chorus or a prologue which comments on the action. Sometimes a character 'takes charge' of the situation. This means that the characters are controlled although they do not realise it. The audience is well aware of the situation and the anticipation of events is heightened. Shakespeare uses a stage manager figure in *The Tempest* and *Measure for Measure*. Another play which makes use of this technique is *Our Town* by Thornton Wilder (1938). This play is rather like a modern soap opera as it traces the ordinary lives of people and the audience follows their hopes and fears and their ups and downs.

The text begins like this:

Act One
No curtain
No scenery.
The audience, arriving, sees an empty stage in half light.
Presently the stage manager, hat on and pipe in mouth, enters and begins placing a table and several chairs stage left, and a table and chairs down stage right.
'Left' and 'right' are from the point of view of the actor facing the audience. 'Up' is towards the back wall.
As the house lights go down he has finished setting the stage and, leaning against the right proscenium pillar, watches the late arrivals in the audience.
When the auditorium is in complete darkness he speaks:

Stage manager
    This play is called 'Our Town.' It was written by Thornton Wilder; produced and directed by A.... in it you will see Miss C ... Miss D ... and Mr F ... Mr G ... Mr H ... and many others. The name of the town is 'Grover's Corners', New Hampshire – just across from the Massachusetts line: Latitude 42 degrees 40 minutes; longitude 70 degrees 37 minutes.
The first act shows a day in our town. The date is 1901. The time is just before dawn.

[He continues describing what the audience has to imagine and even describes the subsequent death of some of the people we are about to meet.]

As the play ends the stage manager remarks:

    'There are the stars – doing their old, old criss-cross journeys in the sky. Scholars haven't settled the matter yet, but they seem to think there are no living beings up there. They're just chalk ... or fire. Only this one is straining away straining away all the time to make something of itself. The strain's so bad that every sixteen hours everybody lies down and gets a rest.
    He winds his watch
    Hm ... eleven o'clock in Grover's Corners – You get a good rest too. Good night.'

The playwright is showing the audience one of the themes of the play here – the inevitability and relentlessness of life and also the pitifully small place man has in the universe.

This is an easy play to produce as there is no scenery at all – you only need an open space. Try to produce a short extract of this play as a group.

ACTIVITY 216

Another play which uses a similar technique is *The Royal Hunt of the Sun* (1946) by Peter Shaffer. The play is about the 'invasion' of Peru by the Spanish in the middle of the sixteenth century. It is a modern play and no doubt shows the inhumanity of the colonisers who try to plunder this land of all its individuality and wealth. It is based on some true events and the main character, Francisco Pizarro, is a real historical figure.

In this play one of the characters in the action tells the story. He is called 'Old Martin' as a narrator . The play acted before us, and which he also watches, is about events from his youth.

In the play he is called Young Martin. He comments on his thoughts now, as an old man, on the action he produces before us which involves himself as a youth. Below is an extract from the beginning of the play.

What effect do you think this would have on the audience or the story?

The idea of a character commenting on the action in this way is intriguing.

From this introduction to the play what do you think the focus of the play might be? What do you think is significant in the only stage scenery that is mentioned here?

Act One
A bare stage. On the back wall, which is of wood, hangs a huge metal medallion, quartered by four black crucifixes, sharpened to resemble swords.

Darkness.
Old Martin, grizzled, in his middle fifties, appears. He wears the black costume of a Spanish hidalgo in the mid sixteenth century.

OLD MARTIN
Save you all. My name is Martin, I'm a soldier of Spain and that's it. Most of my life I've spent fighting for land, treasure and the cross. I'm worth millions. Soon I'll be dead and they'll bury me out here in Peru, the land I helped to ruin as a boy. This story is about ruin. Ruin and gold. More gold than any of you will ever see even if you worked in a counting house. I'm going to tell you how one hundred and sixty seven men conquered an empire of twenty four million. And then things that no-one has ever told: things to make you groan and cry out I'm lying. And perhaps I am. The air of Peru is cold and sour like in a vault, and wits turn easier here even than in Europe. But grant me this: I saw him closer than anyone and had only cause to love him. He was my altar, my bright image of salvation, Franscisco Pizarro. Time was when I'd have died for him, or any worship.

Young Martin enters duelling an invisible opponent with a stick. He is Old Martin as an impetuous boy of fifteen.

ACTIVITY 217

What is the effect of using a character as a stage manager figure? Does this help or hinder the enjoyment of the play? Why do you think some playwrights use this technique? Consider the effect on the character, the audience and the meaning of the play.

Key skills: Communication – discussion

General activities

ACTIVITY 218

Find as many different texts of your set plays as you can and compare the different editions. The editions do not need to be from different times but it would be interesting if you can find any old editions. Does this give you any clue about how they are considered today and if this has changed over time? Look at the information in the introductions. Look at the illustrations if there are any. Find out what the critical reaction was when they were first produced, if any characters were considered unacceptable or unreal, if there was a public outcry about the language used or the morals of the characters. Were the themes particularly topical or are they always relevant? Have there been any significant changes in its reception? For example, has it gone through phases of being unpopular? Has the ending been changed in any way?

ACTIVITY 219

Find and compare some photographs or sketches which show the stage set or costumes of a play you are studying. Which ones best express the way that you feel the play should be staged? You will be able to find this information on the Internet, from programmes written for productions and in books on drama. Present your findings to the group.

Key skills: Information Technology – different sources

ACTIVITY 220

Look at what was happening socially and politically at the time your set play was written. Does this have any effect on the play as it was written or produced? Perhaps you could concentrate on the political situation. Is it at all relevant? Use the Internet, history books, encyclopaedias and the introduction to help you. Write this up as an information sheet for A level students.

Key skills: Information Technology – different sources

ACTIVITY 221

Try to find out how your set play was received when it was first produced and see if the critical reception has changed over time. You may find this in the introduction to your text or in newspaper archives which are available on CD ROM, available in libraries.

Key skills: Information Technology – different sources

ACTIVITY 222

Think in detail about the staging of a play you know well including costumes and set. Choose two main characters and write notes on how the characters should be portrayed.

Further reading

Cambridge Paperback Guide to World Theatre by Sarah Stanton and Martin Banham (1996), Cambridge University Press.

Modern British Drama 1890–1990 by Christopher Innes (1992), Cambridge University Press.

12 Getting It All Together

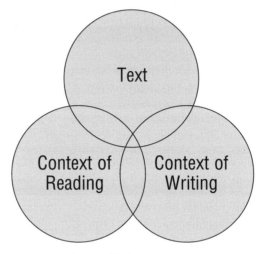

Text

Context of Reading

Context of Writing

I f you have studied most of the preceding chapters you are probably near the end of your course. In this chapter we are going to look at some of the specific tasks that you will be asked to do as you approach the final assessment.

Where does this fit in?

You may be asked to do some or all of these tasks:

1 Writing involving comparison
2 An extended coursework essay
3 Preparation for pre-release material
4 Preparation for unseen texts on a theme you have studied.

The last two items are important as they form the synoptic element of the course – a distinctive feature of A2.

Health Warning!

These tasks seem rather daunting and they are certainly challenging. However, throughout your course you have been preparing for them either implicitly or explicitly. Remember you have learned a lot since page one of this book!

1 Making comparisons

Comparison is something you have to do for A2, as in assessment objective 2ii:

'... Explore and comment on relationships and comparisons between texts'.

Making comparisons between substantial literary works is something that you will have to do if you are to succeed at A level. This section deals with the business of comparing literary works themselves (as opposed to criticism, interviews with writers and early drafts etc). Criticism is compared on page 256 in the section on pre-release materials.

ACTIVITY 223

In a small group discuss exactly what is meant by comparison and how you go about comparing two things. What are the essentials of making a comparison between two things? You might think about these extreme cases:

Compare a matchbox with a tortoise. Compare the United States of America with a frog. Compare a CD with a meal. Which is easiest?

In order to compare two things you need to have similarities and these similarities must be in respect to something else. For example, if you compare a tortoise and a matchbox it is likely that you will think about shape, but unless you are writing a poem the comparison probably stops there. The two are made of different substances, they serve vastly different purposes, one is man-made, the other is natural etc. The differences are so obvious that there is little value in the comparison.

So, one principle for making comparisons in literary studies is: don't choose texts that are too dissimilar, otherwise the comparison will be pointless. Similarities can be seen as points of reference whilst you consider differences. This will be clarified below.

In literary studies you might have to compare two novels, two plays, two or more poems or short stories. Remember to check carefully for details of what you are allowed to compare in your subject specifications as these can vary and can be restrictive!

> Making comparisons between literary works can be divided into three stages:
> 1 Deciding on the basis for the comparison (why compare?)
> 2 The means of comparison (how do you compare?)
> 3 The significance of the comparison (so what?)

Each of these will now be considered in more detail.

1 Deciding on the basis for the comparison (why compare?)

Firstly, you must decide why you want to compare these two works. If you are not clear about this the whole comparison will break down. For example, the two literary works may both be written by women of the same literary movement at around the same time, so they may be worth comparing.

If the examining board choose the texts to compare for you, or provide the context (e.g. Literature about the First World War), you will not need to worry about this stage.

ACTIVITY 224

The texts below have been paired for comparison. By researching using the Internet and encyclopaedia, find out the basis for comparing each pair of texts. An Internet search may lead you to Amazon – an on-line bookstore that provides brief reviews.

Key skills: IT – different sources

Lord of the Flies (William Golding) and *Robinson Crusoe* (Daniel Defoe)

Lord of the Flies and *The Inheritors* (William Golding)

Oranges Are Not the Only Fruit (Jeanette Winterson) and *The Color Purple* (Alice Walker)

Sacred Hunger (Barrie Unsworth) and *Hawksmoor* (Peter Ackroyd)

The Cone Gatherers (Robin Jenkins) and *Of Mice and Men* (John Steinbeck)

Jane Eyre (Charlotte Brontë) and *The Wide Sargasso Sea* (Jean Rhys)

If On A Winter's Night A Traveller (Italo Calvino) and *The Short Stories of Jorge Luis Borges* (Jorge Luis Borges)

North and South (Elizabeth Gaskell) and *Hard Times* (Charles Dickens)

Last Orders (Graham Swift) and *As I Lay Dying* (William Faulkner)

The Handmaid's Tale (Margaret Atwood) and *1984* (George Orwell)

If This Is a Man (Primo Levi) and *Schindler's Ark* (Thomas Keneally)

The Picture of Dorian Gray (Oscar Wilde) and *Wuthering Heights* (Emily Brontë)

Same subject

This is an obvious basis for comparison. If two literary works deal with the same subject then it is usually easy to compare them. For example: *Robinson Crusoe* (Daniel Defoe) and *Lord of the Flies* (William Golding). Both of these novels deal with people being washed up on desert islands (see page 250). You will then need to be able to break down this subject further for comparison.

ACTIVITY 225

Assuming you have not read either of these novels, how do you think it would be possible to compare two novels about people being washed up on desert islands? In a small group, list the aspects of this experience that could be compared.

COMMENTARY Similarity of subject is a good basis for beginning a comparison although you may not know where it is going to take you. If you are in the position of working things out for yourself, it is a good idea to start with the basics and move on from there. You might initially want to consider aspects of the plot: arrival on the island; rescue; survival; conflict; fear; etc. Begin by making notes on how the novels deal with each aspect. For example, you may note that Crusoe has many adventures before he is shipwrecked, whereas Golding seems hardly concerned with how his boys arrived on the island; Crusoe is alone and so Defoe develops his relationship with the hostile environment and with God through Crusoe's diary, but Golding's boys come into conflict mainly with each other – the novel shows us social problems being worked out; Crusoe encounters an island native, Golding's boys do not. Differences such as these should lead you into a deeper consideration of the purposes behind the novels.

You may find later that some of what you discover at this stage is not useful for your final essay – because you may want to shift or narrow your focus. It is not a good idea at this stage to look at what the critics say – this is likely to limit the development of your own ideas because it is difficult for you to disagree with the critics. Once your own ideas have gone some way, look up the two novels in an encyclopaedia to get some basic idea of the contexts in which the two were written:

Robinson Crusoe	*Lord of the Flies*
Written in the 18th century. The exotic setting appeals to readers in a country expanding its colonies. Science was rapidly developing as a means of controlling nature. Pioneering use of diary form to create strong sense of realism.	Written in the 20th century – a time of pessimism regarding human nature. The island setting is by now a recognised technique for exploring new experiences outside the bounds of 'society'.

These broad concepts may then help you to interpret the details of the texts. But don't be tempted into 'going to the critics' at this stage. It cannot be stressed enough that you should spend a great deal of time preparing your essay. Don't rush into writing before you are ready.

ACTIVITY 226

If there are two novels you are thinking of comparing because of their similarity of subject matter, break them down into their components and compare them as in the above example.

Same theme

You may be wondering exactly what the difference is between a subject and a theme. To pursue the above example, the subject is people washed up on desert islands but the theme might be the human spirit of survival or the inherent evil of humanity. In other words, a subject is more superficial. It is a topic or setting that provides a vehicle for exploration of a deeper idea or philosophy. The most obvious comparison to make between literary texts is between ones that treat the same theme. In many ways both *Robinson Crusoe* and *Lord of the Flies* set out to explore human nature using an unfamiliar environment. In the former, humanity rises back to a civilised state after shipwreck; in the latter, Golding's stranded boys sink to the level of savages. So the point of this kind of comparison is to examine the two writers' treatment of a similar theme.

The following table makes clear the distinction between subject and theme in a number of novels:

Title	Subject	Themes
The Inheritors (William Golding)	How the last Neanderthals were wiped out by Homo sapiens	Golding was replying in literary form to H.G. Wells' claim that it was good for evolution when Neanderthals were wiped out; thus, the evil of Homo Sapiens.
Of Mice and Men (John Steinbeck)	Two men employed on a range during the Depression	Loneliness, companionship.
Emma (Jane Austen)	A young woman delights in pairing off her friends. She eventually gets married.	Self-knowledge. The novel is a 'bildungsroman' in that it traces a young person's development to maturity.

ACTIVITY 227

Using novels that you have read or are reading, construct a table like the one above, distinguishing carefully between their subject and theme.

Themes and contexts

There are rich pickings to be had if you choose a theme and then look across many contexts for works that deal with that theme. This allows you to bring into play knowledge of the contexts in which the novels were written and received – the *informed* part of being an independent informed reader.

Here are some suggestions:

- marriage in late 19th century novels and in 20th century short stories
- the theme of transgression – *The Rime of the Ancient Mariner* (Samuel Coleridge) and *Frankenstein* (Mary Shelley)
- reinterpretations – The stories of Angela Carter as re-interpretations of fairy tales
- outspoken women – *The Awakening* (Kate Chopin) and *The French Lieutenant's Woman* (John Fowles)
- experiments in writing – *Tristram Shandy* (Lawrence Sterne) and *If On A Winter's Night A Traveller* (Italo Calvino)

- outsiders in society, in novels from various periods
- the influence of childhood on adulthood in selected novels. Select novels from different genres and periods.

If you have found enough to justify a detailed comparison, now consider the tools you will need to actually make the comparison.

2 The means of comparison (how do you compare?)

If the above is the 'why?' of comparison then the means of comparison is the 'how?' Here you will need linguistic and literary tools to help you with the comparison. Many of the means of comparison have already been mentioned elsewhere in this book – in the chapters on stylistics, the novel, poetry and plays. So, what follows are some basic outlines and reminders.

Frameworks for comparison

In order to compare two things, you need a framework for making the comparison. To some extent this will come ready-made but you will always find that you have to construct your own framework for whatever piece of work you are doing. If you are dealing with the novel you will need to use tools like these, and be able to say how they are relevant to various points in the text:

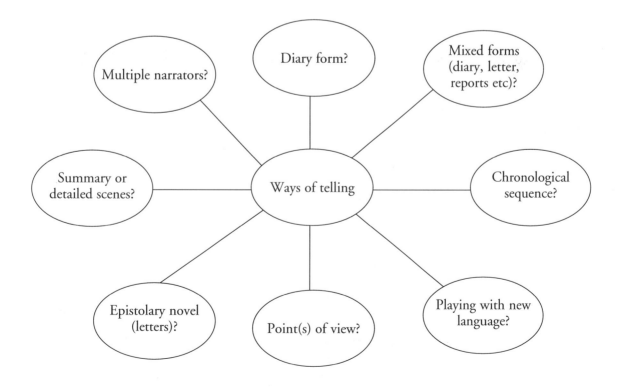

If you are studying two novels, draw a diagram like the one above. Apply the ideas in the diagram to each novel, adding and adapting where necessary.

What you discover here will then need to be developed later in your study.

If you are comparing two poems, the comparison is often a lot easier to manage simply because the texts are likely to be shorter. Here, the analysis will switch to poetry because we are able to reproduce the whole text for you!

Read *In the Theatre: a True Incident* below and *Out Out* – (page 14) which are two poems about someone dying. In a small group before tackling the next activity, discuss how you

would compare them. For example, one point of comparison might be how the moment of death is presented. What are the other points of comparison?

In the Theatre: a True Incident by Danny Abse (born 1923)

'Only a local anaesthetic was given because of the blood pressure problem. The patient, thus, was fully awake throughout the operation. But in those days – in 1938, in Cardiff, when I was Lambert Rogers' dresser – they could not locate a brain tumour with precision. Too much normal brain tissue was destroyed as the surgeon crudely searched for it, before he felt the resistance of it... all somewhat hit and miss. One operation I shall never forget...' (Dr Wilfred Abse)

Sister saying – 'Soon you'll be back in the ward,'
sister thinking – 'Only two more on the list,'
the patient saying – 'Thank you, I feel fine';
small voices, small lies, nothing untoward,
though, soon, he would blink again and again
because of the fingers of Lambert Rogers,
rash as a blind man's, inside his soft brain.

If items of horror can make a man laugh
then laugh at this: one hour later, the growth
still undiscovered, ticking its own wild time;
more brain mashed because of the probe's braille path;
Lambert Rogers desperate, fingering still;
his dresser thinking, 'Christ! Two more on the list,
a cisternal puncture and a neural cyst.'

Then, suddenly, the cracked record in the brain,
a ventriloquist voice that cried, 'You sod,
leave my soul alone, leave my soul alone,' –
the patient's eyes too wide. And shocked,
Lambert Rogers drawing out the probe
with nurses, students, sister, petrified.

'Leave my soul alone, leave my soul alone,'
that voice so arctic and that cry so odd
had nowhere else to go – till the antique
gramophone wound down and the words began
to blur and slow, '... leave ... my ... soul ... alone ...'
to cease at last when something other died.
And silence matched the silence under snow.

ACTIVITY 230

Complete the following table comparing the two poems. The first column names an aspect of the poem. The middle column suggests ways in which the poems are similar and the right-hand columns show how the two poems differ.

Aspect of the poem	Similarities	Differences Out Out	In the Theatre
The start	Begin in the middle of the story		No description of physical scene
Voice – who speaks?	Narrator	Narrator (present in the poem) boy	
Voice – tone	Evoke emotional response		Clipped, addresses reader
Grammar		Past tense. Many 'ands'	
Metaphor		Limited – 'snarled'	
Point of view			
Structure	Lengthy descriptive build-up to climax		
Patterns			Parallel phrases – 'saying', 'thinking', 'saying'.
Background	Both based on true stories		

We are not suggesting that you use the first column slavishly as a checklist. Checklists can be helpful as long as you realise that the list should change for each poem you study!

It is difficult to teach explicitly what you say about these things once you have spotted them. Successful students often seem to know what kinds of things to say without being taught.

ACTIVITY 231

Consider how you might use the observation that parallel phrases are used in the first three lines of *In the Theatre*. Rank order the following points and discuss your order with someone else.

1 To highlight the contrast between what is being said and what is being thought.

2 To create tension.
3 To give the impression that we are in the midst of the action.
4 To reinforce the idea of 'small lies' in the fourth line.
5 To introduce the idea of voices and the thoughts behind them for later in the poem.

Here are some examples of things that can be said about a literary work:

- In this play this definition will not fit easily.
- This allows the readers to empathise with this character.
- This character is stereotyped.

- There are parallels between the author's style and her 'message'.
- This aspect of the novel/poem is important because . . .
- Something reinforces something else (i.e. they serve the same purpose in the work).
- This poem/novel emphasises something for a particular purpose.
- The play fits the definition of an ideal plot.
- The main purpose of the work is . . .
- The writer has used this setting because . . .
- The use of 'bruising' strongly implies that the mix of cultures is not easy.
- Again the beauty of this image comes from its simplicity.
- This poem suggests that . . .
- The poem echoes . . .
- It creates a tense/challenging/atmosphere.
- The effect of this technique is to subvert the expectations of the reader.

ACTIVITY 232

Write a full comparison of the two poems analysed above. Use both the table and the above statements as starting points. Choose the statements that best fit what you are trying to say and adapt them as necessary. You will also want to add your own.

3 The significance of the comparison (so what?)

During stage two you have made the comparison. In stage three you need to decide on what difference the comparison makes to the reader or to the context in which the texts were written. This is the 'so what?' of comparison. If, for example, you have found that two novels are written in very different styles, you may be able to connect that difference with the original intentions of the authors, the circumstances in which the pieces were written or how the reader is meant to respond to the difference. This will be clarified in the examples below.

In this stage you need to connect with stage one. What you say depends on your reason for making the comparison in the first place. If, for example, you are comparing the desert island experiences of Robinson Crusoe and the group of boys in William Golding's *Lord of the Flies*, you are obviously attempting to say something about the wider significance of what happens on the island. This word 'wider' is crucial. It expects you to say something about the attitudes, beliefs and philosophies of the writers, or, if you wish to keep writers out of it, about how those things are implied in the books in question.

This leads you into a consideration of abstract ideas. For example, in connection with *Robinson Crusoe* you might consider the idea of imperialism (the desire for countries to expand their empires) and the survival instinct. *Lord of the Flies* might lead you into territory such as childhood innocence, original sin (the idea that children are born 'evil'), and human nature.

But 'wider' might also have connections with other literature. With *Robinson Crusoe* there are important connections to be made with other novels that could be described as 'adventure', written at about the same time and also with the beginnings of the novel form (this book was one of the very first novels to be written). *Lord of the Flies*, on the other hand, written after the Second World War, makes use of the writer's knowledge of other books about desert islands (such as R.M. Ballantyne's *Coral Island*) and cannot be considered without them.

Final words – microscopes and binoculars

It is useful to see comparison in two ways: Now and then you need to look at your text as if you were looking through a microscope – that is, in detail, particularly when looking at language; but you also need to look at it as if you were looking through binoculars – that is, getting an overview and taking into account context and background.

2 The long, long essay

You may be expected to write one long coursework essay (about 1,500–2,000 words) as one of the AS modules. You may also be asked to write an extended essay for one of the modules in A2 which may be an essay of 2,500–3,000 words. You must be clear before you start what the specified length is. There will be some element of comparison in an essay of this type. Producing a good essay will show your development as an independent and skilful reader and critic. Hopefully you will be surprised at how much you know and how interested you can become in an extended piece of individual work. Your teacher will help, advise and encourage you!

Before you write

What you already know

You have been writing essays from the very beginning of your course. This one is just a 'biggy'.

ACTIVITY 233

Individually write down what you do **first** when you have an essay to write. Add other activities which you think would improve your preparation. As a group, pool your ideas and come up with a list of ideas about how to begin essay writing based on your own experience.

Look back at your earlier essays and notice what mistakes you made and how you could improve. As a group come up with a list of common weaknesses and devise strategies for solving them. Be aware of your own weaknesses in particular.

Key skills: It may be possible to use this for evidence of key skills – **working with others** and **improving your own performance**.

Pitfall

Rushing or leaving things to the last minute – long essays evolve. They cannot be written all in one sitting the night before they have to be handed in.

What are you trying to prove?

Take a good look at the criteria by which your work will be judged:

You obviously have to communicate well.

You will probably have to show that you can compare. There may be restrictions about which texts can be compared. For example, the texts chosen for comparison may need to be either a different genre or a different literary period (not less than 30 years). One of them may have to be prose.

You have to:

- look at language
- look at the interpretation of the texts by others and add your own
- use critical concepts and terminology
- look at genre
- look at context
- integrate the response to the texts as much as you can.

If you know what the assessor is looking for there is a good chance that you will be able to provide the features that will attract a good mark. If you can, as a group, mark a long essay by another student, using the assessment criteria as a guide.

Choosing the topic

It is obviously important to be interested in what you are going to write about. If you have a free choice, think about the particular texts that have interested you most. You may be able to use one text that you already know well and simply add one or two complementary texts. Ask for advice on this. You should really aim to be writing a comparative study of at least two texts. If you are not given a free choice your teacher will choose appropriate texts for you. Some subject specifications put restrictions on the types of texts and all texts have to be approved by a moderator for your Centre.

Pitfalls

- main idea too broad or narrow
- nothing new or of interest to say
- idea too simple or too difficult
- not enough evidence to prove your points
- not enough knowledge of previous critical comment

Choosing the title

You may not have any choice! But if you do …

This is a pretty vital aspect of your preliminary work. If you choose to do something that is too challenging or not challenging enough, you will find it difficult to do well. You might like to begin with a working title and then make it more precise once you have got into the essay itself. The main thing is to be clear about what you are doing and then do it! The main theme of an essay is called the hypothesis. You should try to develop a hypothesis and then prove it. Remember you should play to your strengths and write about something that interests you.

Notice what you are asked to do. What **precisely** is the task? Is it general or specific? Are you asked for your personal opinion or are you asked about the views of others? Are you asked to compare/contrast, discuss or evaluate? You should do as you are asked. Write out the title and annotate it in such a way as to identify all its aspects.

ACTIVITY 234

You may be faced with the following instructions in your title:

- discuss
- compare
- contrast
- evaluate

In a group try to distinguish between these tasks and write your own definition of each of these words. To help you a brief list of definitions is given below. Identify which definition fits which instruction.

- Identify all the aspects of a topic in detail and explain the significance of these aspects
- Identify and develop the similarities in texts
- Identify and develop the differences between texts
- Identify the features of the texts and judge their worth.

Pitfalls

- title too vague or too specific
- no real purpose to your essay

Reading

The main source of information will probably be the text itself but you should read critical works on these texts to add some standing to your personal response. Keep good records of what you read and detailed notes about anything you wish to quote. It is most frustrating if you find you need to refer to something and cannot find it! Although you do need, at some point, to read what others have said, do not rely on the words of famous critics. The assessors are also looking for a personal informed response. Jot down ideas whenever they occur to you – don't think, 'Oh, I'll remember that' because you probably won't!

Remember: the palest ink is better than the most retentive memory.

Getting the information

Make notes and charts to help you see what you are finding out. For example, list the similarities and differences in the style, characters, setting and structure. Make sure that your original title is still appropriate. Follow the activities and ideas at the beginning of this chapter.

Pitfall

Using an idea simply because you think it is interesting or clever even though it is not relevant.

Writing

Getting started

ACTIVITY 235

Here are some things you must do.
Put these activities in the order in which you think they should be done.

a write conclusion
b brainstorm ideas
c check spelling
d study the texts
e write an introduction
f make sure you have enough material
g write a detailed paragraph plan
h change the title
i change the texts
j read critical works

Pitfall

Continuing with an essay that is not 'working' rather than cutting your losses and rethinking.

Drafting

When writing an essay of this length, i.e. over about 1,500 words, it is essential to be prepared to re-write. Obviously the most efficient way to do this is on a computer. The final version is also then more pleasing to both you and the examiner. Try moving whole paragraphs about and writing several different introductions and conclusions. Write for 20 minutes and then stop. Start again from an entirely different viewpoint.

Revising

Try reading your essay and noting the main point of each paragraph in the margin. Through using these notes, see if there is a logical progression in your essay. Change it if necessary. You should be able to re-write the original plan of your essay from reading the essay itself. You should also be able to reconstruct the title from a reading of your essay. You may be able to get some one else to test this for you.

Linking words: Make sure you have guided your reader through the essay by using linking words or 'signposts'. These are words which show the relationship of one section of your writing to another. Make a list of words which might serve this function, for example 'therefore', 'however'. See if they would help to show the logical development of your essay.

Technical accuracy: Read the essay through carefully and check the spelling. Do this when you have not looked at the essay for a while so that you see what is actually written and not what you already expect to be there.

Completing

Introduction and conclusion: It may be that you left the introduction and conclusion until last. Think what function the introduction and conclusion should fulfil. Check that they really do their job. Read the essay through, simply to check that the beginning and the end are good. The first and last impression given to the examiner are important. You may be able to get a friend to do this for you – if you reciprocate the favour!

The formalities

Quotations, bibliography: Check that you have acknowledged what you have read. Include all you have read even if you did not refer to it directly. Check that any quotations from critical works are acknowledged. Check that you have quoted sensibly and accurately from the texts themselves.

Cutting your losses/damage limitation

If you have spent quite a long time working on an essay which still is not fitting together, you should seriously consider cutting your losses and starting again on a new topic with different texts. This may seem rather drastic but in the end it is worth it, as sometimes failure is unavoidable if the original idea does not 'work'. Discuss this with your teacher to check for agreement and come up with a more acceptable topic. Remember to check the subject specifications again!

Checklist

- Have you read your work specifically for spelling and punctuation?
- Have you acknowledged quotations from other sources?
- Have you used quotations from the texts?
- Have you integrated the texts? Perhaps you could do this even more now you know them well.
- Is the development of your argument clear or do you need to add more signposts?
- Is every paragraph absolutely relevant to the question?

Long essays are often the most rewarding work that you do. This is because you quickly become experts in your chosen topic. You are in control: you can really show how good you are.

Further reading

Learn How to Study by Derek Rowntree (1970, Reprinted 1984) Macdonald.

Writing an Essay, How to Improve your Performance for Coursework and Examinations by Brendon Hennessy (1997) (How to Books).

Writing a Thesis. A Guide to Long Essays and Dissertations by George Watson (1987) Longman.

Synoptic assessment: where does this fit in?

Synoptic assessment means that for this part of the course all of the Assessment Objectives are assessed at the same time! This assessment will take place at the end of your course. But it's not as bad as it sounds:

'Synoptic assessment will involve the explicit synthesis of insights gained from a close and detailed study of a range of texts for the development of English Literature. It will require candidates to show evidence of the ways in which contextual factors and different interpretations of texts illuminate their own readings, and ensure that candidates demonstrate their skills of interpretation and expression to give accurate, well-argued responses'. (QCA)

Two of the ways in which this can be assessed are through pre-release materials, and through the exploration of a theme given well in advance of the exam. These will be explained in the next two sections.

3 Pre-release materials

Pre-release materials are issued some time in advance of the actual exam so that you get a chance to study them before being faced with a question about them. They consist of several texts that are related in some way, perhaps centring around a literary work. They might be: extracts from literary works (fiction, drama or poetry), articles and reviews, biography and autobiography, historical information and interpretation. Inevitably, comparison between the texts – though not all of them at the same time – is an important part of the tasks you will be required to do. Remember that pre-release materials are designed to test your performance on all of the Assessment Objectives. Remind yourself of them now! (page 4).

ACTIVITY 236

Preparation: If you don't prepare your materials before the exam then the whole point of this style of examination is lost. In a pair discuss which of the following would be worth doing as preparation (answers at the end of the chapter):

1 predict the likely questions
2 group the texts together in various ways
3 read them through once
4 thoroughly research every writer mentioned in the texts
5 cross-reference the texts
6 highlight key points
7 use different colours for nouns, verbs, adjectives, etc.
8 skim-read the texts several times
9 read actively by asking questions and making links between texts as you read
10 consider your personal response to the texts
11 colour code concepts that repeatedly occur
12 guess the meanings of words you don't understand
13 if the extracts are based on a literary text, buy and read a copy of that text before the exam.

The following activity takes black British literature as its topic. All of the pieces are critical writing taken from journals and books. Two questions are considered using these materials. The first is done for you and the second is over to you.

ACTIVITY 237

Compare and contrast the views of black British literature presented in Texts 1 and 2. Which do you find most persuasive and why? Here are some guidelines:

■ Use a dictionary to look up unfamiliar words. For some key words a literary encyclopaedia would also be useful.
■ The opening sentences of paragraphs often tell you what will appear in that paragraph. Look for sentences that qualify the opening sentence in some way.

■ Look for words that suggest a value or a judgement on the part of the writer, like 'oppressive' and 'impossibility' in Text 1.
■ Pick out the key words that indicate the writer's focus.
■ Look at the way the writer attempts to convince you. For example, use of: questions, examples, jargon, comparisons, etc.
■ Make a list of similarities and differences between the two extracts.

Text 1
(*Notes*: 'Reterritorialisation' means claiming something (in this case a language/place) as one's own. 'Linguistic impoverishment' means that a language is considered to be inferior.)

... Some black writers have only standard English available as a medium of expression; there is also the dominance of standard linguistic and literary forms which can make any thought of deviance seem an impossibility. In her introduction to *Gifts from My Grandmother,* Meiling Jin talks of her struggle with Wordsworthian forms and sentiments which continued, against her will, to structure her poetry, and of her present truce with them, and the English language in general.

For poets of Caribbean descent, there is usually the possibility of an alternative means of expression in Creole, but here there is still the oppressive weight of the dominant forms to be removed or come to terms with. For them, the use of Creole is a deliberate attempt at reterritorialisation, and some of them, like Valerie Bloom in *Yuh Hear 'Bout?,* make forceful use of it. ...

This use of Creole is apparently so uncompromising that it is deemed necessary (even in a book on Black women writers) to provide a 'translation' alongside it! Grace Nichols, on the other hand, uses Creole in a way which is more restrained and contrastive, combining it with standard English in the same poem. Thus, for example, in the sequence *The Fat Black Woman's Poems*, descriptions in standard English are interspersed with sections in Creole which represent the Fat Black Woman's thoughts and utterances. This produces humorous effects, yet at the same time serves to highlight the Fat Black Woman's separation from the white, standard English speaking, world around her. Amryl Johnson's eponymous granny in *Granny in de Market Place* is a self-possessed individual like the Fat Black Woman, and her hilarious encounters with the market stall-holders are conducted entirely in Creole.

The persistent but ill-formed idea that use of Creole represents a form of linguistic impoverishment or deprivation on the part of the speaker is satirised in Merle Collins's *No Dialects Please* as are the hypocrisy and ignorance which accompany such ideas, and the efforts of the dominant culture to impose a unified model of language ...

The felt need to print 'translations' of poems written in Creole also raises questions of whom the poems and the books address – performance audience and reading public – and the implied difference between them. The use of translation does, however, reinforce preconceptions about Black English as alien and/or defective; no one suggests providing translations of the arguably much more impenetrable Glaswegian dialect of Tom Leonard, for example.

(Patrick Williams, *Difficult Subjects: Black British Women's Poetry*, page 115)

Text 2

(*Notes*: In this text the metaphor 'wearing the ship on the head' is a reference to a 19th century beggar who wore a replica of a ship on his head as a 'badge of his immigrant status'; 'anglophillic' literally means 'loving the English')

Times have changed and the children of the earlier generation, born in England and often to biracial parents, do not carry the ship comfortably on their heads. They are introducing something of a dilemma in the British literary scene because they are often either unwilling to or incapable of wearing that ship that points to an immigrant identity or an identity of 'otherness'. Many of them will reject any lineage with the writers of the sixties and quite arrogantly (if understandably), and, perhaps foolishly, assert a new invention: the black British voice.

In addition to a large group of writers who inhabit and explore an international and in-between identity, there is a second group fixated on home – a geographical home, and in this, they are no different from the 'exile' writers of the sixties – the Braithwaites, Selvons, Salkeys, et al. The difference, of course, is that home is no longer the Caribbean or Africa – home is Britain. In other words, they are connecting with the 'homeness' of Britain. It is an uncomfortable contention and one that does not always lead to the same conclusion, but it begins at the same fundamental place: we are citizens in this country, some of us were born here, have lived here all or most of our lives; this is home. Why does it not feel like home? Should we look here or elsewhere? What does it mean that this home does not feel like home?

There is, then, a serious engagement with nationalism that may be quite new for Britain. These novels are seeking to redefine the national character of Britain and to achieve this by expanding the conception of Englishness or Britishness. Their loyalties are no longer the kind of grovelling Anglophillic adoration for the Mother Country that may have characterised the attitude of colonial blacks who were coming to live in England. No, these are English people and they are struggling to understand what this means. Such individuals have always existed in England; however, the numbers are significant now, and their colours are dark, thus producing a curious problematic in the English literary world. I am making a somewhat slight distinction between these writers and 'immigrant' writers like James Berry, John Agard and Grace Nichols, who, while being recognised as prominent British authors, still carry with them, and in their work, an undaunted connectedness to their place of birth. But their work is distinct, I think, from S.I. Martin, a Bedford born novelist; Courtia Newland, a twenty-three year old West Londoner; Bernardine Evaristo, a London born novelist and poet; Andrea Levy, also a native Londoner, and Q, an enigmatic pop figure who wears his credentials with daring and aggression. What all these writers share is a belief that they are writing British literature even as they tell the story of the blacks who are British.

(slightly adapted from Kwame Dawes, *Negotiating the Ship on the Head: Black British Fiction*, in *Wasafiri*, page 18, 1999)

COMMENTARY Build your answer around the following ideas:

Text 1	Text 2
Focus: the language used by black writers	**Focus**: the 'nationality' of black writers
Dominance of the English language and of traditional literary forms	The new 'voice' of British black writers
Use of Creole to combat this	The idea of 'home'
Issue of audience and translation	The new nationalism
Creole as an inferior language	'Immigrant' writers versus natives

Elements you might consider to be persuasive:

Text 1	Text 2
Use of words that arouse emotion: 'deviance', 'impossibility', 'struggle', etc.	Use of metaphor ('the ship on the head')
Use of examples	The writer expresses his own doubts
Reference to writers' lives	Paragraph 1 ends with a key idea
Use of jargon ('reterritorialisation')	Use of examples
Writer's emotional involvement (exclamation mark)	Patterned build up of argument (lines 14–15)
Consideration of alternative positions	Use of open-ended questions (lines 15–17)
Reference to literature that supports argument	Use of exaggeration ('grovelling Anglophillic adoration')
Comparison with other literature (Tom Leonard)	More personal approach to the whole argument
	Final point summarises with impact

You may, of course, also wish to produce your own arguments. Note too that you may feel some of the above points are dissuasive rather than persuasive!

ACTIVITY 238

1 Answer the same question using Text 3 and one other. You will find that it helps to be systematic – use highlighters and construct tables.

2 Using Text 3 and either Text 1 or 2, explain the themes that arise in Caribbean writing and how they are used in the critics' arguments.

Text 3

At this stage, to my mind, Caribbean literature meant either V.S. Naipaul, whose politics I found difficult to digest, or books in the Heinemann Caribbean Series, whose texts had the annoying habit of continually making reference to fruits and flowers and trees which bore no relationship to those I grew up with in Leeds. The truth was, I would no more have known a breadfruit from a plantain, or a mango from a papaya. A hibiscus may as well have been a flamboyant tree for all I knew, and a palm tree was a palm tree was a palm tree. Who cared that there were a dozen varieties of palm trees, all with their own specific names and histories? Caribbean literature in its broadest sense baffled me. And then I came upon Samuel Selvon and George Lamming.

Sam Selvon's *The Lonely Londoners* was a revelation to me. I recognised the urban landscape, even though it was presented to me in the most striking Caribbean vernacular. However, more important than this, I also recognised the contradictory tension engendered by Selvon's attraction to and rejection by England. In Selvon's fiction there was a sense of being both inside and outside of Britain at the same time. The literature was shot through with the most uncomfortable anxieties of belonging and not belonging, and these same anxieties underscored my life and the lives of many people of my generation in the Britain of the seventies and early eighties.

Selvon also wrote about love, and the concomitant emotion which is betrayal. What made his work at times almost painful to read was the love he expressed for a city which, deep in his heart, he knew would betray him. Sam Selvon's ability to paint a portrait of the gritty inner city, make it attractive, and at the same time people it with characters who were migrating to office from home, from desk to tube, from country to country, people on the move, in between, ambivalent, and lonely, eventually had a larger impact on me than the African-American literature that I had been reading. And then I happened upon the work of his fellow emigrant, George Lamming.

The first book of Lamming's that I read was a remarkable novel from 1972 entitled *Natives of My Person*. As densely textured as Faulkner, and possessing formal ambitions of Joycean proportions, it was clear to me that I need no longer be afraid of Caribbean literature alienating me on the grounds that I couldn't tell a mango from a paw-paw. This literature was drawing me in, teasing me with its deeply historical sensibility, challenging me with its structural gamesmanship. Lamming was in a different league to the vast majority of the other Caribbean writers that I had been attempting to read.

(slightly adapted from *Following On: The Legacy of Lamming and Selvon*, Caryl Phillips, in *Wasafiri*, 1999)

4 Synoptic theme: war in literature

In some subject specifications you will be asked to comment in an examination on unseen texts. This will enable you to show that you have understood and assimilated all the knowledge you have gained during the course. The texts will probably be taken from a chosen literary movement or a chosen theme in literature. There will be no prescribed texts but over the course you will study literature that will help familiarise you with the specific aspect you need to study. The texts you study may form part of your coursework assessment. You will be expected to draw on the reading you have done during the course when you answer the examination questions.

A typical theme may be 'War in Literature' and this will be discussed here.

Oh What a lovely war!

ACTIVITY 239

In small groups discuss and make a list of **people** who could write about war. For example – a historian.

Now look at the **purpose** for which it could be written. For example a historian would be writing for informative purposes.

Now look at the **time** a text could be written. For example – a historian would be writing at least a generation later, after the end of a war.

Combine these ideas. For example – a soldier could write a diary during the war or he could write an autobiography later in his life. His purpose could be for his own satisfaction or to inform others later.

Key skills: Communication – discussion

You have probably come up with a complex set of possibilities which will include combinations of the following **people**:

civilians
soldiers (from privates to generals)
politicians
historians

journalists
novelists
playwrights
poets

and these **purposes**:
letter home
a personal diary
actual written instructions
propaganda
information for historians
biography/autobiography

and this **time**:
contemporary
immediately after the end of the war
a generation later
a century later.

The same event would look very different when recounted by different people at a different time.

Genre

ACTIVITY 240

The texts on the theme of war may be of any genre – poetry, prose (fiction and non-fiction) and drama. Find several examples of each of these. You will need to look in your library or departmental stock cupboard. Look at when they were written in relation to the subject matter. Can you draw any conclusions from this? Were any of the genres particularly difficult to find?

World War One

ACTIVITY 241

There are a great number of anthologies of poetry from World War One. A selection appears at the end of this chapter. As a class activity, choose several poets and divide them between the group. Do some research about the background of these poets and study two of their poems. Present your findings to the group. Identify the common themes you have found, for example, the waste of war, the helplessness of the ordinary soldiers.

Key skills: Communication – presentation

Read these two texts written after the death of
Rupert Brooke, a First World War poet, and
the two poems which follow.

Winston Churchill (1915)

Rupert Brooke is dead. A telegram from the Admiral at Lemnos tells us that this life
has closed at the moment when it seemed to have reached its springtime. A voice
had become audible, a note had been struck, more true, more thrilling, more able to
do justice to the nobility of our youth in arms engaged in this war, than any other –
more able to express their thoughts of self-surrender, and with a power to carry
comfort to those who watch them so intently from afar. The voice has been swiftly
stilled. Only the echoes and the memory remains; but they will linger.

During the last few months of his life, months of preparation in gallant comradeship
and open air, the poet-soldier told with all the simple force of genius the sorrow of
youth about to die and the sure triumphant consolations of a sincere and valiant
spirit. He expected to die: he was willing to die for the dear England whose beauty
and majesty he knew: and he advanced towards the brink in perfect serenity, with
absolute conviction of the rightness of his country's cause and a heart devoid of hate
for fellow-men.

The thoughts to which he gave expression in the very few incomparable war sonnets
which he has left behind will be shared by many thousands of young men moving
resolutely and blithely forward in this, the hardest, the cruellest, and the least-
rewarded of all the wars that men have fought. They are a whole history and
revelation of Rupert Brooke himself. Joyous, fearless, versatile, deeply instructed,
with classic symmetry of mind and body, ruled by high undoubting purpose, he was
all that one would wish England's noblest sons to be in the days when no sacrifice
but the most precious is acceptable, and the most precious is that which is most
freely-proffered.

(Source: obituary note in *The Times, 26* April 1915).

Charles Sorley (1915)

. . . I saw Rupert Brooke's death in *the Morning Post. The Morning Post,* which has
always hitherto disapproved of him, is now loud in his praises because he has
conformed to their stupid axiom of literary criticism that the only stuff of poetry is
violent physical experience, by dying on active service. I think Brooke's earlier poems
especially notably 'The Fish' and 'Grantchester', which you can find in *Georgian
Poetry* – are his best. That last sonnet-sequence of his, of which you sent me the
review in the *Times Lit. Supp.,* and which has been so praised, I find (with the
exception of that beginning 'These hearts were woven of human joys and cares,
Washed marvellously with sorrow' which is not about himself) overpraised. He is far
too obsessed with his own sacrifice, regarding the going to war of himself (and
others) as a highly intense, remarkable and sacrificial exploit, whereas it is merely the
conduct demanded of him (and others) by the turn of circumstances, where non-
compliance with this demand would have made life intolerable. It was not that 'they'
gave up anything of that list he gives in one sonnet: but that the essence of these
things had been endangered by circumstances over which he had no control, and he
must fight to recapture them. He has clothed his attitude in fine words: but he has
taken the sentimental attitude.

(Source: extract from letter of 28 April 1915, in the *Collected Letters of Charles Sorley,*
Cambridge 1919)

The Soldier

If I should die, think only this of me:
That there's some corner of foreign field
That is for ever England. There shall be
In that rich earth a richer dust concealed;
A dust whom England bore, shaped, made aware,
Gave, once, her flowers to her love, her ways to roam.
A body of England's, breathing English air,
Washed by the river, blest by the suns of home.

And think, this heart, all evil shed away,
A pulse in the eternal mind, no less
Gives somewhere back the thoughts by England given;
Her sights and sounds; dreams happy as her day;
And laughter, learnt of friends; and gentleness,
In hearts at peace, under an English heaven.

                                                                    Rupert Brooke

Sonnet

When you see millions of the mouthless dead
Across your dreams in pale battalions go,
Say not soft things, as other men have said,
That you'll remember. For you need not so.
Give them not praise. For, deaf, how should they know
It is not curses heaped on each gashed head?
Nor tears. Their blind eyes see not your tears flow.
Nor honour. It is easy to be dead.
Say only this, 'They are dead'. Then add thereto,
'Yet many a better one has died before'.
Then, scanning all the o'ercrowded mass, should you
Perceive one face that you loved heretofore,
It is a spook. None wears the face you knew.
Great death has made all his for evermore.

                                                                    Charles Sorley

Find out something about Winston Churchill and Charles Sorley.

Examine the attitude of Winston Churchill and Charles Sorley to Rupert Brooke's death. Look carefully at the language they use to express their attitudes in these obituaries. Are these attitudes familiar to you from your reading of war poetry? Refer to specific poets and poems if you can.

Examine the poems of Brooke and Sorley. Look at how these poets have expressed their feelings. Compare their attitudes and the way they are expressed. Find other examples of poets who feel like Brooke and Sorley.

World War Two

The First World War was not the only one to inspire poetry. There are anthologies of poetry from the Second World War too.

Here is a poem that focuses on the battles in the
air. Read it and examine the use of contrast and
its effect.

Zum Waffen Garten

To sail my boat, to fly my kite,
To fill my jar with fish,
To laze away the livelong day,
What more could any boy wish.

'Bandits, skipper, starboard high,
Coming fast in a dive,
Turn right, turn right, turn – now
If we want to stay alive.'

I remember those summer days,
Without a worry or care,
The afternoon on the sinking raft.
The excitement and the scare.

'How long to the target now?'
'Fifteen minutes will see us there.'
'Look out for the flak and the searchlights,
And watch for the marker flare.'

White flannels and a sunlit pitch
The crack of bat against ball
The golden days of eternal youth,
Gone, alas, beyond recall.

'There's the marker and the flak!
Oh target, bright and clear,
Left steady – bombs away,
Get the hell out of here.'

To sail my boat; 'Christ we're hit!'
Searing flames, curses and screams,
A blazing torch across the sky,
Turns to ashes all my dreams.

(Somewhere in the night 1943)
John Durnford (Commissioned Royal Artillery; India, North Malaya, POW 1942–45 in Siam.
Post-war Regular Commission, Royal Artillery, Holder Army Flying Brevet).

You don't have to be a poet to write about war!

Spike Milligan is best known as a comedian but he was moved to write serious poetry in the Second World War.

How I Wrote My First Poem

It was January, 1944, Italy – a small group of Gunners had come forward to a small decimated wood outside the village of Lauro – overlooking the Garigliano plain. We were to dig gun positions for our Battery to occupy (19 Bty 56 Heavy Artillery) for the forthcoming attack across the Garigliano river to coincide with the attack on Cassino, we being the left flank – owing to our close proximity to the enemy, work had to be done (digging gun pits, command post etc) with great stealth – mostly at night, it was bitter cold weather – a mixture of icy rain and hoar frost in the mornings – one night when we had completed the work I was in my dug-out, it was a quiet night – occasional harassing fire – and sporadic small arms fire from various sentries – or patrols meeting in some area between the lines, I could hear digging – nearby – and thought it was a similar operation to ours – I remember saying to my trench-mate 'Thank Christ we've finished ours – but the digging I could hear was a much grimmer affair. It was the London Scottish (or The Scabs Fusiliers) burying their dead – suddenly to the sound of rain a lone piper struck up 'Over the Sea to Skye', the words of the song come to mind 'Carry the boy who's born to be king' – it was a haunting experience. Then 10 days later – by which time our guns had moved in – came a midnight disaster – a German gun found our range and a direct hit on Sgt. Wilson's gun position – the camouflage net caught fire – the charges started to explode – all were killed – or burnt to death except 2. Next day we buried them – we had no piper – just the sound of the guns around us – and I felt moved to write what was in fact my first poem –

Spike Milligan

The Soldiers At Lauro

Young are our dead
Like babies they lie
The wombs they blest once
Not healed dry
And yet – too soon
Into each space
A cold earth falls
On colder face.
Quite still they lie
These fresh-cut reeds
Clutched in earth
Like winter seeds
But they will not bloom
When called by spring
To burst with leaf
And blossoming
They sleep on
In silent dust
As crosses rot
And helmets rust.

Spike Milligan Italy, January 1943.

Do you think this is a good poem? What are its good/bad qualities?

You don't have to be a soldier to write poetry about war!

In 1854 Alfred Lord Tennyson (1809–1892) wrote *The Charge of the Light Brigade* in 'celebration' of an event in the Crimean War a few months earlier. He did this as part of his duties as poet laureate. Although in 1830 he had joined the Spanish revolutionary army, he had not taken part in any fighting! Here are some of the things that have been said about him:

W.H. Auden: 'He had the finest ear, perhaps of any English poet but he was undoubtedly the stupidest'.

Poet and critic Tom Paulin: 'Imperialist, racist, reactionary, sexist. Tennyson is in brilliant command of a dead language. The words he marshals belong to a brigade of cheap, brittle alloys which lack any natural spring or give'.

T.S Eliot: 'Tennyson is a great poet, for reasons that are perfectly clear. He has three qualities which are seldom found together except in the greatest poets: abundance, variety, and complete competence'.

Read *The Charge of the Light Brigade* and discuss which of the above opinions you have some agreement with.

The Charge of the Light Brigade

I
Half a league, half a league,
Half a league onward,
All in the valley of Death
Rode the six hundred.
'Forward, the Light Brigade!
Charge for the guns!' he said:
Into the valley of Death
Rode the six hundred.

II
'Forward, the Light Brigade!'
Was there a man dismayed?
Not though the soldier knew
Some one had blundered:
Their's not to make reply,
Their's not to reason why,
Their's but to do and die:
Into the valley of Death
Rode the six hundred.

III
Cannon to right of them,
Cannon to left of them,
Cannon in front of them
Volleyed and thundered;
Stormed at with shot and shell,
Boldly they rode and well,
Into the jaws of Death,
Into the mouth of Hell
Rode the six hundred.

IV
Flashed all their sabres bare,
Flashed as they turned in air
Sabring the gunners there,
Charging an army, while
All the world wondered:
Plunged in the battery-smoke
Right through the line they broke;
Cossack and Russian
Reeled from the sabre-stroke
Shattered and sundered.
Then they rode back, but not
Not the six hundred.

V
Cannon to right of them,
Cannon to left of them,
Cannon behind them
Volleyed and thundered;
Stormed at with shot and shell,
While horse and hero fell,
They that had fought so well
Came through the jaws of Death,
Back from the mouth of Hell,
All that was left of them,
Left of six hundred.

VI
When can their glory fade?
0 the wild charge they made!
All the world wondered.
Honour the charge they made!
Honour the Light Brigade,
Noble six hundred!

                                                        Alfred Lord Tennyson

ACTIVITY 246

The same event was described by W.H. Russell for *The Times* on 14th November 1854. How effective is this as an account? Which account do you think best describes the situation? Why?

At ten minutes past eleven our Light Cavalry Brigade advanced. . . . They swept proudly past, glittering in the morning sun in all the pride and splendour of war. . . . At the distance of 1,200 yards the whole line of the enemy belched forth, from thirty iron mouths, a flood of smoke and flame. The flight was marked by instant gaps in our ranks, by dead men and horses, by steeds flying wounded or riderless across the plain. In diminished ranks, with a halo of steel above their heads, and with a cheer which was many a noble fellow's death cry, they flew into the smoke of the batteries; but ere they were lost from view the plain was strewn with their bodies. Through the clouds of smoke we could see their sabres flashing as they rode between the guns, cutting down the gunners as they stood. We saw them riding through, returning, after breaking through a column of Russians and scattering them like chaff, when the flank fire of the batteries on the hill swept them down. Wounded men and dismounted troopers flying towards us told the sad tale. . . . At thirty-five minutes past eleven not a British soldier, except the dead and the dying, was left in front of the Muscovite guns.

You don't have to write about war in the form of poetry!

Some excellent contemporary accounts by ordinary soldiers in their own words can be found in *Voices and Images of the Great War* and *Somme* by Lyn Macdonald.

War has been the subject of many novels, for example the popular *Birdsong* and *Charlotte Gray* by Sebastian Faulks

Most of Robert Graves' autobiography *Goodbye to All That* is about his experiences in the First World War.

You can write about war when it's over!

Micheal Ondaatje's *The English Patient* is about the Second World War. It was published in 1992 and won the Booker Prize.

Historical accounts are written many years after the end of hostilities.

ACTIVITY 247

Below are four extracts from texts concerning war. Read them and decide what sort of text they are (for example novel, autobiography) and give detailed reasons about how you came to this decision. When you have done this, decide which ones give the most vivid impression of what war is like and say why. You should comment on specific language use and how the thoughts and feelings are expressed.

Extract A

One piece of shell went through my left thigh, high up, near the groin; I must have been at the full stretch of my stride to escape emasculation. The wound over the eye was made by a little chip marble, possibly from one of the Bazentin cemetery headstones. (Later, I had it cut out, but a smaller piece has since risen to the surface under my right eyebrow, where I keep it for a souvenir.) This, and a finger-wound which split the bone, probably came from another shell bursting in front of me. But a piece of shell had also gone two inches below the point of my right shoulder-blade and came out through my chest two inches above the right nipple.

My memory of what happened then is vague. Apparently Dr Dunn came up through the barrage with a stretcher-party, dressed my wound, and got me down to the old German dressing-station at the north end of Mametz Wood. I remember being put on the stretcher and winking at the stretcher-bearer sergeant who had just said: 'Old Gravy's got it, all right!' They laid my stretcher in a corner of the dressing-station, where I remained unconscious for more than twenty-four hours.

Late that night, Colonel Crawshay came back from High Wood and visited the dressing-station; he saw me lying in the corner, they told him I was done for. The next morning, July 21st, clearing away the dead, they found me still breathing and put me on an ambulance for Heilly, the nearest field hospital. The pain of being jolted down the Happy Valley, with a shell hole at every three or four yards of the road, woke me up. I remember screaming. But back on the better roads I became unconscious again. That morning, Crawshay wrote the usual formal letters of condolence to the next-of-kin of the six or seven officers who had been killed. This was his letter to my mother:

22.7.16

Dear Mrs Graves,

I very much regret to have to write and tell you your son has died of wounds. He was very gallant, and was doing so well and is a great loss. He was hit by a shell and very badly wounded, and died on the way down to the base I believe. He was not in bad pain, and our doctor managed to get across and attend to him at once.

We have had a very hard time, and our casualties have been large. Believe me you have all our sympathy in your loss, and we have lost a very gallant soldier.

Please write to me if I can tell you or do anything.

Yours sincerely,

C. Crawshay, Lt-Col.

Then he made out the official casualty list – a long one because only eighty men were left in the battalion – and reported me 'died of wounds'.

Extract B

Close to collapse, he staggered downhill towards the river, to the drink he had craved since noon. He left his rifle on the bank and stumbled down into the water. He dropped his head beneath the sluggish flow and felt it rush down into the pores of his skin. He opened his mouth like a fish.

He stood on the river bed, trying to hold himself together. He trailed his hands with the palms turned up as though in supplication. The noise pressed against his skull on both banks of the river, it would not diminish. He thought of Byrne, like a flapping crow on the wire. Would they pour water down the hole of his neck? How would he drink?

He tried to calm his thoughts. Byrne was dead: he had no need of water. It was not his death that mattered; it was the way the world had been dislocated. It was not all the tens of thousands of deaths that mattered; it was the way they had proved that you could be human yet act in a way that was beyond nature.

He tried to move to the shore, but the current was stronger than he had thought, and as his body neared its final exhaustion, he lost his footing and was carried downstream.

He was surrounded by Germans in the water. A man's face next to his shouting foreign words. Stephen held on to him. Others clasped each other, fighting to get out. All around him the people who had killed his friends, his men. Close to, in their pitted skin and wide eyes, he saw men like himself. An old, grey-haired corporal screaming. A boy, like so many, dark-complexioned, weeping. Stephen tried to hate them now as he had hated them before.

The press of German flesh, wet in the river, all around him, their clogged tunics pressing him, not caring who he was. The whining mêlée of their uncomprehended voices, shouting for their lives.

Extract C

The next year (1916) is especially memorable in the western fighting for two battles on French soil, one extending over seven and the other over four months. The attack and defence of Verdun and the Battle of the Somme rank among the greatest achievements of human endurance and the saddest tragedies of human waste. At the end of the year little seemed to have been accomplished. The French had repelled their enemy and recaptured almost all the positions which they had held in the earliest phases of the attack. The British, who had lost 60,000 men in the first day's fighting in the Somme, had failed to break the studied and intricate defences of the

German line. Yet in reality the two appalling butcheries had altered the balances of fortune. When the French had repelled the invader from Verdun in July and the sustained and heroic effort of the new British levies on the Somme had died down in October, the old German army, the best trained and most highly skilled body of fighting men which the world has ever seen was no more. Hereafter the Germans were compelled for the most part to depend upon youthful levies whose military qualities were no greater than those of their French or British adversaries.

Extract D

You were between the devil and the deep blue sea. If you go forward, you'll likely be shot, if you go back you'll be court-martialled and shot. So what the hell do you do? What can you do? You just go forward because that's the only bloke you can take your knife in, that's the bloke you're facing.

We were sent in to High Wood in broad daylight in the face of heavy machine-gun fire and shell fire, and everywhere there was dead bodies all over the place where previous battalions and regiments had taken part in their previous attacks. We went in there and C Company got a terrible bashing there. It was criminal to send men in broad daylight, into machine-gun fire, without any cover of any sort whatsoever. There was no need for it; they could have hung on and made an attack on the flanks somewhere or other, but we had to carry out our orders.

But there was one particular place just before we got to High Wood which was a crossroads, and it was really hell there, they shelled it like anything, you couldn't get past it, it was almost impossible. There were men everywhere, heaps of men, not one or two men, but heaps of men everywhere, all dead. Then afterwards, when our battle was all over, after our attack on High Wood, there was other battalions went up and they got the same! They went on and on. They just seemed to be pushing men in to be killed and no reason. There didn't seem to be any reason. They couldn't possibly take the position, not on a frontal attack. Not at High Wood.

Most of the chaps, actually, they were afraid to go in because they knew it was death. Before we went in, we knew what would happen, some of the blokes that had survived from previous attacks knew what they'd been through. It was hell, it was impossible, utterly impossible. The only possible way to take High Wood was if the Germans ran short of ammunition, they might be able to take it then. They couldn't take it against machine-guns, just ridiculous, It was absolute slaughter. We always blamed the people up above. We had a saying in the Army, 'The higher, the fewer'. They meant the higher the rank, the fewer the brains.

Check your answers at the end of the chapter.

You can write plays about war.

Many of Shakespeare's plays have references to war and there are also some battle scenes. Because of the nature of theatre, these scenes are short in action but often described in detail. Film versions of these plays often extend the coverage of battle scenes in order to add to the excitement.

ACTIVITY 248

Here is an extract from *Richard II*. What aspect of war is Shakespeare stressing here and what do you learn about Richard's character? This is where Richard is about to leave to quell the problems in Ireland.

RICHARD
We will ourself in person to this war,
And for our coffers with too great a court
And liberal largess are grown somewhat light
We are enforced to farm our royal realm
The revenue whereof shall furnish us
For our affairs in hand. If that comes short,
Our substitutes at home shall have blank charters;
Whereto, who when they shall know what men are rich,
They shall subscribe them for large sums of gold,
And send them after to supply our wants,
For we will make for Ireland presently.

Enter Bushy
Bushy, what news?

BUSHY
Old John of Gaunt is grievous sick, my lord,
Suddenly taken, and hath sent posthaste
To intreat your Majesty to visit him.

RICHARD:
Where lies he?

BUSHY:
At Ely house.

RICHARD:.
Now put it, God, in the physician's mind
To help him to his grave immediately!
The lining of his coffers shall make coats
To deck our soldiers for these Irish wars.
Come gentlemen, let's all go visit him;
Pray God we may make haste and come too late!

ACTIVITY 249

Here is an extract form *Journey's End* (1928) by R.C. Sherriff, a play set in the trenches of the First World War. Read it and write about it showing your understanding of how the playwright has created the sadness and waste of war. You can consider the relationship of the two men and what impact this ending would have on an audience. Are the ideas here an echo of other war literature you have read?

STANHOPE *(turning quickly):* What is it, sergeant-major?
S.-M.:   Mr. Raleigh, sir –
STANHOPE: What!
S.-M.:   Mr. Raleigh's been 'it, sir. Bit of shell's got 'im in the
  back.
STANHOPE: Badly?
S.-M.:   'Fraid it's broke 'is spine, sir; can't move 'is legs.

STANHOPE: Bring him down here.

S.-M.:   Down 'ere, sir?

STANHOPE *(shouting):* Yes! Down here – quickly!

>   The SERGEANT-MAJOR *hurries up the steps. A shell screams and bursts very near.*
>   *The* SERGEANT-MAJOR *shrinks back and throws his hand across his face, as though a*
>   *human hand could ward off the hot flying pieces. He stumbles on again into the*
>   *trench, and hurriedly away.*
>   STANHOPE *is by* OSBORNE's *bed, fumbling a blanket over it. He takes a trench coat off*
>   *the wall and rolls it for a pillow. He goes to his own bed, takes up his blanket, and*
>   *turns as the* SERGEANT-MAJOR *comes carefully down the steps carrying* RALEIGH *like*
>   *a child in his huge arms.*
>   *(With blanket ready.)* Lay him down there.

S.-M.:   'E's fainted, sir. 'E was conscious when I picked 'im up.

>   *The* SERGEANT-MAJOR *lays the boy gently on the bed; he draws away his hands,*
>   *looks furtively at the palms, and wipes the blood on the sides of his trousers.*
>   STANHOPE *covers* RALEIGH *with his blanket, looks intently at the boy, and turns to the*
>   SERGEANT-MAJOR

STANHOPE: Have they dressed the wound?

S.-M.:   They've just put a pad on it, sir. Can't do no more.

STANHOPE: Go at once and bring two men with a stretcher.

S.-M.:   We'll never get 'im down, sir, with them shells falling on Lancer's Alley.

STANHOPE: Did you hear what I said? Go and get two men with a stretcher.

S.-M. *(after a moment's hesitation)*:   Very good, sir.

>   *The* SERGEANT-MAJOR *goes slowly away.*
>   STANHOPE *turns to* RALEIGH *once more, then goes to the table, pushes his*
>   *handkerchief into the water-jug, and brings it, wringing* wet, *to* RALEIGH's *bed. He*
>   *bathes the boy's face. Presently* RALEIGH *gives a little moan, opens his eyes, and*
>   *turns his head.*

RALEIGH: Hullo – Dennis –

STANHOPE: Well, Jimmy – *(he smiles)* – you got one quickly.

>   *There* is *silence for a while.* STANHOPE *is sitting on a box beside* RALEIGH. *Presently*
>   RALEIGH *speaks again – in a wondering voice.*

RALEIGH: Why – how did I get down here?

STANHOPE: Sergeant-major brought you down.

>   RALEIGH *speaks again, vaguely, trying to recollect.*

RALEIGH: Something – hit me in the back – knocked me clean over – sort of –
winded me. I'm all right now. *(He tries to rise.)*

STANHOPE: Steady, old boy. Just lie there quietly for a bit.

RALEIGH: I'll be better if I get up and walk about. It happened once before – I got
kicked in just the same place at Rugger; it – it soon wore off. It – it just numbs you
for a bit. *(There is a pause.)* What's that rumbling noise?

STANHOPE: The guns are making a bit of a row.

RALEIGH: Our guns?

STANHOPE: No. Mostly theirs.

>   *Again there is silence in the dug-out. A very faint rose light is*
>   *beginning to glow in the dawn sky.* RALEIGH *speaks again – uneasily.*

RALEIGH: I say – Dennis –

STANHOPE: Yes, old boy?

RALEIGH: It – it hasn't gone through, has it? it only just hit me? – and knocked me
down?

STANHOPE: It's just gone through a bit, Jimmy.

RALEIGH: I won't have to – go on lying here?

STANHOPE: I'm going to have you taken away.

RALEIGH: Away? Where?

STANHOPE: Down to the dressing-station – then hospital – then home. *(He smiles.)* You've got a Blighty one, Jimmy.

RALEIGH: But I – I can't go home just for – for a knock in the back. *(He stirs restlessly.)* I'm certain I'll be better if – if I get up. *(He tries to raise himself and gives a sudden cry.)* Oh – God! It does hurt!

STANHOPE: It's bound to hurt, Jimmy.

RALEIGH: What's – on my legs? Something holding them down –

STANHOPE: It's all right, old chap; it's just the shock – numbed them.

Again there is a pause. When RALEIGH *speaks, there is a different note in his voice.*

RALEIGH: It's awfully decent of you to bother, Dennis. I feel rotten lying here – everybody else – up there.

STANHOPE: It's not your fault, Jimmy.

RALEIGH: So – damn – silly – getting hit. *(Pause.)* Is there – just a drop of water?

STANHOPE *(rising quickly)*: Sure. I've got some here.

He pours some water into the mug and brings it to RALEIGH.

(Cheerfully.) Got some tea-leaves in it. D'you mind?

RALEIGH: No. That's all right – thanks

STANHOPE *holds the mug to* RALEIGH'S *lips, and the boy drinks.*

I say, Dennis, don't you wait – if – if you want to be getting on.

STANHOPE: It's quite all right, Jimmy.

RALEIGH: Can you stay for a bit?

STANHOPE: Of course I can.

RALEIGH *(faintly)*: Thanks awfully.

There is quiet in the dug-out for a long time. STANHOPE *sits with one hand on* RALEIGH'S *arm, and* RALEIGH *lies very still. Presently he speaks again – hardly above a whisper.*

Dennis –

STANHOPE: Yes, old boy?

RALEIGH: Could we have a light? It's – it's so frightfully dark and cold.

STANHOPE *(rising)*: Sure! I'll bring a candle and get another blanket.

STANHOPE *goes to the left-hand dug-out, and* RALEIGH *is alone, very still and quiet, on* OSBORNE'S *bed. The faint rosy glow of the dawn is deepening to an angry red. The grey night sky is dissolving, and the stars begin to go. A tiny sound comes from where* RALEIGH *is lying – something between a sob and a moan.* STANHOPE *comes back with a blanket. He takes a candle from the table and carries it to* RALEIGH'S *bed. He puts it on the box beside* RALEIGH *and speaks cheerfully.*

Is that better, Jimmy? (RALEIGH *makes no sign.)* Jimmy –

Still RALEIGH *is quiet.* STANHOPE *gently takes his hand. There is a long silence.*

STANHOPE *lowers* RALEIGH'S *hand to the bed, rises, and takes the candle back to the table. He sits on the bench behind the table with his back to the wall, and stares listlessly across at the boy on* OSBORNE'S *bed. The solitary candle-flame throws up the lines on his pale, drawn face, and the dark shadows under his tired eyes. The thudding of the shells rises and falls like an angry sea.*

A PRIVATE SOLDIER *comes scrambling down the steps, his round, red face wet with perspiration, his chest heaving for breath.*

SOLDIER: Message from Mr. Trotter, sir – will you come at once.

STANHOPE *gazes round at the* SOLDIER *– and makes no other sign.*

Mr. Trotter, sir – says will you come at once!

STANHOPE *rises stiffly and takes his helmet from the table.*

STANHOPE: All right, Broughton, I'm coming.

The SOLDIER *turns and goes away.*

STANHOPE *pauses for a moment by* OSBORNE'S *bed and lightly runs his fingers over* RALEIGH'S *tousled hair. He goes stiffly up the steps, his tall figure black against the dawn sky.*

The shelling has risen to a great fury. The solitary candle burns with a steady flame, and RALEIGH *lies in the shadows. The whine of a shell rises to a shriek and bursts on the dug-out roof. The shock stabs out the candle-flame; the timber props of the door cave slowly in, sandbags fall and block the passage to the open air. There is darkness in the dug-out. Here and there the red dawn glows through the jagged holes of the broken doorway.*
Very faintly there comes the dull rattle of machine-guns and the fevered spatter of rifle fire.

The End
You should be grateful you only have A levels to contend with!

Answer to Activity 236: Suggested preparation of pre-release materials: 1, 2, 5, 6, 9, 10, 11.

Answers to Activity 247:

A   Autobiography. Robert Graves *Goodbye to All That*
B   Novel *Birdsong* by Sebastian Faulks
C   *A History of Europe* by H.A.L. Fisher
D   Personal Account from *Somme* by Lyn Macdonald

Further reading

Birdsong (1994) Vintage and *Charlotte Gray* (1990) Vintage, both by Sebastian Faulks.

Regeneration by Pat Barker (1991) Penguin.

Catch 22 by Joseph Heller (1964) Corgi.

Somme (1983) and *1914–1918 Voices and Imges of the Great War* (1991) Penguin Books, both by Lyn Macdonald.
A combination of military history and personal recollections of survivors.

The Voice of War. Poems of the Second World War Edited by Vicor Selwyn (1987) Dent.

Poetry of the Great War, an Anthology Edited by Dominic Hibberd and John Onions (1986) Macmillan.

The Penguin Book of First World War Poetry Edited by Jon Silkin (1979) Penguin.

Never Such Innocence. A New Anthology of Great War Verse Edited by Martin Stephen (1991) Everyman.

Poetry Of The First World War Casebook Series Edited by Dominic Hibberd (1992) Macmillan.

English Poetry of the First World War: Contexts and Themes by George Parfitt (1990) Harvester/Wheatsheaf.

Video *The Battle of the Somme* narrated by James Fox, W.H. Smith.

Acknowledgements

The publishers would like to thank the following for their kind permission to reproduce copyright material:

Copyright Text

p13 *A Martian Sends a Postcard Home* © Craig Raine, Oxford University Press, 1983; pp14, 21–2 'Out Out' from *The Poetry of Robert Frost*, edited by Edward Connery Latham, Jonathan Cape Ltd and by permission of the estate of Robert Frost; pp14–15 'Five Ways to Kill a Man' © Edwin Brock; p17 *Men are from Mars, Women are from Venus* © John Grey, Thorsons; p18 *Cider with Rosie* © Laurie Lee, Penguin, 1970; p23 'The Wheel' © Amryl Johnson from *The Long Road to Nowhere*, Virago, 1985; p25 'Thaw' from *Collected Poems* © Edward Thomas, Faber & Faber; p27 'Daniel' © Martin Turner from *Trespasses*, Faber & Faber, 1992; p28 'Bedtime Story' by Jeffrey Whitmore reprinted with permission from *The World's Shortest Stories*, edited by Steve Moss, copyright © 1998, 1995 by Steve Moss, published by Running Press, Philadelphia and London; p34 'Days' from *The Whitsun Weddings* © Philip Larkin, Faber & Faber, 1964; The extract on page 39 is reproduced from *Talking Heads* by Allan Bennett with permission of BBC Worldwide Limited, © Alan Bennett 1988; p53 *A Dangerous Knowing* edited by Barbara Burford et al., Sheba Feminist Publishers, 1985; p71 'Pattern' © Fred Brown from *Angels and Spaceships*; pp85–7 'Sonnet XLI' © Edna St Vincent Millay; p101 'Your Dad Did What?' © Sophie Hannah from *Leaving and Leaving You*, Carcanet; p103 'Writing Block' from *Beastiary* © Helen Dunmore, Bloodaxe Books; p104 'The Rain Stick' © Seamus Heaney, *The Spirit Level*, Faber & Faber; p141 *Canterbury Tales*, translated by Nevill Coghill, Penguin; p174 'The Tyre' from *CloudCuckooLand* © Simon Armitage, Faber & Faber, 1997; pp178, 183 'Hare in the Snow' from *Beastiary* © Helen Dunmore, Bloodaxe Books; p179 'Suicide in the Trenches' © Siegfried Sassoon; p183 'Going to Extremes' from Light Armour, © Richard Armour, McGraw Hill, 1954; p186 'Swan Song' by F.S. Flint; pp193–4 *Enduring Love* © Ian McEwan, Vintage; pp195–6 *Cold Mountain* © Charles Frazier, Headline; pp224–5 *Educating Rita* © Willy Russell, Longman 1980; pp234 *Look Back in Anger* © John Osborne, Faber & Faber; pp235–8 *A Streetcar Named Desire* © Tennesse Williams, Methuen; pp240 *Royal Hunt of the Sun* © Peter Shaffer, Penguin 1946; pp258–9 *Negotiating the Ship on the Head: Black British Fiction* © Kwame Dawes in *Wasafiri* edited by Susheila Nasta, 1999; p260 *Following On: The Legacy of Lamming and Selvon* © Caryl Phillips, in *Wasafiri* edited by Susheila Nasta, 1999; p263 'Obituary note for Winston Churchill', *The Times*, 26 April 1915; p265 'Zum Waffen Garten' © John Durnford, 1943; p266 'How I Wrote My First Poem' ©

Index